Students at Risk
in At-Risk Schools

Students at Risk in At-Risk Schools

Improving Environments for Learning

☐

Editors
Hersholt C. Waxman
Judith Walker de Felix
James E. Anderson
H. Prentice Baptiste, Jr.

CORWIN PRESS, INC.
A Sage Publications Company
Newbury Park, California

Copyright © 1992 by Corwin Press, Inc.

All rights reserved. No part of this book may be reproduced or utilized in any form or by any means, electronic or mechanical, including photocopying, recording, or by any information storage and retrieval system, without permission in writing from the publisher.

For information address:

Corwin Press, Inc.
A Sage Publications Company
2455 Teller Road
Newbury Park, California 91320

SAGE Publications Ltd.
6 Bonhill Street
London EC2A 4PU
United Kingdom

SAGE Publications India Pvt. Ltd.
M-32 Market
Greater Kailash I
New Delhi 110 048 India

Printed in the United States of America

Library of Congress Cataloging-in-Publication Data

Students at risk in at-risk schools : improving environments for
  learning / edited by Hersholt C. Waxman . . . [et al.].
      p.   cm.
  Includes bibliographical references and index.
  ISBN 0-8039-4003-3
  1. Socially handicapped children—Education—United States.
  2. Underachievers—Education—United States.   I. Waxman, Hersholt
C.
  LC4091.S737   1992
  371.96'7—dc20   91-38882
                                                                       CIP

92 93 94 95 10 9 8 7 6 5 4 3 2 1

Corwin Press Production Editor: Tara S. Mead

Contents

Foreword
CHRISTIAN J. FALTIS vii

About the Authors x

1. INTRODUCTION
Reversing the Cycle of Educational Failure for Students in At-Risk School Environments
HERSHOLT C. WAXMAN 1

PART I: Conceptual and Theoretical Issues
H. PRENTICE BAPTISTE, JR., Part Editor 11

2. Philosophical and Conceptual Issues Related to Students at Risk
PAUL F. BITTING, PAULA A. CORDEIRO, and
H. PRENTICE BAPTISTE, JR. 17

3. Marginality, Community, and the Responsibility of Educators for Students Who Do Not Succeed in School
ROBERT L. SINCLAIR and WARD J. GHORY 33

4. The Dropout Issue and School Reform
RAY GARCIA and JUDITH WALKER DE FELIX 43

PART II: Issues Confronting At-Risk Students
JUDITH WALKER DE FELIX, Part Editor 61

5. Linguistically and Culturally Diverse Children: Effective Instructional Practices and Related Policy Issues
EUGENE E. GARCIA 65

6. Learning Technology Contexts for At-Risk Children
RICHARD T. JOHNSON 87

7. Learning Differences Among At-Risk Minority Students
OLIVIA N. SARACHO and
CYNTHIA KOREN GERSTL 105

PART III: Leadership and Training Programs for Educational Improvement
JAMES E. ANDERSON, Part Editor 137

8. Leadership That Promotes Instability: A Hope for At-Risk Students
EUGENE E. EUBANKS and RALPH PARISH 143

9. Thinking Differently About Leadership Development in a Culturally Plural Society
A. REYNALDO CONTRERAS 160

10. Multicultural Teacher Education: A Proposal for Change
MARILYNNE BOYLE-BAISE and CARL A. GRANT 174

PART IV: Effective Programs for Students in At-Risk School Environments
HERSHOLT C. WAXMAN, Part Editor 195

11. Toward a Model of Elementary Grades Chapter 1 Effectiveness
SAM STRINGFIELD and NANCY YODER 203

12. Instructional Programs That Improve the Reading Comprehension of Students at Risk
YOLANDA N. PADRON 222

13. Implementation of an Urban School-Within-a-School Approach
DANIEL U. LEVINE 233

14. Accelerated Schools for Students in At-Risk Situations
JANE McCARTHY and HENRY M. LEVIN 250

15. Conclusion: Future Directions for Educating Students at Risk
JUDITH WALKER DE FELIX, H. PRENTICE BAPTISTE, JR., and JAMES E. ANDERSON 264

Index 273

Foreword

This book is about organizing schools to prevent at-risk children from falling behind and eventually dropping out of school before achieving full socialization in the values, skills, and knowledge needed for successful participation in society. Leaving school without an adequate education cheats these students out of a chance for a better life as adults. Moreover, in the eyes of many, it places their brothers and sisters and, later on, their sons and daughters at risk of failing in school as well. The editors of this book have assembled an impressive cadre of authors to write about positive steps that school leaders and teachers together can take to improve education for at-risk students and put an end to the cycle of failure that has touched too many of our students' lives.

As I see it, the organizing principle of this book is that solving the problems of at-risk students is first and foremost a matter of understanding the school's role, at both the classroom and the administrative levels, in addressing the socioacademic needs of students who have tended not to succeed in school. From this perspective, students are deemed to be at risk not only because others who came before them failed in school but also because the existing school conditions are inadequate to ensure their success. This critical perspective is in stark contrast to the more popular one that places all of the blame of being at risk squarely on the shoulders of the student and, by extension, on the student's cultural background. According to this widely held perspective, ethnic and language-minority students are at risk because they belong to a low socioeconomic class or to castelike ethnic groups, or because they live in an impoverished home environment, or because they have limited English proficiency, or because they rely too heavily on a relational learning style. It is plain to see that those who hold this perspective believe that neither the school environment nor the instructional practices used by teachers has anything to do with why students are at risk of leaving school inadequately prepared for the socioacademic demands of society. The position taken in this book is that preexisting conditions may very well contribute to part of why certain students are at risk, but the major reason that these students are not doing well in school is because schools have not provided the kinds of leadership and learning environments that students of diverse cultural backgrounds require.

The collection of chapters in this book are arranged to introduce the reader, first, to some of the key theoretical issues concerning the education of at-risk students, using a triangular approach. That is, the editors, Waxman, Walker de Felix, Anderson, and Baptiste, have selected authors who present theoretical concerns from the perspectives of the educational leader, the classroom teacher, and the at-risk student. This multifaceted approach not only promotes cross-validation of the issues, it also encourages educational leaders and teachers to see the issues from different perspectives and, in the process, to develop a complementary understanding of each other's roles in improving educational conditions for at-risk students.

As the title indicates, however, this book is about much more than theoretical issues and the ways that different interest groups view them. The book's major focus is on what educational leaders and teachers, working together, can do to improve the conditions of teaching and learning for at-risk students. Accordingly, the lion's share of the chapters in this book are dedicated to showing the kinds of success that can be achieved in diverse school contexts and classroom settings. School people will especially appreciate the way that the editors have tied effective practices to theoretical concerns and vice versa. For example, after a comprehensive discussion on the relationship between school policy and issues of educational leadership within schools attended by large numbers of at-risk students, the readers are treated to a variety of chapters that suggest ways to create positive changes in the existing environment. In most cases, the suggestions are made based on the accomplishments of high-quality programs that have been especially successful in keeping at-risk students in school. To reinforce the premise that schools can make a real difference in the lives of at-risk students, a number of chapters also outline specific strategies for retooling and training both educational leaders and teachers to work with at-risk students. The combination of these chapters with the ones on effective school environments provide powerful evidence that schools can indeed affect the success of all

Forward

students, regardless of their language, cultural, or socioeconomic backgrounds.

The editors of this book are to be commended for their efforts in assembling and publishing this collection of thoughtful and useful works. While it is most obvious that educational leaders and classroom teachers will benefit directly from studying the issues and effective practices presented in this book, it is the at-risk students who may very well be the greatest beneficiaries.

Christian J. Faltis
Arizona State University, Tempe

About the Authors

James E. Anderson received his Ph.D. from The Ohio State University. His areas of specialization are cultural dynamics in education, teacher education, minority leadership, and educational administration in multicultural settings. His writing and research are related to "education that is multicultural." He was the co-editor of the *Journal of Educational Equity and Leadership* for several years. He consults nation-wide in his areas of specialization. He is a faculty member in the Department of Educational Leadership and Cultural Studies and Director of the International Multicultural Education Institute at the University of Houston.

H. Prentice Baptiste, Jr. currently is Professor and Chair of the Department of Educational Leadership and Cultural Studies at the University of Houston. He earned his B.S. from Lamar State College of Technology and his M.A.T. and Ed.D. degrees from Indiana University. His research has centered on multicultural education, effective school indicators, and science magnet schools. He has served as coeditor of the *Journal of Educational Equity and Leadership* and publishes regularly in the field. He has worked extensively in staff development for urban schools faculty, and has edited a trainer's guide. He has written numerous articles, chapters, and papers regarding the infusion of multicultural concepts to curriculum.

Paul F. Bitting began his professional career in the public schools of New York City serving as a classroom teacher, counselor, and administrator. He holds a Master degrees from the City University of New York (Educational Administration), St. John's College (Liberal Education), and the University of North Carolina at Chapel Hill (Philosophy). He received his Ph.D. from the University of North Carolina at Chapel Hill in the Social Foundations of Education specializing in the Philosophy of Education. He has published in the areas of Critical Thinking, Philosophy for Children, and Multicultural

Philosophy and the Schools. He is presently an Assistant Professor in the College of Education and Psychology at North Carolina State University.

Marilynne Boyle-Baise received her Ph.D. from the University of Wisconsin—Madison in Curriculum and Instruction. She is an Assistant Professor in the Teacher Education Program at Sangamon State University in Springfield, Illinois. She teaches courses in language arts and social studies methods, teaching and learning, and multicultural education. She is the head of the Coalition for Education That is Multicultural, which is a school-university collaboration effort.

A. Reynaldo Contreras is Associate Professor of Educational Leadership and Policy Studies at Indiana University, Bloomington. Currently, he is on special assignment in the Office of the Associate Vice President for Research and Dean of the University Graduate School; a Research Associate in the Indiana Education Policy Center' and a professor of Educational Leadership. Prior to this, he was on the faculties of California State University at Los Angeles and San Diego State University. He received his Doctor of Philosophy degree in Administration and Policy analysis from Stanford University, and his research interests include policy studies in education, state educational policy development, minority educational leadership and education in urban settings.

Paula A. Cordeiro is an Assistant Professor at the University of Connecticut in the Department of Educational Leadership. She taught overseas for six years and is the former Head of the American School of Las Palmas, Spain. Her major areas of specialization are the administration of schools in culturally diverse settings, the principalship, and urban education. She is the university's facilitator for the Danforth Principal Preparation Program.

Eugene E. Eubanks is Professor of Education and Urban Affairs at the University of Missouri—Kansas City. An analyst of issues of big city education and desegregation, his most recent writings have dealt with the effective organization of schools and the change process in the educational reform movement. A former mathematics teacher, principal and deputy superintendent at the K-12 levels, he was Dean of the School of Education at UMKC for nine years. Since 1987, he has served as chair of the Desegregation Monitoring Committee appointed by the District Court to ensure the implementation of a major and comprehensive desegregation order in Kansas City, Missouri.

Christian Faltis is Associate Professor of Bilingual Education in the College of Education at Arizona State University, Tempe. He completed his Ph.D. in Bilingual-Cross Cultural Education at Stanford University. He has published extensively on the topics of bilingual education, second-language education, and equity issues in education.

Cynthia Koren Gerstl is a doctoral student in the Department of Curriculum and Instruction at the University of Maryland, College Park. She specializes in English as a Second Language and has extensive teaching experience in this area.

Ward J. Ghory, over the past 20 years, has taught (high school, graduate school, kindergarten), administered (public, alternative, and independent schools), consulted (12 states), and written (one book and numerous articles) in an ongoing effort to understand and resolve the myriad difficulties experienced by young people who are not successful in school.

Eugene E. Garcia is Dean of the Division of Social Sciences and Professor of Education and Psychology at the University of California, Santa Cruz. He is involved in various community activities and has served as an elected member or a board of education. He has published extensively in the area of language teaching and bilingual development. He holds leadership positions in professional organizations and continues to serve in an editorial capacity for psychological, linguistic, and educational journals and serves regularly as a proposal panel reviewer for federal, state, and foundation agencies. He presently serves as Co-Director of the National Center of Research in Cultural Diversity and Second Language Learning funded by the U.S. Department of Education. He is conducting research in the areas of effective schooling for linguistically and culturally diverse student populations.

Ray Garcia is Assistant Professor of Educational Leadership and Cultural Studies at the University of Houston. His research interests are academic performance of at-risk students, dropout prevention strategies, and administrative practices in effective schools. He has an extensive background in administrator training programs, project management, staff development, and program evaluation. He has been a classroom teacher as well as a school principal. Prior to joining the university faculty, he was project manager and educational consultant with Region IV (Texas) Education Service Center. He has published articles recently on at-risk students. He is currently conducting research focusing ont he role of the school principal in at-risk programming.

About the Authors

Carl A. Grant is a Professor in the Department of Curriculum and Instruction at the University of Wisconsin—Madison. He was selected in 1990 as one of the top leaders in teacher education by the Association of Teacher Educators. His major professional interests include multicultural education; race, social class and gender, and school life; and preservice and inservice education. His article "Race, class, gender, and abandoned dreams" published in *Teacher's College Record* was selected as one of the three top articles by Educational Press Association of America for 1988. Among his books are *After the School Bell Rings* with Christine Sleeter (1986), which was selected by the American Educational Studies Association (AESA) Critics Choice Selection Panel in 1987 as one of the most outstanding books in the area of educational studies; *Turning on learning* with Sleeter (1988); *Preparing for Reflective Teaching* (1984); *Bringing Teaching to Life* (1982); and *Community Participation in Education* (1979).

Richard T. Johnson is an Assistant Professor in the College of Education at the University of Hawaii at Manoa. He has published many articles in the areas of early childhood education, interactive videodisk technology, and students at risk.

Henry M. Levin is Professor of Education and Affiliated Professor of Economics at Stanford University where he also serves as the director of the Center for Educational Research. He is the founder and director of the Accelerated Schools Project, which currently includes more than 100 school nationwide. He is a specialist in the economics of human resources and serves as the Editor of the *Review of Education Research*.

Daniel U. Levine is Professor of Educational Administration at the University of Missouri—Kansas City. A former high school teacher in Chicago, he has conducted numerous studies dealing with urban education, compensatory education, school effectiveness, desegregation, and other topics, and has written textbooks in educational sociology and in the foundations of education. His most recent publications include the eighth edition of *Society and Education*, a monograph on *Unusually Effective Schools* summarizing two decades of school effectiveness research, and an analytic paper examining the potential of school-based management. He currently serves as an advisor to school improvement projects in Kansas City and other school districts.

Jane McCarthy is an Associate Professor in the Department of Instructional and Curricular Studies, College of Education, University of Nevada—Las

Vegas. She serves as the director of the UNLV Accelerated Schools Satellite Center and formerly directed the Accelerated Schools Satellite Center Project at Stanford University.

Yolanda N. Padron is an Assistant Professor in the School of Education at the University of Houston—Clear Lake. She has published many articles in the areas of cognitive reading strategies for second language learners, bilingual education, multicultural education, parent education programs, and improving the education of students at risk.

Ralph Parish is Professor of Education Administration at the University of Missouri—Kansas City. He engages in ethnographic research concerning change by performing actual roles in school districts and leadership groups and has written extensively regarding school reform, school organizations as cultures, and change as a cultural process. He has been a director of elementary education, magnet middle school principal and teacher, high school principal and teacher, State Facilitator in the National Diffusion Network, and developer/director of a nationally validated cooperative learning program. He received a Ph.D. in curriculum and instruction from the University of Oregon.

Olivia N. Saracho is Professor of Education in the Department of Curriculum and Instruction at the University of Maryland, College Park. She has had experience with bilingual children. Her major research interest is in cognitive style. She is the co-editor of the book *Understanding the Multicultural Experience* published by the National Association for the Education of Young Children.

Robert L. Sinclair is Professor of Education at the University of Massachusetts, Amherst and Director of the National Coalition for Equality in Learning, which is funded by the Danforth Foundation. This effort focuses on ensuring that all students have access to quality learning on equal terms. He is a graduate of the University of California at Los Angeles. He and his students are known for their willingness to attack knotty, difficult problems. He strongly believes that the strengths of our schools should serve as a platform for making education an even more powerful means for helping all children learn at high levels of accomplishment. Rather, he strongly believes that teachers, administrators, parents, and members of the local community can join together to improve conditions in local schools so that students increase their learning. He is particularly concerned about students on the margins because they are as deserving as those in the mainstream. His book

About the Authors

written with Ward Ghory, *Reaching Marginal Students: A Primary Concern for School Renewal*, advances his ideas about constructive ways to help students who are struggling in school to become productive learners.

Sam Stringfield is a Principal Research Scientist with the Center for Research on Effective Schooling for Disadvantaged Students at the Johns Hopkins University. His research interests include compensatory education, school and teacher effectiveness, educational program improvement processes, and international studies of the educations provided to disadvantaged children.

Judith Walker de Felix is Chair of the Curriculum and Instruction Department at the University of Houston, where she teachers bilingual/second language education. She was the coeditor of *Leadership, equity, and school effectiveness* and has written several articles on bilingual education. She is currently involved in research projects implementing interactive videodisc technology in language learning.

Hersholt C. Waxman is the Associate Dean for Research in the College of Education at the University of Houston. He is also a Senior Research Associate at the National Center on Education in Inner Cities at Temple University. He is a former president of the Southwest Educational Research Association and a recent recipient of the Distinguished Alumni Award for the College of Education at the University of Illinois at Chicago. He has conducted many studies in the areas of classroom instruction, teacher education, school effectiveness, classroom learning environments, student learning, and students in at-risk environments.

Nancy Yoder is a former Title I teacher who has worked in Chapter 1 program improvement with both the Evaluation and Rural Chapter 1 Technical Assistance Centers in the Southeast. She now teaches at Ben Franklin Academy, an alternative high school in Atlanta for students who want individual instruction in an accepting, family environment.

• 1 •

INTRODUCTION
Reversing the Cycle of Educational Failure for Students in At-Risk School Environments

HERSHOLT C. WAXMAN

In recent years, the number of students who could be considered at risk of school failure or "educationally disadvantaged" has increased and their degree of "disadvantage" has also increased (Levin, 1989; Pallas, Natriello, & McDill, 1989). In the 1988 National Education Longitudinal Study (Hafner, Ingels, Schneider, & Stevenson, 1990), for example, about 41% of Black eighth graders and 37% of Hispanic eighth graders were characterized as having two or more risk factors (e.g., from single-parent homes, having a sibling who dropped out of school, or home alone after school three or more hours a day). In their national study of "typical" elementary, middle, and high school students, Frymier and Gansneder (1989) found that nearly one third of the students in their study were identified as having 6 or more risk factors (out of a possible 45 factors that they identified from prior research). Furthermore, the Carnegie Council on Adolescent Development (1989) estimated that about 25% of 10- to 17-year-olds may be extremely vulnerable to multiple high-risk behaviors (e.g., school failure and substance abuse) and another 25% may be at moderate risk.

These findings and other indicators, such as (a) the high dropout rates for Hispanics, Blacks, and students in central cities (Kaufman & Frase, 1990), (b) the large number of students who live in poverty (LaRosa & Maw, 1990; Reed & Sautter, 1990), and (c) the failure of students to do well on higher-level applications, complex reasoning, and problem solving (Mullis, Owen,

& Phillips, 1990), illustrate the critical status of students who are currently at risk of failure in our nation's schools.

Large, urban school districts face special challenges caused by factors like poverty and crime that make the solution of their educational problems very complex (Walberg, Bakalis, Bast, & Baer, 1988). In his critical analysis of the "truly disadvantaged underclass," for example, Wilson (1987) specifically describes how the life of students in inner-city or ghetto schools has deteriorated in recent years. He argues that "inner-city social isolation" is the major problem facing the large number of socially disadvantaged students who live in highly concentrated poverty areas. This social isolation is due to the flight of families to the suburbs and metropolitan fringes as well as to more affluent families who live in the inner city but choose to send their children to parochial or private schools. Consequently, most of the large, urban school districts are becoming overwhelmingly populated with working- or lower-class minority students. Wilson (1987) argues that this "social isolation" prevents these minority students from interacting with individuals and institutions that represent mainstream society, which creates further structural constraints and limits opportunities for social mobility.

Addressing the problems of inner-city schools is one of the most important national educational issues (Cuban, 1989b). Nowhere are the social implications of increasing numbers of disadvantaged families in inner cities more prevalent than in the large, urban school districts, where the deleterious conditions of underachievement, student and teacher alienation, and high dropout rates exist. Furthermore, many of the physical structures and facilities in inner-city schools are abysmal and in desperate need of rehabilitation (Piccigallo, 1989). Those students attending inner-city or ghetto schools represent the most imperiled group of our increasing numbers of students at risk of failure (Boyd, 1991).

Reversing the Deficit Model of Public Policy

More than a decade ago, Bronfenbrenner (1979) criticized the deficit model of public policy, which, he argued, is the public's common perspective on social and educational problems. The deficit model suggests that it is the individual child, his or her family, or his or her ethnic group that is deficient and that therefore we need to focus on the individual, not on the circumstances that produce the problem (Bronfenbrenner, 1979). From this deficit model, the public focuses on specific programs for these "problem children" rather than on trying to prevent the problem circumstances. Because the model assumes a deficiency, the solution is determining the source of the problem and then trying to correct it.

Alternative strategies or approaches for reforming schools call for changing the circumstance under which children go to schools, not trying to change the children themselves. Since the beginning of public education, low-achieving students and school dropouts have been defined as problems of individual children or families (Cuban, 1989a). We need to avoid such "deficit models" and avoid labels that suggest that there are deficiencies on the part of students.

Defining or Labeling At-Risk Students

We must be cautious in terms of the overlap and ambiguity of constructs that have been used to define these at-risk students. On the one hand, educators describe the term *at risk* as a new label for a phenomena that is as old as public school itself (Richardson, Casanova, Placier, & Guilfoyle, 1989). On the other hand, others argue that the term *at-risk student* is the latest of a series of popular labels that focuses on individual characteristics and therefore stigmatizes the student. This term is often criticized because it suggests that the student has the characteristic of being "at risk" instead of being in a place or circumstance that is considered to be at risk.

One common definition of the term *at-risk students* is a category of students who are unlikely to graduate from high school (Slavin, 1989). Other criteria, however, have also been selected as determining or defining at-risk students. Students who have failed one or more grades, have been assigned to special education, or speak a language other than English may also be considered at risk. Others have identified at-risk students in terms of poverty, drug abuse, sexual activity, race, and ethnicity (Pellicano, 1987).

Levin (1989, p. 47) describes at-risk students as "those who lack the home and community resources to benefit from conventional schooling practices." Pallas et al. (1989) formulate a definition for the term *educationally disadvantaged* to describe students who have been exposed to inappropriate education in the school, family, or community. Comer (1987) calls this group "high-risk children" and defines them as students who underachieve in school and consequently will underachieve as adults.

Whatever definition or term is used to describe these students, we need to be cautious not to allow the term to be used to label or stigmatize students. We also need to be aware that these labels often mask the diversity of those students whose situations we are defining (Wehlage, Rutter, Smith, Lesko, & Fernandez, 1989). A wide range of students are categorized as "at risk," and we need to be aware that this diversity requires diversity in schools and school interventions. This diversity among students also suggests that schools affect students differently. The next two sections of this chapter describe two school-related problems that affect students at risk: (a) Matthew effects and (b) at-risk school environments.

Matthew Effects for Students at Risk

Although we know that students from disadvantaged backgrounds typically begin school already behind their nondisadvantaged classmates (Levin, 1990), a fact that could be considered more critical, however, is that schools also contribute to these students' learning problems (Wang, 1990). Consequently, another factor that needs to be considered in the education of students from at-risk school environments is the "Matthew effect" (Reynolds, 1989; Stanovich, 1986; Walberg & Tsai, 1983; Wang, 1990). The Matthew effect suggests that these disadvantaged students who are behind at the beginning of school or who learn at a slower rate will likely show a "progressive retardation" as they continue in school (Reynolds, 1989; Walberg, 1988).

Evidence of the Matthew effect has important implications for the education of students in at-risk school environments. Programmatic issues, for example, may need to be focused specifically on students at risk because school-based programs or instructional programs that are beneficial for all students may have more positive effects for those students who are initially advantaged (Walberg, 1988). Consequently, students at risk may even fall further behind their advantaged peers.

One of our greatest educational problems is that we often teach at-risk or disadvantaged students less than they are capable of learning (Knapp & Shields, 1990). Another aspect of the Matthew effect occurs when teachers interact with or treat low-achieving or special needs students differently. This occurs, for example, when teachers only call on at-risk students to answer low-level knowledge questions or when teachers wait less time for low-achieving students to answer questions. Furthermore, several studies have found that teachers have differential expectations for students at risk. Edmonds (1986), for example, found that there were differential expectations for students in "ineffective schools" and teachers varied their instruction according to students' sex, race, or social class.

At-Risk School Environments

Recently, several educators have reframed the problem of "blaming the victim" to argue that school systems, school programs, organizational and institutional features of school, the structure of schools, or the school environment contribute to the conditions that influence students' academic failure (Boyd, 1991; Cuban, 1989a, 1989b; Kagan, 1990; Meacham, 1990; Pellicano, 1987; Sinclair & Ghory, 1987; Wehlage et al., 1989). From this perspective, it could also be argued that many features of schools and classrooms are alienating and consequently drive students out of school rather than keep them in (Kagan, 1990; Newman, 1989).

Teacher alienation is another issue that needs to be addressed when we consider at-risk school environments. There are many teachers, for example, who feel isolated, alienated, and burnt out (Dworkin, 1986; Firestone, 1989). Teachers in urban schools especially experience a high degree of physical, psychological, and professional isolation (Wehlage, Rutter, & Turnbaugh, 1987). Because teacher disengagement feeds the alienation of students, there is consequently a cycle of alienation that exists in schools too. As Firestone (1989, p. 42) describes it, "because teachers and students share the school environment and because each group is dependent upon the other to meet its needs and achieve its successes, teacher alienation and student alienation feed each other."

The school environment is the broader context or climate of the school that either facilitates or constrains classroom instruction and student learning (Shields, 1991). Sinclair and Ghory (1987) also maintain that it is the school environment that either encourages or discourages student learning through a series of interactions. The term *at-risk school environment* suggests that it is the school that should be considered at risk. School environments that (a) alienate students and teachers, (b) provide low standards and a low quality of education, (c) have differential expectations for students, (d) have high noncompletion rates for students, (e) are unresponsive to students, (f) have high truancy and disciplinary problems, or (g) do not adequately prepare students for the future are considered to be "at risk." Students who participate in these at-risk school environments merit our special attention because, if we can alter their learning environment, we will improve both their education and their overall chances for success in society.

Overview of the Book

We know that students can be exposed to inappropriate educational experiences in the family, school, or community (Pallas et al., 1989). Community demographics and family conditions, however, cannot be greatly changed by educators, while educational policy and practice can be modified to improve the education of students at risk (Comer, 1987). In addition, researchers have found that the school effect is more powerful than the (a) family effect, (b) teacher effect, (c) neighborhood effect, and (d) the cultural environment that describes the community (Edmonds, 1986). In this book, we specifically focus on students in at-risk school environments and how educators can alter or modify these environments to improve students' cognitive and affective outcomes.

This book is divided into four parts: Part I, Conceptual and Theoretical Issues, provides insight into some of the recent concerns and problems of students at risk. Part II, Issues Confronting At-Risk Students, specifically addresses three recent concerns that educators have investigated: (a) instructional practices, (b) learning technology contexts, and (c) learning differences. In particular, this part focuses on how current schooling experiences, and not the students' cultural or linguistic backgrounds, put students at risk of failing.

Part III, Leadership and Training Programs for Educational Improvement, focuses on how educational leaders and practitioners can be developed and prepared in the future to avoid repeating the failures of the past and extending the "cycle" of at-risk students. Finally, Part IV, Effective Programs for Students in At-Risk School Environments, illustrates how instructional programs can effectively improve the education of students at risk. In the final chapter, "Conclusion: Future Directions for Educating Students at Risk," some of the future trends and directions for educating students in at-risk school environments are discussed. In addition, some of the dilemmas facing us and these students are addressed.

Reversing the Cycle

This book illustrates ways we can reverse the cycle of educational failure for students from at-risk school environments. The purpose of this book is to make available information for improving our understanding of the problems as well as solutions to problems for students in at-risk school environments. We are especially concerned about inner-city or urban schools because they serve a disproportionate and socially significant share of these students (Boyd, 1991). Educators need to be aware of the concerns and problems facing these students and how schools contribute to the degree of risk. In conclusion, it is apparent that some of the risks associated with students' failure in school are due to the particular school the student attends.

This book attempts to describe some of the research-based approaches that successfully work in improving the education of students in at-risk school environments. Although recognition of the uniqueness of each school and classroom situation will always need to be considered, the accumulation of research evidence over time and across several studies may provide consistent findings that enhance our understanding of schools and classrooms in inner-city or ghetto settings.

Improving the education of students in at-risk school environments, however, will take more than just awareness of the problems and knowledge of some solutions. As Futrell (1988, p. 31) puts it, "Interrupting the cycle of desperation that defines the life of the at-risk child will require the concerted efforts of all educators." She also maintains that it will require an alliance among (a) teachers; (b) administrators; (c) university professors, deans, and presidents; (d) parents; and (e) the government. This will also require a call to action and collaboration among educators. This process will also require a change in attitudes that will make all of us aware of the severity of the problems *and* seriously committed to reversing the cycle of educational failure for students in at-risk school environments.

References

Boyd, W. L. (1991). What makes ghetto schools succeed or fail? *Teachers College Record, 92,* 331-362.

Bronfenbrenner, U. (1979). Beyond the deficit model in child and family policy. *Teachers College Press, 81,* 95-104.

Carnegie Council on Adolescent Development. (1989). *Turning points: Preparing American youth for the 21st century.* New York: Carnegie Corporation.

Comer, J. P. (1987). New Haven's school community connection. *Educational Leadership, 44*(6), 13-16.

Cuban, L. (1989a). The "at-risk" label and the problem of urban school reform. *Phi Delta Kappan, 70,* 780-784, 799-801.

Cuban, L. (1989b). At-risk students: What teachers and principals can do. *Educational Leadership, 46*(5), 29-32.

Dworkin, A. G. (1986). *Teacher burnout in the public schools: Structural causes and consequences for children.* Albany: State University of New York Press.

Edmonds, R. (1986). Characteristics of effective schools. In U. Neisser (Ed.), *The school achievement of minority children* (pp. 93-104). Hillsdale, NJ: Lawrence Erlbaum.

Firestone, W. A. (1989). Beyond order and expectations in high schools serving at-risk youth. *Educational Leadership, 46*(5), 41-45.

Frymier, J., & Gansneder, B. (1989). The Phi Delta Kappa study of students at risk. *Phi Delta Kappan, 71,* 142-146.

Futrell, M. H. (1988). At-risk students: The economic implications, the moral challenge. In R. Yount & N. Magum (Eds.), *School/college collaboration: Teaching at-risk youth* (pp. 31-36). Washington, DC: Council of Chief State School Officers.

Hafner, A., Ingels, S., Schneider, B., & Stevenson, D. (1990). *A profile of the American eighth grader: NELS:88 Student descriptive summary.* Washington, DC: U.S. Department of Education, National Center for Educational Statistics.

Kagan, D. M. (1990). How schools alienate students at risk: A model for examining proximal classroom variables. *Educational Psychology, 25,* 105-125.

Kaufman, P., & Frase, M. J. (1990). *Dropout rates in the United States: 1989.* Washington, DC: U.S. Department of Education, National Center for Educational Statistics.

Knapp, M. S., & Shields, P. M. (1990). Reconceiving academic instruction for the children of poverty. *Phi Delta Kappan, 71,* 753-758.

LaRosa, D., & Maw, C. E. (1990). *Hispanic education: A statistical portrait 1990.* Washington, DC: National Council of La Raza.

Levin, H. M. (1989). Financing the education of at-risk students. *Educational Evaluation and Policy Analysis, 11,* 47-60.

Levin, H. M. (1990). The educationally disadvantaged are still among us. In J. G. Bain & J. L. Herman (Eds.), *Making schools work for underachieving minority students* (pp. 3-11). New York: Greenwood.

Meacham, A. W. (1990). Curriculum and the at-risk student. *Baylor Educator, 15*(2), 17-26.

Mullis, I. V. S., Owen, E. H., & Phillips, G. W. (1990). *Accelerating academic achievement: A summary of findings from 20 years of NAEP.* Princeton, NJ: National Assessment of Educational Progress.

Natriello, G., McDill, E. L., & Pallas, A. M. (1990). *Schooling disadvantaged children: Racing against catastrophe.* New York: Teachers College Press.

Newman, F. M. (1989). Student engagement and high school reform. *Educational Leadership, 46*(5), 34-36.

Pallas, A. M., Natriello, G., & McDill, E. L. (1989). The changing nature of the disadvantaged: Current dimensions and future trends. *Educational Researcher, 18*(5), 16-22.

Pellicano, R. R. (1987). At risk: A view of "social advantage." *Educational Leadership, 44*(6), 47-49.

Piccigallo, P. R. (1989). Renovating urban schools is fundamental to improving them. *Phi Delta Kappan, 70,* 402-406.

Reed, S., & Sautter, R. C. (1990). Children of poverty: The status of 12 million young Americans. *Phi Delta Kappan, 71,* k1-k12.

Reynolds, M. C. (1989). Students with special needs. In M. C. Reynolds (Ed.), *Knowledge base of the beginning teacher* (pp. 129-142). Oxford: Pergamon.

Richardson, V., Casanova, U., Placier, P., & Guilfoyle, K. (1989). *School children at-risk.* London: Falmer.

Shields, P. M. (1991). School and community influences on effective academic instruction. In M. S. Knapp & P. M. Shields (Eds.), *Better schooling for the children of poverty: Alternatives to conventional wisdom* (pp. 313-328). Berkeley, CA: McCutchan.

Sinclair, R. L., & Ghory, W. J. (1987). *Reaching marginal students: A primary concern for school renewal.* Berkeley, CA: McCutchan.

Slavin, R. E. (1989). Students at risk of school failure: The problem and its dimensions. In R. E. Slavin, N. L. Karweit, & N. A. Madden (Eds.), *Effective programs for students at risk* (pp. 3-19). Boston: Allyn & Bacon.

Stanovich, K. (1986). Matthew effects in reading: Some consequences of individual differences in the acquisitions of literacy. *Reading Research Quarterly, 21,* 360-407.

Walberg, H. J. (1988). Synthesis of research on time and learning. *Educational Leadership, 45*(6), 76-85.

Walberg, H. J., Bakalis, M. J., Bast, J. L., & Baer, S. (1988). *We can rescue our children.* Chicago: Heartland Institute.

Walberg, H. J., & Tsai, S. L. (1983). Matthew effects in education. *American Educational Research Journal, 20,* 359-373.

Wang, M. (1990). Programs that promote educational equity. In H. P. Baptiste, H. C. Waxman, J. Walker de Felix, & J. E. Anderson (Eds.), *Leadership, equity, and school effectiveness* (pp. 132-154). Newbury Park, CA: Sage.

Wehlage, G. G., Rutter, R. A., Smith, G. A., Lesko, N., & Fernandez, R. R. (1989). *Reducing the risk: Schools as communities of support.* London: Falmer.

Wehlage, G. G., Rutter, R. A., & Turnbaugh, A. (1987). A program model for at-risk high school students. *Educational Leadership, 44*(6), 70-73.

Wilson, W. J. (1987). *The truly disadvantaged.* Chicago: University of Chicago Press.

PART I

Conceptual and Theoretical Issues

H. PRENTICE BAPTISTE, JR., EDITOR

From the very beginning, Americans have depended upon their schools to provide an opportunity for all citizens to receive an education. This education allows them to participate more fully in our democratic society. For many members of our society, education has provided the only means available to the "American dream." Unfortunately, our country is developing a class of young people who are undereducated, unskilled, and doomed to poverty status. These young people are our current and future dropouts.

Today's technological society demands an educated and skilled work force to compete in the global community in which we now live. James S. Catterall (1985) estimates that each year's class of dropouts will cost over $200 billion in both lost earnings and unrealized tax revenues during their lifetimes. Additionally, billions will be spent for welfare, medical aid programs, and expenses in the criminal justice system. These are expenses that can and should be avoided. Keeping a teenager in school by providing him or her with a quality education that will prepare that youth for gainful employment after graduation is much more cost-effective than providing welfare payments and other forms of public assistance for a lifetime.

There has been much research done on a group of students who are currently being called "at risk." Throughout this book, you will find a number of terms used for the "at-risk" student population. These students have previously been called *dropouts, disadvantaged, marginal, impoverished, alienated, low achievers, disenfranchised, low income, culturally deprived,* and so on. Whatever the terminology, these students are disadvantaged because schools are not meeting their specific educational needs.

The literature suggests that children may be at risk due to factors related to their socioeconomic status (poverty), family background (single-parent home), or community (drugs or youth gangs). In reality, children are at risk because they are unable to take full advantage of the educational opportunities available to them. The schools are failing these children.

The educational success of the at-risk student is dependent upon four groups currently working separately, which may account for the lack of success on the part of the at-risk student. The groups are educators, schools, parents, and the community. These groups must function in an integrative way to accomplish the goal of successfully educating the at-risk student population.

Role of Educators

Administrators, teachers, and other school personnel share the responsibility of providing effective and efficient instruction for all students. The teacher is the leader of the classroom and, as such, should lead by example. A major concern of the classroom teacher should be to help build a positive self-concept for all students. Each student should be treated with respect, and his or her worth as a person should be validated in the classroom on a regular basis. Many dropouts have a negative self-concept and very low self-esteem. In their study, Wehlage and Rutter (1986) found that school factors related to discipline were significant in contributing to the decision to drop out. They measured the level of teacher interest in students as perceived by students, student perceptions of the effectiveness of discipline, and student perceptions of disciplinary unfairness. At-risk students tended to perceive as low the effectiveness and fairness of discipline.

At-risk students need administrators and teachers who are willing to take risks in providing new and innovative programs. They must be committed to the task of minimizing the negative effects of race, poverty, and other social, economic, and cultural variables and maximizing their efforts toward enhancing the quality of educational programs available for those students at risk. Jonathon Kozol, George McKenna, Jaime Escalante, and Marva Collins all provide positive role models for educators. These individuals believed that, for education to be effective, those charged with the task should be caring and supportive persons who have high expectations for their students.

The classroom environment must be one that is nonthreatening to the students, and the interactions between student and teacher and student and student should be based on respect.

Educators must accept students with all their problems in a nonjudgmental manner. They must identify those characteristics of students that cause them to be at risk; these factors may be a result of academic, social, or economic conditions. Once identified, administrators and teachers must devise curricula and teaching strategies that will be effective with all students including at-risk students. A measure of success for all students should be assured by teaching strategies and the curricula. This success can then be rewarded and used as positive reinforcement. In addition, the classroom teacher must work with the school and the parents to make referrals either directly or through the school counseling office to assist the at-risk student with other types of services and support that may be required. Essentially, educators are responsible for making the educational experience meaningful and related to future goals and objectives while simultaneously helping to address some of the school needs that may help to keep the student in school.

The School

Today's schools are ill-equipped and ill-designed to accommodate today's students. Although almost every aspect of U.S. society has entered into the technological age, the U.S. school system remains in the industrial age. The programs, curriculum, and even buildings are essentially the same as they were 100 years ago. Probably the only thing that has changed is the learner. Because of the social conditions that exist for youth, they bring to the schools a completely different set of problems and concerns that schools need to address.

According to researchers, school size may have an effect on school dropping-out behaviors. Large schools with poor and minority enrollments tend to alienate students. The students have little contact with teachers or other adults and fail to become a part of the school community (Wehlage & Rutter, 1986).

The school should provide a supportive environment for *all* students. This requires the school to embrace each student as an individual. Students should feel that they are part of the school community. The school should provide a positive environment for the students. The pupils should be involved in developing school spirit, and a strong activity program should be established for them. Both academic and social expectations for the student should be high. Prizes and awards for which all students have equal access should be provided. The awards should be based on a variety of accomplishments, thus allowing students who may not be the top achievers to experience success and receive recognition for their success. A number of authors feel that students should be involved in cooperative learning activities. Cooperative learning improves achievement for students and develops social skills that students can use in the school environment and society (Slavin, 1983). Johnson and Bany (1970, p. 169) state that "competition undermines cooperation." Schools should encourage cooperation among the students.

The Parents

Parents need to become partners with the schools in the education of their children. They have the responsibility of being the "overseers" of their children's education. Educators must stress to them that it is not enough to send the child to school well rested, fed, clean and neat, and with proper school supplies (and many parents even fail to fulfill one or more of these requirements). The parent needs to know that he or she has a responsibility to spend time with the child at the end of the school day. This interaction should involve questioning the child on the day's events. Such questions might include the following: How did you like school today? Will you describe something interesting that happened? Was your teacher in school today? Do you have homework?

This type of questioning activity shows the child that the parent is interested in what he or she does in school. It gives the child an opportunity to discuss any accomplishments. Further, it alerts the parent to any homework assignments. Parents should ask to see notebooks, assignments, tests, and other schoolwork. This will let the student know that the parent is monitoring the child's school progress.

Parents should be encouraged to attend school-sponsored activities such as Parent's Night and PTO meetings. If the parents attend school sporting events, concerts, plays, and programs with the child, it often encourages the student to participate in such extracurricular activities. Children become involved in academics as well as social activities if they know that their parents are interested and supportive of these efforts. Even if the child does not participate, the student and parent are both showing school support by being spectators, fans, or members of the audience.

The Community

Quality education is a prerequisite for a society that intends to compete internationally and globally in today's complex society. Every segment of the society, the family, schools, business, and government is going to have to cooperate to halt the upward trend in school dropouts. It is estimated that every $1 invested today will save $4.75 in the future cost of welfare, remedial education programs, health care, and crime (Staff Report of the Select Committee, 1985).

Business has been successful in the past in cooperating with schools to meet certain objectives. They must now devote time, money, and energy to developing programs that will entice the at-risk population to stay in school and assist them in gaining some success in their learning careers. At-risk students need more resources, services, and innovative programs that relate to the "real world." A Committee for Economic Development (1987, p. 16) report states:

> [For] effective partnership, each side must fully understand what the other has to offer and develop a realistic view of what can be accomplished. The goals of partnerships should be to engage children, teachers, administrators, parents, and business executives in efforts designed to improve the children's performance, broaden their horizons, and demonstrate an ongoing commitment from the community.

The chapters in Part I address in more detail the problems of at-risk students and ways to improve their educational experience. The chapter by Paul Bitting, Paula Cordeiro, and H. Prentice Baptiste, Jr., discusses the stigma of labeling students "at risk." Their chapter rejects the current approach of trying to determine what causes failure. Rather, this chapter chooses to focus on what occurs with those students who fall into the category of at-risk students but who succeed. The authors of this chapter share three case histories of "at-risk" students who have succeeded, and they further describe some positive factors that are common to all three students.

In their chapter, Robert L. Sinclair and Ward J. Ghory present a definition and discussion of the "marginal" student. They describe the work being done by the National Coalition for Reaching Marginal Students and its efforts to assist educators and the community in recognizing and addressing the needs of the marginal student.

The chapter by Ray Garcia and Judith Walker de Felix discusses the dropout dilemma from a national perspective. It describes the problem of getting accurate information on the number of dropouts annually due to confusion in how states compile their reports. Garcia and Felix also detail socioeconomic and demographic information on those students at risk for dropping out. They conclude their chapter by describing interventions that may provide the best results for successfully keeping at-risk students in the system and providing them with educational programs that work.

We hope that these chapters will give some insight into the problems of at-risk students and provide suggestions for possible solutions at every level: family, school, and community.

References

Catterall, J. S. (1985). *On the social costs of dropping out of schools* (Report No. 86-SEPT-3). Stanford, CA: Stanford University, Center for Educational Research.

Committee for Economic Development. (1987). *Children in need: Investment strategies for the educationally disadvantaged.* New York: Research and Policy Committee.

Johnson, L. V., & Bany, M. A. (1970). *Classroom management: Theory and skill training.* New York: Macmillan.

Slavin, R. E. (1983). When does cooperative learning increase student achievement? *Psychological Bulletin, 94,* 429-445.

Staff Report of the Select Committee on Children, Youth, and Families. (1985). *Opportunities for success: Cost-effective programs for children.* Washington, DC: U.S. House of Representatives, Government Printing Office.

Wehlage, G. G., & Rutter, R. A. (1986). *Evaluation of a model program for at-risk high school students.* Paper presented at the annual meeting of the American Educational Research Association, San Francisco.

• 2 •

Philosophical and Conceptual Issues Related to Students at Risk

PAUL F. BITTING

PAULA A. CORDEIRO

H. PRENTICE BAPTISTE, JR.

Issues Related to Identifying At-Risk Students

There is a story about a philosopher who rose up from his deathbed to announce to his assembled friends, "I have it! I have found the answer!" only to sink back into a coma before sharing it with anyone. Hours later he rose again, this time to ask, "What was the question?" Our culture has generally tended to solve its problems without experiencing its questions. That is our genius as a civilization, but it is also our pathology. Now the pathology is overtaking the genius, and educators are beginning to sense this everywhere. The way questions are framed and discussed by academicians both reflects and helps shape how issues are approached in the real world, no matter how otherworldly academic debate may sometimes seem. Warren Bennis (1989, p. 112), in his insightful and often humorous book *Why Leaders Can't Lead*, states,

> There are too many predicaments, too many grievances, too many ironies, polarities, dichotomies, dualities, ambivalences, paradoxes, contradictions, confusions, complexities, and messes, and so we naturally incline toward people with answers—without even bothering to wonder what the questions, the real questions, are.

Academicians and practitioners addressing the issues and problems of what is now referred to as the "at-risk" student have often lost touch with the questions, expending enormous resources to generate the right answers, or at least partially right answers, for what we consider to be the wrong questions. We mean particularly that the organizing question for most of the past two decades has been this: Why cannot children who are poor and dark learn as other children do? It may have been a question worth asking, but, in retrospect, it was clearly not the most efficient way to promote positive change. A great deal of trouble could have been saved and innumerable children might have been helped had we spent somewhat less time investigating failure and more time trying to understand success, however statistically rare success might be.

There have always been students who do well in schools who are no different than those who are otherwise failing. Until very recently, however, such students had been relegated to the margins of the ongoing discussion, treated as interesting but as outliers, not meaningful exceptions to the all-important general pattern. Like many perspectives, academicians have created a cult of failure, a cult whose doctrine held that variations in school resources have limited effects on learning; that schools themselves really have little to do with who learns how much; that the child's background is what matters; and that reform is meaningless with such students.

In the past few years, that has begun to change. Since 1980, many major journals and books have published discussions of effective urban schools. Even more popular books, articles, and studies have been written highlighting individual achievements against tremendous odds (Firestone & Rosenblum, 1988; Louis & Miles, 1990; Oakes, 1987; Werner & Smith, 1989; Wilson & Corcoran, 1988). Whether this new attention given to the successes, rather than the failures, of "at-risk" students will lead to real changes, we cannot say, but it opens possibilities that have not existed before. Ronald Edmonds, Lawrence Lezotte, Michael Rutter, and others have played a particularly important role in raising the level of questioning and discussion to the more success-oriented mode. Edmonds (1979), for example, pointed out that who learns what is a matter of political choice. Perhaps in the future we will choose not to educate students designated as "at risk." But it is worthwhile to know that it is a choice we have made, and we are not merely accepting miseducation because we just do not know how to do it better.

In the first part of this chapter, we begin by examining the philosophical and educational ramifications of the concept of being "at risk." We then go on to examine what could possibly be learned from those who fit the sociological "at-risk" profile but have achieved academic success. What worked? Why did it work? That is, if "at-risk" students can be taught successfully anywhere, then why not everywhere?

The Stigma of "at Risk"

In his central work *Souls of Black Folk*, W. E. B. DuBois complained about sociologists gleefully counting Black bastards and prostitutes (1961, p. 20). For a large part of the twentieth century, DuBois's characterization remained accurate in describing how the social sciences addressed matters of economic and social inequalities. Such an approach assumed that understanding inequality is essentially a matter of describing those who suffer from it.

Those who continue to understand the concept of "at risk" in this way contend that the problem results from cultural or genetic or psychological inadequacies in the preschool lives of the students. There may be arguments as to just which preschool factors are critical, but there is an underlying agreement that the problem with the "at-risk" student is within the "at-risk" student. Such factors take on the status of stigma.

According to Goffman (1963, p. 1), the Greeks originated the term *stigma* to refer to "bodily signs designed to expose something unusual and bad about the moral status of the signified. . . . Today the term is widely used in something like the original literal sense, but is applied more to the disgrace itself than to the bodily evidence of it." People often create what Goffman (1963, p. 5) calls a "stigma-theory" about people who are thought of as not quite normal. This stigma-theory explains a person's inferiority and accounts for the possible danger she or he represents. As a result, various types of discrimination, oftentimes unthinkingly, occur. In schools, these stigmas are intertwined with a plethora of labels: *LD, BD, special ed, latchkey, limited English proficient, underprivileged, disadvantaged, at risk,* and so on. Often, if these labels are imposed at an early age, the stigma remains throughout the student's school years.

Consider the sheer range and variety of questions on which social scientists, "counting bastards," have traditionally ended up explaining stigma with stigma. Why are some people poor? Because they have not developed the relentless future-time orientation of "normal" people or because their essentially matriarchal backgrounds failed to give them the achievement orientation so necessary in our competitive society. Why can't some children learn to read? Because their home backgrounds do not offer the intellectual nourishment conducive to learning.

Consider further the attributes of "at-risk" students with the following stigmatizations:

1. quite commonly come from a broken home;
2. are nonverbal and concrete minded;
3. are physically less healthy than his or her middle-class peers;
4. lack stable identification figures (role models);
5. lack stable community ties because of constant migration;
6. are often handicapped by his or her color, which provides him or her with a negative self-image;
7. are handicapped in the expression and comprehension of language;
8. tend to be extroverted rather than introverted. (Rosehan, 1967, p. 40)

Perhaps the classic statement on explaining the stigma of "at risk" was expressed by political scientist Edward Banfield. In *The Heavenly City* (1970), Banfield stated that most social problems cannot be solved because they depend on changing one's psychology or culture of poverty. Banfield believes the government is incapable of changing the culture of poverty. He wrote that, for the poor, schooling is unnecessary because they lack ability:

> The answer is that the children who are stimulated into mobility in school are ones whose initial class culture permits or encourages—perhaps even demands—mobility. The more nearly upper class the child's initial culture, the more susceptible s/he is to being "set in motion" by the school. At the other end of the continuum, the lower class child's culture does not even recognize—much less value—the possibility of rising or, rather, of doing those things, all of which require some sacrifice of present for future gratification, without which rising is impossible. (Banfield as quoted in Berube, 1984, p. 126)

Banfield's solution is to allow these children to leave school.

The characteristic educational policy implication logically flowing from such stigma theories, of course, is that the "at-risk" student must be changed, not the relationship between the student and the school. Of late, researchers have begun to shift their focus of inquiry. For example, in his book on at-risk, inner-city, high school students, Farrell (1990, p. 147) explores some intriguing questions regarding the lives of these students. He argues that high schools, even if they remove the many "academic handicaps," will not be effective for these students "unless they [students] can see a link between school and work." Farrell argues for both content and process changes in schools. He questions the ability of the high school to reform itself sufficiently to educate at-risk students. Farrell states that this is impossible unless the educational system starting from kindergarten is reformed.

Stigma Elimination Through Educational Change

Visitors to our contemporary culture from another place and time whose inhabitants were all intellectually superior to us would no doubt find in the way we educate the least advantaged of our citizenry much cause for wonder. Their wonder would not flow from our ignorance of the inefficiency of the system. Rather, the cause for wonder would be the method by which we seek to come to grips with that inefficiency. Over and over again, we have reverted to remediation as a means of changing the student rather than altering the student-school relationship through educational change. And when the remediation turns out to be inefficient, compensatory approaches proliferate in an effort to remedy the ineffectual remediation. The fundamental source of such inefficiency in distributing education effectively to all its students—the faultiness of its basic design—remains unexamined, and increasingly vast sums are poured into efforts to compensate for the inefficiency of the compensatory efforts, and this process continues on in the direction of futility. Evaluation of traditional compensatory education programs has shown only modest positive effects on achievement. The majority of these gains have been in the first three years of school. In addition, once a child leaves a Chapter 1 compensatory education program, these modest gains are rarely maintained. In reviewing the research on Chapter 1 programs, Archambault (1989) found little support for the pullout programs that are considered synonymous with Chapter 1. He pointed out that even those Chapter 1 compensatory education programs that are in class rather than pullout do not necessarily reduce the stigma on the student or the lesson fragmentation. Archambault argues that stigmatization is not a function of setting but that sensitivity or insensitivity in the setting is the determining factor for whether or not the student feels different.

Inefficient remediation and its concomitant compensatory approach to such inefficiency reflects a relationship between the student and the school that suggests that the student must change or, as Banfield argues, leave. Many opt to leave. The alternative to such continuous stigmatization is for schooling to change in response to the interests, needs, and concerns of the students. That is, if we always do what we have always done, will we always get what we have always gotten? What we have always gotten through this continuous process of remediation and compensation is a large cadre of disconnected, stigmatized students we now designate as "at risk."

The Harm That Schools Do

Whatever the problems of an educational system, it is apparent that they most severely and harshly affect precisely those portions of the population that are already educationally disadvantaged. The system thus affects the student population differentially, so that there is significant student vulnerability to systematic problems. It seems that students vary greatly in their susceptibility to the harmfulness of ineffectual educational processes. Some cultural groups are not much harmed by inadequate public education, and many of their members may succeed in spite of it; the system can thus not take credit for their success. Other cultural groups may succumb to the harm very readily, and the system bears some responsibility for their failure. In any event, consideration of the factors to be taken into account in changing education must involve the harm committed by the current educational process that makes compensatory education appear necessary. An analysis of such harmful characteristics holds more promise than taking as a starting point the stigmatizations of differences in cognitive capacities based upon ethnic or socioeconomic backgrounds.

The theory implicit in current practice with respect to compensatory education is that the most extreme and obnoxious symptoms of an inadequate educational experience may be remedied or redressed by means of a countervailing educational thrust that would make up for the ground lost and would bring the lagging population up to par with others. Unfortunately, the methods employed in compensatory education generally turn out to be much the same as those in the existing system itself. One obvious example might be the long-standing practice of grade retention. There appears to be little warrant for the belief that grade retention will bring about student achievement when, through such practices, we use the same methods and materials that were initially unsuccessful. So the question arises as to the extent such practices actually contribute to the "at-risk" stigmatization. Grisson and Shephard (1989, p. 60) offer evidence to suggest the possibility of such a relationship: They argue that "whenever high school dropouts and graduates are compared, it is always the case that a substantially larger proportion of the dropouts have repeated a grade." They go on to suggest that "statistical controls help to assure us that the apparent relationship between retention and dropping out is not merely a correlational artifact" (p. 58). Grade retention thus may contribute in subtle and interactive ways to an already complex constellation of causes for school leaving.

With no clear understanding of the causes of the miseducation now prevalent, such compensatory practices tend to be preoccupied with little more than the alleviation of symptoms and in reality turn out to be more punitive than effective. Slavin (1987) calls for alternatives to traditional compensatory approaches. One alternative he advocates for at-risk students is cooperative learning. Another attack on these programs, albeit implicit, has come from Levin (1988), who advocates "accelerated schools." These schools call for collaborative teacher leaders who reexamine and modify school practices. Levin argues that labeling children and offering them boring drill and practice instruction will ensure they never catch up with the mainstream children.

If the educational process were to be changed to reflect the needs of students stigmatized as "at risk," what criteria could be used to determine that the change would be of optimum serviceability? One does not usually attempt to change something unless one first knows what one expects of it or what one is trying to accomplish by means of it. We argue that the overall objective of such change would be an educational system of maximum intrinsic value (as contrasted with a system of purely instrumental and extrinsic value) and maximum meaningfulness.

The Significance of Meaning

Aristotle begins his *Metaphysics* with the rather sweeping generalization: "All men by nature desire to know" (Book I.1, 980a21-7 in McKeon, 1940). Aristotle is attributing to us a desire, a force, that urges us on toward knowledge. From earliest childhood, humans display an innate curiosity.

Indeed, the British psychoanalyst Melanie Klein (1981, p. 87) once called this childhood curiosity "epistemphilia"—love of episteme. But curiosity is not, we believe, the best way to conceptualize what drives us on. Perhaps it is better to think of the human's natural capacity to be puzzled, to search for meaning in observed phenomena; we want to know why they occur.

It is out of this search for meaning, this sense of wonder, Aristotle says, that humans first begin to philosophize. That is, philosophy grows out of the natural human capacity to feel puzzlement and awe. We cannot remain content until we have an explanation of why some observed entity is as it is. This discontent causes us to desire to know; it propels us toward exploration, the search for meanings, and the formation of explanations.

All of us have known what it is for things to lack meaning. It is a deeply disturbing experience, much more than simply being puzzled. Our capacity for puzzlement and awe leads us to suspect there is an answer somewhere that will yield understanding. But meaninglessness can be terrifying. Stigmatized children who sit at their desks inundated with factual information that seems jumbled, pointless, and unconnected to their lives have a direct sense of the meaninglessness of their school experiences. Meaninglessness is a much more fundamental problem than simply being puzzled as to what to believe or do.

Barone (1989, p. 147) tells us about Billy Charles, the boy from the hills of Tennessee who is repeating seventh grade. He tells us about Bill Charles, who is "at risk" according to his school; Billy Charles, who expresses his intention of dropping out of school; Billy Charles, whom teachers and administrators call "slow" and "hard to talk to." Barone also tells us about the Billy Charles who details the act of "juggling"; who hunts, fishes, and traps; who loves the outdoors. Billy Charles reminds us of Barbara Porro's Bob, who has "real teachers" and "pretend teachers." She describes how students and teachers play "real school" and "pretend school." While Bob plays the "low achiever's game" in some classes, in "real school" (those classes where instruction is geared to students' academic ability), he works rather than goofs off. Bob and his fellow students adapt to each class; thus they find their own way of adapting to the system. According to Porro (1985, p. 270), Claremont high school "appears to be running smoothly . . . the way in which it operates is not necessarily related to educating. The system merely sets us an opportunity for education to take place. Whether or not real education happens is up to individual teachers and students." Barone (1889, p. 149) tells us that, while "Billy Charles is rarely present in spirit at school, he drifts less often out of social studies and reading classes." This is because the teacher in his social studies class is doing what teachers in Porro's "real school" are doing—gearing instruction to the student. They are teachers who provide stimulus variation and use diverse models of teaching. Barone, like Farrell, calls for the reforming—the restructuring—of our schools. The lives of these children in most cases differ from those of their teachers. Teachers' understanding and appreciation of that diversity is a necessary precondition to good teaching. As Tyler (1949) told us years ago, the needs of the learner are crucial to the development of curriculum. Likewise, Dewey (1902) discussed the importance of starting where the student is now and leading outward from that point. Yet our schools continue to ignore the individuality of the learner.

Apologists for our current educational practices are able to ground their conclusions in stigma-theory, enabling them to define the problem in terms of bored, unmotivated, and apathetic children influenced by a less than adequate home environment. But if the home environment were not at least initially stimulating, these children would come to preschool and kindergarten bored and apathetic. They do not! Whatever their environment, nearly all children initially enter their school experiences with this sense of wonder and awe of which Aristotle reminds us. They are bright-eyed, curious, and ready to learn. By third grade, however, we begin to see a dissipation of such inquisitiveness and, by the middle school years, they are beginning to suspect the meaninglessness of disjointed facts having no clearly discernible connection to their lives. In the last 10 years, in reaction to the national reports, there has been considerable focus on curriculum revision. But, as Farrell (1990, p. 149) points out, "What makes a class boring seems to be how it is taught rather than what is taught." Goodlad (1984, p. 108) found the classroom tone to be "neither harsh and punitive nor warm and joyful; it might be described most accurately as flat." Ethically, can we continue to expect "boring" and "flat" classes to have meaning for students?

The connection between education and meaning should be considered inviolable. Whenever meaning accrues, there is education. This may happen in school, at home, or on the playground. The relationship between such meaning making and schooling, however, is a highly contingent one. But schools that consider education their mission and purpose are schools that dedicate themselves to helping children find meanings relevant to their conditions.

Therefore we begin with a premise different than the prevalent one. We begin by assuming that the only way to make compensatory practices meaningful is not to approach them as compensatory devices at all but to design them so as to promise meaningful experiences for all young people. Just as there exists no "compensatory medicine," compensatory education should not exist. Just as the intensive care facilities available in hospitals to those who are seriously ill are the model of lesser facilities elsewhere for those whose medical needs are less severe, so the care and attention we give to the educational development of the highly vulnerable members of our society should be a model of meaningfulness and excellence, representing the best services available to all. The success stories we describe here are evidence that human capacity can be created. Teachers and students are not merely the victims of an environment or hereditary capacity, they are important factors in producing it (Combs, 1979). There is no effective strategy for compensatory education that is not at the same time an effective strategy for all education.

What is clear is that schooling must change itself so that socioeconomic conditions can never be the excuse for purely educational deficiencies. It must change itself so that cultural diversity will be regarded as an opportunity for the system to give proof of its excellence rather than as an excuse for its collapse. It must change itself so that no significant fraction of those affected by it should ever be able to say, "It failed to help me to discover the full range of options available to me." Or, "I grew. But I would have grown by synchronizing my abilities so that they would reinforce each other rather than cancel each other out." Or, "When I entered the system of schooling I brought curiosity, imagination, and creativity to a world I found awe inspiring and open to me. Thanks to my school experiences I have left all these behind. Now I find the world to be a closed system of disjointed facts with little room in it for curiosity, imagination, and creativity."

An education that has been structured for meaningfulness promises to be an academically superior one. But there are benefits in addition to such intrinsic delights. That is, when educational experiences are contextually structured so as to make available to the student a rich and tempting array of meaning, it intensifies the student's sense of purpose and direction. It is rather pointless to exhort students to be proud of themselves (to have a "positive self-image") while presenting to them a world that appears to lack purpose and meaning. It is similarly pointless to assure them that they have the dignity and worth of human beings when what students more immediately and precisely need is to be helped to express the individuality of their experience and uniqueness of their point of view. This applies with all the more forcefulness to students who, for any number of complex reasons, have lost their sense of purpose and direction, for they have few other resources to call upon in life than their wits and, when these are disparaged, what else are they to rely on?

At-Risk Scholars

We describe here three high school students who possessed the identified correlates of being at risk yet were academic successes (Cordeiro, 1991). Just as we study those schools that are successful despite being made up of a majority of students who have the stigma of being "at risk," so too can we learn from the "outliers." There are those students who possess some, or all, of the risk characteristics identified in the literature but somehow not only have stayed in school and not failed but have excelled.

The three students discussed here were all honors/magnet students in high school and were accepted to four-year institutions upon graduation in June 1990. Because successful completion of high school and entrance to college are usually indicators of school success, we have labeled these students successes.

Upon entering school, these students fit the sociological profiles of "at-risk" students. They came from low socioeconomic backgrounds. They were from a minority group and lived in single-parent homes or with guardians. Spanish was their first language; they spoke little English upon entering school. None of these children had parents who graduated from high school; in fact, their parents were elementary school dropouts. They came from large families with five or more children. They all had siblings who had dropped out of school. So too had many of their peers dropped out. From the age of 14 or 15, they worked 15-20 hours per week. During their junior and senior years, they worked more than 25 hours a week. They lived in 'barrios' in the inner city and moved homes at least four times in the elementary grades, changing schools a minimum of three times. Often bantered about in the literature or found in school district profiles about students in danger of dropping out are these characteristics that all three possessed. Yet, despite possessing them, they excelled. If we are to accept these "risk" profiles, then what made these students excel? What factors played a role in their success?

Did they lose their stigmatization along the way or were they never labeled? Can we learn anything from their success that might provide insight into possible instructional or environmental adaptations that might increase the proportion of students who complete high school?

Anna was the fourth child of seven from a Mexican American family. Her parents came to the United States while in their early twenties. Upon entering school, Anna spoke no English. At the time of the study, her father was unemployed and occasionally lived with her mother, who cleaned houses part-time. Despite struggling in elementary school until fifth grade, Anna spoke positively about those years. She remembered awards she had won for sports, attendance, and art. She still had most of them and was eager to display them. At one point, she was placed back into third grade; then, three months into the school year, at the insistence of her mother and minister, she was placed in the correct grade for her age. Suddenly her grades began improving. She felt her English language skills were strong by that point. Anna described how her minister helped her attend special language classes. She detailed the important support role he played for her when she was lacking confidence about her academic abilities.

Upon transferring to middle school, Anna entered a magnet program. She had been encouraged to do so by her fifth-grade teacher. Although fearful of the idea and the process of application, she did it because her teacher guided and encouraged her along the way. According to Anna, her father also encouraged her to "get an education" because he did not have one. By high school, Anna rose at 5:30 to take two buses to school each morning. She took a bus to get to work in the afternoon and often did not get home until 8:00 or 9:00 in the evening. Yet Anna graduated in the top 10% of her class.

At the age of 8, Leo came to the United States from El Salvador. Upon arrival, he lived with an aunt because his mother had remained in El Salvador. He had never lived with or known his father. At the age of 16, he moved out and a younger brother came to live with him. Leo said he was retained in elementary school because of problems with English. Leo, like Anna, felt positive about his early years in school despite having several language problems. He talked about and proudly showed the researchers his math awards, certificates, medals, and even the gifts he had received from teachers.

Leo started working at the age of 14. From the age of 16 on, he worked full-time—40 hours per week, year round. He came to the United States speaking no English, yet graduated from the magnet/honors program at his high school. Like Anna, Leo had attended a magnet middle school and magnet high school. He said he had been encouraged to apply to a magnet school by one of his teachers. This teacher, whom Leo had for two consecutive years in middle school, spent considerable time discussing what a good experience this would be for him and helped him to apply. He felt she knew him well and cared about him.

Marcela and her mother were U.S. born and her father was born in Mexico. Marcela had not lived with her mother since the age of 3 because her mother had been declared an unfit parent. Her mother had become a transient and lived under one of the elevated bridges in nearby downtown. Marcela was the eldest of five children and worked part time. At the time of the study, one of her brothers had quit school.

Upon entering school, Marcela spoke some English but, as was evident from her school records, language was a problem for her until fourth grade. She moved nine times during kindergarten through fifth grade, attending five different schools. Then she started doing exceedingly well. She formed a close bond with a person in the Hispanic community who volunteered at the youth center at her church. This woman had encouraged Marcela to apply to a magnet middle school. She got the application forms for Marcela and helped her fill them out. She continuously encouraged Marcela throughout her middle and high school years. Like Leo and Anna, Marcela felt positive about elementary school. Displayed in a case in her bedroom were her dance, art, math, and attendance awards.

Implications for Our Questions

Above are mentioned just a few of the salient points that emerged from analyzing the data collected in these three case studies. Several areas emerged that may be of particular importance. First, each of these children had at least one role model outside the immediate family. For Marcela, it was a woman she knew in the Hispanic community center at her church. By her junior year in high school, she had known this woman for seven years. For Leo, it was an elementary teacher and then a middle school computer teacher who had taught him for two years. For Anna, it was her minister as well as a fifth-grade teacher.

Another salient point, pregnant with possibilities, is the type of school. All three students attended magnet/honors schools during the middle grades and throughout high school. Immediately, questions arise. Were these students that much more ahead of their peers in fifth grade so that attending magnet and honors classes in middle school was more appropriate for them? Or, as the researcher suspected after interviewing administrators and counselors and looking at archival data from that period, was it because they were Hispanic and the district needed to meet racial/ethnic quotas? If placement was not based on academic reasons, then it may be possible that the environment created by these magnet schools and honors classes was conducive to their success. This leads to another question. What about those students who possess the identified characteristics of being "at risk" but are placed in magnet/honors programs from elementary school? Are their chances of success greater?

They participated in as many school activities as was possible despite the numbers of hours they worked. They viewed school as a place to see friends. They did not particularly like secondary school, yet they knew it was something they had to do because they had to leave the barrio. They had to have more than their families had. (They saw school as the only route to possible success.) Despite the system being a gauntlet, they learned to maneuver in and out with amazing alacrity. In the following stanza from a poem written for an English class about what America and Mexico had done for her, one student wrote:

> What has Mexico done for me?
> It gives me relief from the American lifestyle.
> What about America?
> I can't distinguish, other than
> the key to my future . . . Education.
>
> (Cordeiro, 1991, p. 48)

These students bought into the idea that an education was necessary. A high school diploma was only the first stepping stone; it was merely a formality. Getting into college was paramount, because a college diploma was the only way for them to get out of the barrio.

Finally, it is imperative to look at the reward structure for these children. All reported having experienced considerable success in elementary school. The only academic problems mentioned were language related. These students had received certificates, awards, medals, gifts, letters of recognition, and trophies from their earliest years in school. Although they believed everyone got them, they still valued these awards highly.

The writers invite the reader to look at the many questions raised by Werner and Smith in their landmark study of resilient children and youth (Werner & Smith, 1989, pp. 159-164). Many issues they raise also emerged from the data in these cases studies. In particular, educators and educational researchers need to explore several questions the data in these studies suggest. What is the impact of role models who are outside the family circle? What support services should the school offer during elementary and middle school years for these children? Should we more closely examine the roles of cross-age tutoring and peer counselors? How best can the church and ethnic community organizations work with schools? Are there different levels of participation to be found among children in the primary grades that may lead to nonparticipation behaviors as early as second or third grade?

Clearly, we now have evidence showing the inadequacies of many pedagogical methods and approaches. As Walberg (1990) reminds us, the knowledge base regarding teaching is extensive. Just as there is considerable information regarding the descriptors of effective schools, we now have knowledge of effective teaching and effective learning strategies. Dare all of us in the education community ask the questions that only a few, the outliers, have been asking all along? As Ogbu (1989) pointed out

> Many social scientists want Blacks and other subordinate groups to do as well in school as middle-class white people do. This goal is commendable. But in their eagerness to bring about change, they often design their studies not so much to understand the total situation as to discover *what is wrong* and how the situation should be changed. I believe this approach leads to the wrong kinds of questions, the wrong kinds of answers and the wrong kinds of solutions. (p. 400)

Dare we ask why some are supposed to fail yet do not?

References

Archambault, F. X. (1989). Instructional setting and other design features of compensatory education programs. In R. E. Slavin, N. L. Karweti, & N. A. Madden (Eds.), *Effective programs for students at risk* (pp. 220-263). Boston: Allyn & Bacon.

Barone, T. (1989, October). Ways of being at risk: The case of Billy Charles Barnett. *Phi Delta Kappan,* pp. 147-151.

Bennis, W. (1989). *Why leaders can't lead.* San Francisco: Jossey-Bass.

Berube, M. R. (1984). *Education and poverty: Effective schooling in the United States and Cuba.* Westport, CT: Greenwood.

Combs, A. (1979). *Myths in education.* Boston: Allyn & Bacon.

Cordeiro, P. (1991). *Growing away from the barrio: An ethnography of high achieving at risk Hispanic youths at two urban high schools.* Unpublished doctoral dissertation, University of Houston.

Dewey, J. (1902). *The child and the curriculum.* Chicago: University of Chicago Press.

DuBois, W. E. B. (1961). *Souls of Black folks.* Greenwich, CT: Fawcett.

Edmonds, R. (1979, October). Effective schools for the urban poor. *Educational Leadership,* pp. 15-23.

Farrell, E. (1990). *Hanging in and dropping out: Voices of at-risk high school students.* New York: Teachers College Press.

Firestone, W. A., & Rosenblum, S. (1988). The alienation and commitment of students and teachers in urban high schools. *Educational Evaluation and Policy Analysis, 10,* 285-300.

Goffman, E. (1963). *Stigma: Notes on the management of spoiled identity.* New York: Simon & Schuster.

Goodlad, J. I. (1984). *A place called school.* New York: McGraw-Hill.

Grisson, J. B., & Shephard, L. A. (1989). Repeating and dropping out of school. In L. A. Shephard & M. L. Smith (Eds.), *Flunking grades: Research and policies on retention* (pp. 34-63). New York: Falmer.

Klein, M. (1981). *Love, guilt and reparation.* Honolulu, HI: Hogarth.

Levin, H. (1988). *Accelerated schools for at-risk students.* New Brunswick, NJ: Rutgers University, Eagleton Institute of Politics, Center for Policy Research in Education.

Louis, K. S., & Miles, M. B. (1990). *Improving the urban high school.* New York: Teachers College Press.

McKeon, R. (Ed.). (1940). Metaphysics. *The basic works of Aristotle* (pp. 682-926). New York: Random House.

Oakes, J. (1987). *Improving inner city schools: Current directions in urban district reform.* Santa Monica, CA: Rand, Center for Policy Research in Education.

Ogbu, J. (1989). Social stratification and the socialization of competence. In *Education and society* (pp. 390-401). Orlando, FL: Harcourt Brace Jovanovich.

Porro, B. (1985). Playing the school system: The low achiever's game. In E. Eisner (Ed.), *The educational imagination* (2nd ed., pp. 256-274). New York: Macmillan.

Rosehan, D. L. (1967). Cultural deprivation and learning: An examination of methods and theory. In H. L. Miller (Ed.), *Education for the disadvantaged* (pp. 38-42). New York: Free Press.

Slavin, R. (1987). Making Chapter 1 make a difference. *Phi Delta Kappan, 69*(2), 110-119.

Tyler, R. W. (1949). *Basic principles of curriculum and instruction.* Chicago: University of Chicago Press.

Walberg, H. J. (1990, February). Productive teaching and instruction: Assessing the knowledge base. *Phi Delta Kappan,* pp. 470-478.

Werner, E. E., & Smith, R. S. (1989). *Vulnerable but invincible: A longitudinal study of resilient children and youth.* New York: Adams, Bannister & Cox.

Wilson, B., & Corcoran, T. (1988). *Successful secondary schools: Visions of excellence in American public schools.* East Sussex, England: Falmer.

• 3 •

Marginality, Community, and the Responsibility of Educators for Students Who Do Not Succeed in School

ROBERT L. SINCLAIR

WARD J. GHORY

On the fringes of most school environments gathers a shadow population of students whose motivation and achievement are stymied. These are the marginal students who are not being well served by our public schools. Precious little attention is given either to the needs of these young people or to their assets. They are viewed as deviants from the "regular" students, outsiders who are not productive members of the learning community. This persistent problem of increasing numbers of students who are not succeeding must be attacked because youth who fail on the margins are as deserving as those who thrive in the mainstream.

In a democratic society, educators have the major responsibility of ensuring that the opportunity to obtain a quality education is made available on equal terms to all youth of all families. Equal access to learning has come into sharp focus repeatedly in the last 35 years because it is here where education and civil rights merge. In their ruling against segregation of students in schools according to race, the Supreme Court of the United States reminds us of the complexity of equality. They state:

AUTHORS' NOTE: Another version of this chapter appeared in *Wingspan*. (1991, February). Tampa: Pedamorphosis.

> Does segregation of children in public schools solely on the basis of race, even though the physical facilities and other "tangible" factors may be equal, deprive the children of equal educational opportunities? We believe that it does.... To separate them from others of similar age and qualifications solely because of their race generates a feeling of inferiority as to their status in the community that may affect their hearts and minds in a way unlikely ever to be undone. (*Brown v. Board of Education*, 1954)

Unfortunately, too many students still do not benefit from their educational experiences. While attempting to survive on the fringes, marginal students do not obtain equal access to quality learning. Simply put, they are at risk of not realizing their personal and academic promise.

The National Coalition for Equality in Learning was formed to provide greater equality in public schools by attacking the problem of educating students who become separated from constructive learning. This effort in ten varied locations across the United States encourages collective inquiry and action in 80 diverse schools and their immediate communities to improve the status of young people who are not succeeding. The work is an important response to the challenge of helping all students learn well. The experience of the National Coalition helps us reflect on marginality as a persistent problem that hinders equality and to consider community as a promising means for fostering equality.

Problem of Marginality

Marginality—that is, disconnection between students and the conditions designed for their learning—is a complex situation arising from many sources and taking many forms. Various types of students become marginal in schools, such as the learner not working up to potential, the understimulated exceptional learner, the one with a long history of academic failure or substandard achievement, or the one suddenly performing poorly despite previous success. Students can become marginal regardless of sex, race, family structure, or economic background, although these variables do seem to influence the likelihood of problems with school. Marginal learners can include "children at risk" from low-income homes as well as troubled youths from well-to-do families. Gifted students may become marginal. Marginal students may live in urban, rural, or suburban locations. For some, the experience of marginality will be short-lived. Yet, for many, disconnection will be a critical step in developing habits and attitudes that make marginality a way of life.[1]

To be "marginal" is to be caught in a *condition* of strained relations with school and persistent struggles with learning. As a result, marginal students are located in a *position* on the outskirts of the school environment, alienated from the setting designed to promote learning. It is tempting to blame the marginal student for this disconnection. But this common approach of blaming the victim fails to account for the role of the environment in influencing behavior. All students are a product of family and community settings that have predisposed them to patterns of behavior that are more or less functional in a particular school environment. The school typically builds on, refines, or causes reconsideration of these patterns. Although some students suffer from severely damaged personalities or from serious physical or mental handicaps, it is estimated that fewer than 5% of young people enter school with relatively unalterable problems in learning (Bloom, 1976). Student origins by themselves account for only a small fraction of delinquent acts, and origins have a negligible impact on students becoming marginal (Natriello, 1982). This means that, when a student becomes marginal, it is crucial to consider how the school environment may force a disconnection and hinder learning.

It is disturbing to realize that all students may be at risk of becoming at least temporarily disconnected from full and productive involvement in classrooms and schools. To analyze the responsibility of educators for students who do not succeed in school, it is critical to realize that differences in learning result from two-sided interactions between an individual and an environment. To solve problems of marginal students, educators need ways of thinking and acting that help us hold both ends of the individual-school equation in balance. Use of the term *marginal* to explain student learning shifts the perspective from deeply seated problems rooted in individuals to problematic relationships between individuals and school environments. After all, differences among students are not the real problem! The prime issue is the ability of educators to respond to variations among students that result from their previous and current experiences. If we perceive only that individual students are responsible for the problems they have in learning, it is easier to cast the responsibility of the educator in distant and benevolent terms. But if we begin to see ways in which school environments tolerate and even promote the difficulties students experience, the responsibilities of educators become more urgent and responsive.

When students are seen moving to the margins, it is necessary to determine what aspects of the school-student relationships are not working. It is a fundamental responsibility of educators to identify problems students are having in their learning and acknowledge difficulties schools are having responding to human variability. The marginality of an individual is always relative and changeable, a matter of degree. The degree of marginality depends not only on the characteristics of the actor or action but on the way the student or behavior is viewed and treated by educators. Problematic behaviors are not an individual's total personality and behavioral repertoire; they are responses to how a student perceives his or her environment and to how he or she is being treated. In the National Coalition, we are finding that marginal learners can change even deep-seated, unproductive habits, just as constructive adjustments can be made in relatively static educational environments. As Dewey emphasized, it is the role of the educator to change conditions until opportunities for action and reflection are created that promote student learning (Dewey, 1963).

Improvement in conditions for learning will not be accomplished by simply intensifying current features of school environments that have proven problematic to the very people we hope to assist. Attempts to ease disconnected and uninspired learners into compliance with a more demanding version of the conditions that drove them to the edge in the first place will not be enough. A shift in perspective is needed. School and nonschool settings must become joined so that a more responsive environment for learning may be crafted. In plain terms, a community for learning must be designed to serve marginal students better. It is useful to explore the promise of community as a means for educators to meet their responsibilities with marginal students.

Promise of Community

A community is a formal or informal group of people who have common views and values, who tolerate a range of differences, and who actively support one another in pursuit of a common end that transcends their individual needs. People in a community believe in something shared, get together regularly to deepen their commitment and understanding, and develop mutual aspirations. A community consists of primary relationships among people who help each other accomplish individual and common goals.

Humans are social animals. They are stimulus seeking, so being without community often results in loneliness. Life without community, if it persists, may contribute to mental instability or deviant behavior. Living in a large apartment complex and not knowing anyone is to experience a loss of community. Being at a sporting event and not having any association with others may result in a failure to develop community. Similarly, not understanding one's schoolwork or persistently misinterpreting group expectations for acceptable behavior in the classroom also lead to loss of a sense of community.

Loss of community then is loss of group reinforcement for desirable goals. We are discovering that students who are marginal often do not have people in their immediate circle who prize academic accomplishments or encourage attitudes and habits that are necessary to being successful in school. While all parents want their children to do well in school, many marginal students are subtly socialized to adopt behaviors that conflict with school expectations. They become caught between wanting to do well in school and not wanting to be seen as untrue to the cultural and behavioral norms learned in the home and expected on the streets. Marginal students face contradictory pressures without the clear direction that comes from significant others who can model and support behavior that leads to school success without the loss of personal integrity. In this sense, the creation of an intentional community for learning where none exists shows promise as a means for resolving the disconnection or alienation that marginal students experience. The community becomes a sanctuary for learning, a welcoming starting point rather than an alienating pressure point.

The work of the National Coalition shows that some students are skilled at building or joining a community to correct a void in their human interactions and to help them accomplish desired learning. It may be productive for marginal learners to master this skill. The ability to recognize and seek membership in communities with constructive ends is important. Some communities are dysfunctional. We know, for example, that students who are severely marginal often seek membership in a community of marginal colleagues whose goals may be opposed to learning in school. This, of course, makes constructive intervention extremely difficult. Robert Merton helps us understand that, the more permanently an individual has internalized his or her marginal status, the more powerful the intervention must become (see the seminal study of deviance in social systems by Merton, 1938).

Professional educators, parents, and students can develop a powerful community for learning by creating supportive enclaves within a larger environment. For example, parents and teachers can join together to help each other assist their children and other students obtain desired skills and competencies. These educative communities start with parents finding common ground with teachers concerned about their children doing well. Again, a promising approach for reaching marginal students is the stimulating or forming of responsive communities for these youths who are struggling with their learning.

Educators in the National Coalition for Equality in Learning report that marginal students often are presented with the same school environment as other students but become part of a different community—or have no community. Physical, social, and intellectual conditions in school then are not the sole determiners of community. A community is also in the mind, and the perceptions of marginal students decisively influence their behavior. Hence it is important to discover the shape of a student's perceived community so that constructive designing and redesigning of the learning environment can take place.

Even students who are skilled at creating and finding a community must center on a cause or purpose that is meaningful and valued. Students lose command of their knowledge and skills when they do not find a place and a reason to apply what they have learned. For this reason, another promising strategy for reducing marginality is for students to play meaningful roles in forming their own learning community with concerned and supportive adults. This may be accomplished easily as students help to set goals for personal learning, or it may become complex as students help to shape a new school program or to govern an existing one. For many students, it is liberating to realize they do not have to continually adjust their behavior to fit school settings that do not work for them. They can use their knowledge and skills to improve their own school community or to help others. We are finding that increased success for marginal students takes place in a community of significant relationships formed to advance a common purpose for learning.

Responsibility of Educators

By starting with problems of marginal students, it may be possible to define some particular responsibilities educators have for improving learning through community. These responsibilities are found in three features of learning communities.

First, learning communities are built around common goals. Educators must begin by knowing their students well enough to create convincing reasons for them to learn. This implies presenting a rationale for the content and skills contained in the curriculum in terms that makes sense to students who may view the academic world as the province of people who are not like themselves. It means helping skeptical students draw on their own academic strengths and personal backgrounds to understand important ideas and useful information. In some schools, it may mean expanding the curriculum to include multicultural content that makes it more likely for marginal students from different backgrounds to increase their learning. Educators then have a responsibility for translating goals of education into reality that makes sense to marginal students.

While the responsibility for building a community with common learning goals for all students is shared by various educators, this responsibility connects with the role of the school principal in special ways. For example, it is the principal's responsibility to articulate the mission of quality, integrated education for all. Practically speaking, this leadership includes encouraging teachers and school staff to believe in the capacity of their students to learn at high levels of accomplishment and to believe in their own professional abilities to create alternative ways for all students to learn.

Schools that consistently are unsuccessful with some learners tend to be mired in a slough of restraining attitudes and counterproductive practices that defy efforts by marginal students, parents, and educators to break the cycle of failure. The work of the National Coalition suggests it is the principal's responsibility to confront such defeatism in a tactful but direct manner. Specifically, the successful principal finds ways to help teachers, parents, and students reconsider their ways of thinking and acting toward marginal students.[2] Prior to problem solving in any school, but especially in schools that have a sizable population of marginal students, the principal takes the lead in building a platform of shared concerns, positive attitudes, and common goals among educators, parents, and students.[3]

A second feature of learning communities is that they are supportive settings where someone having difficulty is noticed and quickly provided with appropriate resources, similar to the support a family musters without hesitation when one of its members is in need. It is the special role of the teacher to intervene when students start to show signs of becoming marginal. Teachers have an obligation to help students become more powerful learners by teaching them an array of learning skills that will help them succeed in classrooms and other educative settings. Of course, as learning environments and instruction differ, so will the specific skills needed by students. Nevertheless, when students increase their ability to learn in different ways, they stand to benefit. To perfect only one style of learning is to put the student at risk of becoming marginal in environments that call for alternative approaches to learning.

When students consistently have difficulty relating successfully to classroom conditions designed for their learning, the individual teacher has to adjust curriculum and instruction to connect more productively with the characteristics of these marginal students. Teachers report that a learning environment can be adjusted to encourage fuller participation and more success for marginal students. One promising change, for example, is the elimination of ability grouping that sorts learners and the creation of clusters of diverse students who help each other learn. Also, the use of the home and other nonschool settings to encourage learning is starting to get meaningful results with students who have a history of failure. Genuine concern for marginal students will eventually produce constructive changes in classrooms and schools, despite real and perceived constraints. Again, it is the responsibility of educators to develop the determination and creativity necessary to solve problems that stand in the way of reaching out to students who are having difficulty in school.

A third feature of learning communities that links with the responsibilities of educators is that, in a constructive community, each member makes the community a richer place for all. It is a common fallacy of programs for marginal students simply to view the students as weak, flawed vessels that must receive additional services that separate them from the "mainstream" population. On the contrary, we have learned that marginal students need meaningful ways to use their special skills and to apply their growing commitment and increasing knowledge. It is the responsibility of educators, including parents, to identify student strengths and to open doors for students to contribute their talents to the school community. Marginal students often make surprisingly constructive contributions to the problem-solving functions of a school—to its student councils, drug committees, disciplinary boards, community service programs, and so on. Because marginality is related to the way a person is perceived and treated, putting marginal students in responsible roles often causes dramatic improvements in self-esteem, social behavior, and academic learning. Ultimately, it is the responsibility of educators to provide marginal students with opportunities to gain control of their own lives and learning.[4]

Closing

When a significant number of students become marginal and fail in their learning, the society loses the benefit of educated citizens and the individual loses the opportunity to experience a productive and fulfilling life in our democracy. Educators need to reach these marginal students and help them return to productive learning. One crucial priority for educational reform then is to find meaningful ways to serve children and youth who have not found sufficient reasons or means for academic and personal success available to them in the past. We believe that more understanding of the problem of marginality and greater appreciation for the promise of community will help educators meet their responsibilities for creating greater equality in education.

Notes

1. For a comprehensive analysis of the marginal student problem in U.S. public schools, see Sinclair and Ghory (1987).
2. For an analysis of how changing ways of thinking and how redefining roles serve as powerful interventions for increasing student learning, see Cummins (1986).
3. It is possible to overstate the leadership function of the principal to make it appear that the principal is acting alone in school renewal leadership. Frequently, a second change facilitator (an assistant principal, special teacher, or district supervisor) is nearly as active, and in some cases more active, than the principal. See Hord, Stiegelbauer, and Hall (1984).
4. A persuasive analysis of the complex attitudes and skills needed to take command of one's own learning is presented in Marzano, et al. (1988).

References

Bloom, B. S. (1976). *Human characteristics and school learning.* New York: McGraw-Hill.
Brown v. Board of Education of Topeka. (1954, May 17). Earl Warren, Chief Justice for the Supreme Court of the United States.
Cummins, J. (1986). Empowering minority students: A framework for intervention. *Harvard Educational Review,* 56, 18-36.

Dewey, J. (1963). *Experience and education.* New York: Collier.
Hord, S., Stiegelbauer, S., & Hall, G. (1984). How principals work with other change facilitators. *Education and Urban Society, 17,* 89-109.
Marzano, R. J., et al. (1988). *Dimensions of thinking: A framework for curriculum and instruction.* Alexandria, VA: Association for Supervision and Curriculum Development.
Merton, R. K. (1938). Social structure and anomie. *American Sociological Review, 3,* 672-682.
Natriello, G. (1982). *Organizational evaluation systems and student disengagement in secondary schools: Executive summary* (ED 236-066). Washington, DC: National Institute of Education.
Sinclair, R. L., & Ghory, W. J. (1987). *Reaching marginal students: A primary concern for school renewal.* Berkeley, CA: McCutchan.

• 4 •

The Dropout Issue and School Reform

RAY GARCIA
JUDITH WALKER DE FELIX

Since the release of the 1983 National Commission on Excellence in Education's report *A Nation at Risk,* many educators and community members have begun looking at the school dropout and the potential school dropout or student at risk in a somewhat different context. The report described "alarming conditions" of the educational system in the United States. The negative implications outlined in the report led to the development of reactionary agendas on the part of school systems across the nation (Garcia, 1989).

Perhaps due to the economic implications that the dropout syndrome has for the various groups in our society, few issues in U.S. education have generated more public debate or greater activity than the dropout problem. Moved by the report's compelling arguments, the U.S. Congress proposed dropout prevention legislation that authorized federal funds to assist dropout-plagued school districts in meeting the challenge of the dropout dilemma. Dropout prevention efforts have been sailing through state legislatures. The private sector, while devoting energy and resources to keeping adolescents in school until graduation, is focusing its efforts on developing partnerships with the educational establishment to combat the dropout problem (Office of Educational Research and Improvement [OERI], 1987).

This chapter will investigate the status of the national dropout situation through a traditional examination of (a) the magnitude of the dropout problem, (b) the at-risk student population, (c) the complex problems confronting potential dropouts, and (d) approaches to working with at-risk students. Finally, we discuss how these usual views of the dropout syndrome may need to be altered if real reform is to take place.

Scope of the Problem

The magnitude of the dropout problem is difficult to calculate because national statistics, studies, and approaches dealing with dropouts lack standardization. The pool of national data on dropouts is derived from three major sources: the Census Bureau, the U.S. Department of Education's National Center for Education Statistics, and the High School and Beyond Study. Caution is needed when interpreting data from these three primary sources because all three sources use different definitions in attempting to describe a school dropout. These sources calculate national dropout rates ranging from 14% to 28%. Because data collection on dropouts is poor and not standardized, members of the Institute of Educational Leadership argue that it is difficult for educators and policymakers to get a true picture of the scope and nature of the problem nationally (Freeland, 1986).

The High School and Beyond (HS&B) data provide an intriguing estimate of the dropout rate. HS&B was a longitudinal study of students who were sophomores and seniors in 1980. Its base-year survey involved more than 30,000 sophomores and 28,000 seniors from 1,015 high schools throughout the country. It was estimated that about 14% of 1980 sophomores dropped out of school before graduation. Because some students may have abandoned school before they became sophomores, however, it is very likely that the overall dropout rate was underestimated (Peng, 1985).

Although the term *at risk* has become voguish and has been applied in a variety of different ways (DeLone, 1985), concern for the potential dropout can be traced back to the early 1900s. Wehlage, Rutter, Smith, Lesko, and Fernandez (1989) cite two historical cases dealing with youth now labeled "at risk." The researchers note the work of Ayres, which included a 1909 investigation of the problem of nonpromotion and dropouts in the elementary schools. This early study focused on the reasons dropouts abandoned school prematurely and investigated the holding power of schools. The researchers also profile the work of Kliebard, which provided an account of a 1913 study of 500 children working in a factory and their attitudes toward school. Of the 500 youngsters polled, 412 told an investigator that they preferred factory labor to the humiliation and cruelty they encountered in school.

Catterall (1985) argues that a historical profile of school dropouts casts some confusion on what educators should think about the U.S. record for high school completion. There is a consensus among national studies on dropouts that approximately 25% of all youth abandon school prior to graduation (e.g., Peng, 1985). When viewed from a historical perspective, however, the 75% completion rate is high. Approximately 90% of all males did not receive a high school diploma in the 1900s (records were not reported for female students). Around the 1920s, the noncompletion rate remained stagnant at about 80%. This trend seemed to shift in the 1950s, when the noncompletion rate fell below 50%. A stabilizing period occurred during the 1960s, when the graduation rate remained at the current 75% (Wehlage et al., 1989). School completion-rate increases grew steadily from the turn of the century and then stalled at current levels around 1970. Catterall (1985) offers one rationale for this stall, suggesting that as a nation we have reached natural limits in what we can do to attract large numbers to formal schooling. As an alternative view, Catterall suggests that the current dropout rates reflect underdevelopment of our human resources and that ultimately society suffers tangible losses because many young adults are lacking essential basic skills. This is particularly important for educators because inner-city public schools show consistently larger dropout rates, some quoting alarming rates of 50% or higher (U.S. General Accounting Office [USGAO], 1986).

Using another analysis of school dropouts, Wehlage et al. (1989) argue that research has created a rather one-sided view of dropouts. These scholars assert that much of the current research focuses on the characteristics of students, along with their families and cultural backgrounds, as being responsible for their abandoning school prematurely. In their analysis of the school dropout, these researchers allude to a vacuum in the research literature that describes how policies and practices of school systems contribute to the dropout problem.

Another problem with our knowledge base of school attrition is that many of the studies on dropouts in the United States were conducted on the assumption that young people who become dropouts leave school between the ninth and eleventh grades. Not all potential dropouts, however, reached the ninth grade. The Texas School Dropout Project concluded that, in 1980, three out of ten Texas dropouts—152,000 young people—had completed fewer than nine years of schooling when they ultimately dropped out; 27,000 had completed less than five years of formal schooling (Intercultural Development Research Association [IDRA], 1986).

In a 1986 overview of the dropout problem, the Congressional Research Service (CRS) pointed out that there was no single reliable measure of the national dropout rate. The CRS also noted that the use of different definitions and procedures to count the number of dropouts made useful data difficult to obtain (Lyke, 1986). Again, caution should be exercised when interpreting estimates on dropout rates in the nation's schools. Because the nation lacks a standardized definition of what constitutes a dropout, comparisons should be made within this context. No doubt, the lack of a standard definition exacerbates the complexity of the dropout situation. There are said to be at least as many different definitions of a dropout as there are school districts recording dropouts.

School systems also differ in the procedures they use to calculate dropout rates. For example, some school districts count as dropouts students who have moved to other areas and enrolled in other schools; some exclude private school enrollments; others count youth as in school who have transferred to night school and later dropped out. Other school districts look at the number of youth who entered the fifth grade, compare it with the number graduating eight years later, and derive some form of an attrition rate. School district administrative offices many times lose track of the students who leave the school or geographic area or have incomplete information on many students. For this reason, school district data must be analyzed with caution (USGAO, 1986).

Researchers argue that, to begin providing effective instructional services to this population of youngsters, a standard definition is warranted. One problem with discovering ways of alleviating the dropout problem is simply figuring out how many dropouts there are. Others assert that in reality there can be no single definition of an at-risk student because the definition must vary from community to community and from school to school. The basis of a definition, as well as the basis of a school's program for identifying students at risk, then becomes a list of the characteristics of the potential dropout (Brodinsky & Keough, 1989).

Even though there is variance in estimations of dropout rates, the consensus is that the nation's youth dropout rate has progressively become a major educational and societal problem. The implications the dropout problem poses to society are alluded to in much of the literature dealing with this issue. As our technological society has come to require greater skill and knowledge, employment and economic opportunities for youth dropouts have become scarce. Training and production costs in business and industry have seen a consistently increasing trend as industry has become dependent upon a poorly prepared work force to fill entry-level positions. Compounding the problem are the social costs for supporting unemployment benefits for the many who cannot maintain employment. As a result, the projected costs for youth dropouts' lack of educational preparation are enormous, both for the dropouts themselves and for U.S. society at large (OERI, 1987).

Much of the literature on dropouts relates dropping out to increased crime, lower wages, higher unemployment, and diminished life satisfaction. Either directly or indirectly, society is said to suffer in lost economic productivity, a diminished tax base, greater vulnerability to foreign competition, and greater general dissatisfaction in the population (Ramirez & Robledo, 1987).

Advocates of the dropout prevention movement argue that schools must make early intervention a strong priority. Finding a solution to the dropout problem should be a joint venture between the academic arena and society as a whole. After all, society pays directly through the costs of its judicial and correctional system and indirectly in the loss of contributions the individual could have made to the overall society (Ramirez & Robledo, 1987).

The economic productivity lost through the failure of youngsters to finish high school provides another indication of the severity of the dropout problem. At the national level, the cost shown exceeds $200,000 per individual dropout and $200 billion for each school class across the United States. Even if the estimates were reduced by a factor of 10 by adopting extremely pessimistic views of labor markets for young adults or because the time preferences vastly undercut the importance of future earnings, the losses to society remain troublesome: $26,000 or so per dropout and over $20 billion per school class cohort (Catterall, 1985). Although the true economic costs of dropping out are difficult to estimate, Levin and Bachman (1972) 20 years ago projected $71 billion of lost tax revenue from high school dropouts aged 25-34 and welfare and unemployment costs of $3 billion. If current trends continue, business leaders say, the scarcity of well-educated and well-qualified people in the work force will seriously damage this country's competitive position in an increasingly challenging global marketplace (Committee for Economic Development, 1987).

Widespread and varied responses to dropout problems have been triggered by heightened public attention to what is called a crisis in education. These responses range from collaborations between businesses and schools for new program efforts, to targeted state funding and programs, to wholesale changes in a school district's delivery of education services for potential dropouts or students they label at risk. The dropout problem is considered by business and political leaders to be one of the biggest current issues facing the U.S. educational system (OERI, 1987).

Profile of the At-Risk Student Population

With the difficulty of determining the magnitude of the dropout problem comes an equally if not greater difficulty in developing a realistic perception of a profile of our national at-risk student population. Most national surveys provide education progress information from samples of the youth population. Numerous national surveys cited in the research literature provide representative estimates of the extent of the dropout problem among various subgroups. A common element in this pool of research reflects that the nation's at-risk population is disproportionately overrepresented by poor minority students.

Data from High School and Beyond provides a breakdown of dropout rates among minority groups: 13% of the White youth, 17% of the Black youth, and 19% of the Hispanic youth dropped out. Among the Hispanics, the dropout rate for Puerto Ricans in the United States was somewhat higher than for youth of Mexican or Cuban descent (USGAO, 1986).

Similar demographic profiles of dropout rates among ethnic groups are highlighted in the research literature. The Current Population Survey (CPS) data indicate that, in October 1985, there were about 4.3 million dropouts aged 16-24, of whom about 3.5 million were White, about 700,000 were Black, and about 100,000 were other races. The CPS defined school dropouts as persons who neither were enrolled in school nor were high school graduates (USGAO, 1986).

Freeland (1986) reports that estimates from national research on dropout rates range as high as 85% for urban Native Americans and 70%-80% for Puerto Ricans. Blacks abandon school at rates 40% higher than Whites, and Hispanics at rates 50% higher than Whites. In New York City, for example, about 80% of Hispanics leave school. The researcher contends that states with the highest dropout rates tend to be those in the Southeast and West— which generally have high minority populations, fewer English speakers, and more concentrated populations. The lowest dropout rates are in the Midwest, which comprises rural, homogeneous, and older populations.

The High School and Beyond data validate similar profiles. Dropout rates for White youth were higher in the southern and western regions of the United States than in the northeast or north-central regions. Dropout rates were higher in the latter regions for Blacks, however. Among Hispanics, regional differences were small. For each race/ethnic group, the HS&B data indicate that dropout rates were higher in cities than in suburbs and rural areas (USGAO, 1986).

In further validating the racial/ethnic differences, the National Commission on Secondary Education for Hispanics estimated that 45% of the Hispanic high school students in the United States drop out before graduating. This figure constituted more than double the rate for Blacks and three times the rate for Whites. And 40% of Hispanic students never reach tenth grade. Some studies also show that American Indians and Alaskan Natives have very high dropout rates (Peng, 1985). In light of the ethnic profile of dropouts, meeting the educational needs of minority students will no doubt cost money, but it will cost a lot more if they drop out of school (Hill, 1989).

Studies also indicate that dropping out is not evenly distributed economically. In 1979, the dropout rate for 14- to 21-year-olds was 10% among Whites, 15% among Blacks, and 23% among Hispanics (Rumberger, 1981). The lower dropout rate for Whites can be explained entirely by their higher income. In fact, in White families with incomes under $10,000 in 1977, the percentage of 14- and 17-year-olds who were not enrolled in school was nearly twice as high as in Black families (DeLone, 1979). HS&B data also show that the dropout rate for youth from households with low-income, low-skill wage earners and limited educational backgrounds was about three times the rate of those from the highest end of the socioeconomic scale—22% versus 7% (USGAO, 1986).

Although the estimates may vary, they are indicative of the fact that the dropout phenomenon is widespread. Granted that many of these students may eventually return to school, a substantial percentage of a given cohort—more than one out of ten persons—did not receive a high school diploma or its equivalent (Peng, 1985).

Types of At-Risk Students

Just as the issues plaguing at-risk youth are varied and complex, so too are the types of students who compose this population of youngsters. Much of the focus of the research directed at the at-risk population has centered on the negative outcomes resulting from behaviors such as poor grades, truancy, and suicide (Capuzzi & Gross, 1989). A precise typology of early school leavers has not been developed. It is clear, however, that different students leave school under different circumstances and for varied reasons, even for students within the same school (Bickel, Bond, & LeMahieu, 1988).

Ogden and Germinario (1988) suggest that many at-risk youngsters are deficient in the necessary life skills and familial support structures to help them succeed academically. These problems manifest themselves in low self-esteem, poor problem-solving skills, low achievement, high absenteeism, and dysfunctional behavior, among others.

Capuzzi and Gross (1989, p. 367) outline a description of the potential dropout:

> Who are these students? There is no set pattern. Some are brilliant but bored; others have low ability and are undersupported or deterred by their home situation. Some are emotionally troubled, abused, on drugs, or prematurely pregnant; some are male, some are female; some are wealthy but most are poor. Some come from Bill Cosby's TV family, some from my family or your family. And some have no family at all—at 12 years of age or even earlier, they are on the streets, alone.

Other researchers point out that the term *dropout* itself is potentially misleading because it implies a single decision point to leave school, with the student as the sole decision maker. Such is not always the case. Some students merely "fade out" after a period of feeling alienated from school. Others can be subtly or not so subtly "pushed out" by school personnel who do not want to deal with them any longer. Still others are "pulled out" by more important demands on their time such as parenting or supporting elderly family members or by negative community influences such as gangs (Bickel, Bond, & LeMahieu, 1988).

Jones (1988) argues that the educational reform movements have basically ignored the diverse needs of two types of at-risk students: (a) disconnected youth who are alienated from economic and educational opportunities and (b) marginal, at-risk youth who are semiskilled but who cannot read, write, or succeed in the problem-solving skills required in current school practices.

The at-risk problem is further exacerbated by the changing student population. The major demographic change that will challenge tomorrow's schools (Kaufman, 1987) lies in the evolving makeup of the school population compounded by educators' lack of preparation for dealing with this population change.

With the diversity in the types of at-risk students comes a variety of problems researchers have isolated as plaguing this population of youngsters. For example, Cunningham, Putzstuck, and Barberi (n.d.) outline three broad dimensions of the diverse needs of at-risk youth. These researchers classify the problems of at-risk students into educational, cultural, and social domains. Among the educational problems facing potential dropouts include deficiencies in basic skills, lack of study skills, alienation/isolation within the school, and inability to learn from traditional instructional methods. Under the cultural problems of the would-be dropouts, the writers profile poverty, lack of parental support and understanding, need to contribute to family finances, and adolescent parenthood as the most prevalent issues haunting this population of pupils. Identified under the social problems of at-risk students, the researchers describe such characteristic needs as poor problem-solving skills, lack of interpersonal skills, negative self-concept, and peer pressure and conformity.

Hurdles Confronting At-Risk Youth

The education reform movement that has occurred in many states highlights another dimension of the dropout problem. Many state legislatures have attempted to upgrade their educational systems by increasing the academic standards for their school-age population. The emphasis on higher standards for students has adversely affected at-risk students, many of whom did not meet the previous minimum standards. This could be attributed to the fact that most of the reform initiatives contain very few provisions to help these students meet the newly legislated standards (Levin, 1985; Palaich & Mosqueda, 1987).

Research on the impact of higher achievement standards on potential dropouts is mixed. Natriello and Dornbusch (1984) found that students in classrooms with very low standards were more likely to cut class than students in classrooms with more demanding standards. The researchers also noted that a higher demand level in the classroom was found to be associated with greater student effort even when the students' ability level was controlled. A high percentage of students in the low-demand classrooms reported that they felt the teacher should make them work harder.

The Committee for Economic Development (1987) called for broad-scale prevention efforts for at-risk children in light of the education reform movements. They claimed that 30% of U.S. children who are at risk educationally have been largely bypassed by the education reform movement of the past five years. Nationwide, the committee estimates that 1 million young people will continue to drop out each year and up to 700,000 will graduate lacking the skills to qualify for productive employment or higher education if schools impose higher standards without providing the special help needed to meet those standards.

One example is the State of Texas, where the increased academic standards and their impact on the state's at-risk population has caused concern. In 1983, the passage of House Bill 72—with its provisions for mandatory retaining of students at grade level, mandatory test scores on standardized tests, increased homework for students who cannot do it and have no one at home to assist, and no-pass-no-play (sports) provisions—has had an adverse effect on the number of school dropouts. It is estimated that the percentage of students dropping out of school has increased by 10% each year following the implementation of HB 72 (IDRA, 1986).

In Texas, San Antonio Independent School District is one example of this trend. A summary of their ongoing dropout identification and prevention program suggests that the state's public education reform efforts may be prompting students to drop out of school. The adverse effect of the sweeping educational reforms under HB 72 and Chapter 75 (which specified the curriculum) was highlighted following several public hearings held by a district dropout prevention task force. The increased and inflexible demands brought about by the two education reform bills were perceived as having an adverse effect on students who were at risk of not completing high school (Staff, 1987).

There are, then, dual effects of raising achievement standards: Sometimes they challenge students, and sometimes they frustrate them. If academic standards are raised and students are not provided substantial remediation within the limited time they can devote to school tasks, socially and academically disadvantaged students will be more likely to experience frustration and failure, which can result in notable increases in dropping out (Natriello, McDill, & Pallas, 1985).

The growth and scope of state initiatives for increasing academic standards lend support to earlier predictions that programs for at-risk children would constitute a "third wave" of education reform. The increased attention is a by-product, some experts have said, of the educational excellence movement's tendency to push the students most in need of an education out of the classroom (Viadero, 1988).

Approaches to Working With At-Risk Youth

Regardless of the fluctuating dropout rates profiled by a historical sketch, most researchers agree that today's rates may be attributed to outdated school practices and the diminishing holding power of schools for an increasingly diverse student population. Unchanging school conditions seem to be a major contributing factor in a student's decision to leave school. Success in school generally depends on reading and writing skills in which the at-risk students are weak. When school districts survey potential dropouts about early abandonment of school, common responses include the following: "Textbooks are too hard to understand"; "I have trouble writing reports"; and "I have to take subjects I don't like" (Brodinsky & Keough, 1989). Indeed, there are students who are thrown, pushed, or shamed out of the educational system by school policies that keep some youngsters in the ninth grade for as long as three years (Presseisen, 1988).

Research indicates that the problems confronting at-risk youth are so diverse and so complex that single approaches to tackling this problem have experienced little success. An Office of Educational Research and Improvement (OERI) report profiled a compelling recommendation by the Urban Superintendent's Network that no single, magical formula exists to hold potential dropouts in school or to attract those who have already left back to school. Because students leave school for a variety of reasons, educational programs must be comprehensive, tailored to meet individual needs and address the multiple factors that cause students to drop out (OERI, 1987).

Similarly, Bailin (1985) argues that no single intervention will provide the entire answer in addressing the problems of educationally disadvantaged or at-risk students. He outlines three broad approaches to working with at-risk youth inclusive of institutional strategies, programmatic strategies, and instructional strategies.

In advocating multifaceted approaches to dealing with the dropout problem, Brodinsky and Keough (1989, p. 44) make the following point:

Since there is no one definition of "at-risk," there is no one solution. The schools that have been most successful are generally those that attack the problem on a holistic basis. They see it as a problem that begins before the child enters kindergarten and then increasingly manifests itself as the child advances (or fails to advance) through school. Therefore, successful strategies attack the problem at many levels.

Hodgkinson (1985) identified promising programs for keeping students with diverse characteristics in school. He advocates "intensive, individualized training in basic skills" and work-related projects. Orr (1987) asserts that, until recently, three general approaches to serving potential dropouts existed: compensatory education, alternative education, and employment and training programs.

Similarly, Ogden and Germinario (1988, p. 26) advocate a team approach to teaching at-risk students.

> A student assistance team composed of an administrator, school nurse and several teachers can be established. Annually, all teachers can assess the students in their class in terms of learning-distractive behavior. The individual teacher can use the information to focus on the children currently enrolled in his/her class. The student assistance team can look for patterns of behavior or high-risk situations which may interfere with a child's ability to reach his/her potential.

In a national survey, Isenhart and Bechard (1987) identified 190 programs directly related to dropout prevention. Using a combination of research and practical experience to design their programs, 46 states had addressed the issue of dropout prevention. Ten strategies appear most frequently in the research literature: definition and identification, networks, academic support, special curricula, incentives and rewards, counseling, school policy changes, alternative school, restructuring, and comprehensive state plans. Most promising plans have been initiated only in the past few years, hence there is little evidence available on the effectiveness of these efforts (Ogden & Germinario, 1988).

There is a tendency to view the dropout problem as belonging to secondary schools primarily because a large percentage of dropouts do so in high school. This view, however, is changing as elementary prevention programs are beginning to show signs of success (OERI, 1987). While measures to deal with the dropout problem must occur at all grade levels in schools, preventive programs at the elementary level appear to have the most promise in the long run (Southwest Education Development Laboratory, 1987).

Intervention in secondary schools may be too late to deal effectively with the dropouts because the factors that lead to their dropping out are already established ("Researchers Find Early Indicators," 1987). Indeed, researchers suggest early prevention programs at the elementary level to increase the early academic performance of at-risk children. DeLone (1985) identified a number of factors that are important at all levels of schooling. Early childhood education, time on task, parent involvement, and effective school leadership seem to pay off. Reynold's (1989) more recent research using sophisticated statistical models points specifically to early school practices, particularly grade retention, as having the most significant impact on later academic failure.

Dropout prevention research indicates that the dropout situation, as it is currently defined, is an extremely complex societal issue and not just an educational problem. Schools, however, continue to be the primary focus of responsibility for finding solutions to this complicated problem. Clearly one of the greatest challenges posed to educators in the United States is the development of a multitiered approach to integrating dropout prevention programs into school systems (Garcia, 1989).

Discussion

The year 1987 was one of hope. It was called "The Year of the Dropout," and several studies of dropouts appeared, including the book *Dropouts in America: Enough is known for action*. In it, Hahn, Danzberger, and Lefkowitz provide clear descriptions of the problems facing the schools and of programs that have helped students succeed academically. Why then does the dropout issue persist?

There appear to be several reasons. First, as discussed previously, there are many diverse definitions of dropouts and little data on them. With all the funds in research program development to assist with the dropout syndrome, it is inexcusable that there is no one definition. The at-risk label, as distasteful as it is, persists because of its wide acceptance and research base. It is time for agreement on how school districts should define their school leavers. We would propose the definition adopted by the Current Population Survey

(CPS) because it is all inclusive. If a person is neither enrolled in school nor a high school graduate, he or she is considered a dropout.

Similarly, there is no excuse for the lack of long-term school records in today's computerized society. As Hahn (1987, p. 256) noted, "Most social initiatives build on a foundation of accurate, verifiable data." Dropout prevention program implementation, however, is lacking much of the essential data. To Hahn, the national statistics reported previously are of little use to educators who want to implement effective local programs. It is on the local level that the records are missing or inaccurate. Graphic examples of this were reported by Phelan (1987), Williams (1986), and Valverde (1986). All these scholars documented that students got "lost" in their own schools. School records in these studies were so mismanaged that students were not able to graduate and/or school officials were unable to locate students.

A second, related reason the dropout syndrome continues is that educators have done little to respond to the realities of dropouts. The greatest predictors of dropping out continue to be the lack of school achievement and its related variables (e.g., being overage, repeating a grade; Reynolds, 1989). Students living in poverty are much more likely to drop out. While there is little school personnel can do to address socioeconomic realities of students, it is the relation between SES and students' academic record that educators can—and should—resolve.

There are numerous studies of effective school programs that have stimulated early academic success among students normally considered at risk of dropping out. Levin's (1988) Accelerated Schools Projects have demonstrated that individual schools can respond to the particular needs of their own students by incorporating strategies known to be effective. Slavin, Leighton, and Yampolsky's (1991) research on Mastery for All report successful techniques for assuring early success. Ramirez (1991) reported on successful programs for Chicano/Latino limited-English-proficient children. Children in those schools that developed the Spanish language throughout the elementary school had significantly higher academic growth profiles than those in schools that forced students into English faster.

By focusing on at-risk students rather than on effective practices, school districts have often avoided their responsibility. Cuban (1990) helps to explain how this happens. First, he provides evidence that the dominant groups in society that set directions for major social policies tend to focus on school change rather than on the deep ills that affect society. Because schools change slowly, no grave economic, social, or political upheavals will occur, thus preserving the elite classes' dominance. His review of recurrent school reform suggests that, while institutional change must be packaged in such a way as to reinforce things as they are, schools and practitioners can effect change. It is in each classroom that teachers, isolated from their supervisors and colleagues, can respond to individual student needs, ignore children, or brutally abuse them. Cuban believes that calls for school reform will continue until the reforms make it into the classroom.

Passow's (1984) analysis of the current reform movement is less optimistic. Passow characterizes *A Nation at Risk* as a major media event. He notes that U.S. education, as portrayed by the media, has been in a "crisis" since at least the 1930s. Passow notes that the reforms of the 1970s seemed to be based on a high school population that was White, middle class, male, and suburban. He continues, "The reports of the Eighties, even more than the earlier ones, fail to attend to the particular problems and needs of schools with large populations of poor and minority children" (Passow, 1984, p. 680). Because "reforms" may move more quickly now that the current political climate has supported the reports' calls for "radical reform," we should be cautious of those changes.

Hlebowitsh (1989, p. 57) also warns thoughtful educators about the current reform climate:

> There has always been a kind of 'knee-jerk' reaction to change when powerful nationalistic forces creep into educational dialog. These forces can cause the school to exercise change on a quantitative and narrowly conceived level. In this way, influential participants can show they have gotten serious without really getting serious at all.

We have attempted here to present a picture of the dropout "crisis" as defined in the major reform reports as well as in research reports. It is clear that much of the rhetoric has little to do with a concern for the changing school population. Blaming the victims and their families continues with the at-risk label and definition of about 25% of the student population as a problem.

As Passow (1984, p. 683) concludes, "Reforming schools, however, is very different from reforming society. Yet both must occur simultaneously if real reform of the education system is to take place." Hahn (1987) is right: Educators do know how to prevent dropouts. A first step appears to be to develop equitable programs to assure academic achievement for all children.

References

Bailin, M. A. (1985). Preface. In H. M. Levin (Ed.), *The educationally disadvantaged: A national crisis* (Working Paper No. 6). Philadelphia: State Youth Initiatives Project, Public/Private Ventures Corp.

Bickel, W. E., Bond, L., & LeMahieu, P. G. (1988). *Students at risk of not completing high school.* Unpublished report, University of Pittsburgh.

Brodinsky, B., & Keough, K. E. (1989). *Students at risk: Problems and solutions.* Arlington, VA: American Association of School Administrators.

Capuzzi, D., & Gross, D. R. (1989). *Youth at risk: A resource for counselors, teachers and parents.* Alexandria, VA: American Association for Counseling and Development.

Catterall, J. S. (1985). *On the social costs of dropping out of school* (Report No. 86-SEPI-3). Stanford, CA: Stanford University, Center for Educational Research.

Committee for Economic Development. (1987). *Children in need: Investment strategies for the educationally disadvantaged.* New York: Research and Policy Committee.

Cuban, L. (1990). Reforming again, again, and again. *Educational Researcher, 19*(1), 3-13.

Cunningham, D., Putzstuck, C., & Barberi, M. (n.d.). *Working together to support at-risk youth.* Denton: North Texas State University.

DeLone, R. H. (1979). *Carnegie Council on children, inequity, and limits of liberal reform.* New York: Harcourt Brace Jovanovich.

DeLone, R. H. (1985). *Education, employment, and the at-risk youth.* Philadelphia: Research for Better Schools.

Freeland, S. (1986, January 6). Dropouts: Who and why? *Education USA*, p. 139-141.

Garcia, R. (1989). *Implementation of the alternatives to social promotion program in Texas.* Unpublished doctoral dissertation, University of Houston.

Hahn, A. (1987). Reaching out to America's dropouts: What to do? *Phi Delta Kappan, 69*(4), 256-263.

Hahn, A., Danzberger, J., & Lefkowitz, B. (1987). *Dropouts in America: Enough is known for action.* Washington, DC: Institute for Educational Leadership.

Hill, H. D. (1989). *Effective strategies for teaching minority students.* Bloomington, IN: National Educational Service.

Hlebowitsh, P. S. (1989, December/January). International school comparisons and the linkage to school reform. *The High School Journal*, 54-59.

Hodgkinson, H. (1985). *All one system: Demographics of education, kindergarten through graduate school.* Washington, DC: Institute for Educational Leadership.

Intercultural Development Research Association (IDRA). (1986, October). Texas school dropout survey project: A summary of findings. San Antonio, TX: Author. (Available from the Intercultural Development Research Association, 5835 Callaghan Road, Suite 350, San Antonio, TX)

Isenhart, L., & Bechard, S. (1987). *Dropout prevention* (Publication No. AR-87-S1). Denver, CO: Education Commission of the States Survey of State Initiatives for Youth at Risk.

Jones, B. F. (1988). Toward redefining models of curriculum and instruction for students at-risk. In B. Z. Presseisen (Ed.), *At-risk students and thinking: Perspectives from research.* Washington, DC: National Education Association.

Kaufman, P. (1987). Trends in elementary and secondary public school enrollment. In J. D. Stern & M. F. Williams (Eds.), *The condition of education.* Washington, DC: Government Printing Office.

Levin, H. M. (1985). *The educationally disadvantaged: A national crisis* (Working Paper No. 6). Philadelphia: State Youth Initiatives Project, Public/Private Ventures Corp.

Levin, H. M. (1988). *Accelerated schools for at-risk students.* News Brunswick, NJ: Center for Policy Research in Education.

Levin, H. M., & Bachman, J. G. (1972). *The effects of dropping out* (U.S. Congress, Senate Select Committee on Equal Educational Opportunity). Washington, DC: Government Printing Office.

Lyke, B. (1986). *High school dropouts* (Issue Brief IB86003). Washington, DC: Library of Congress, Congressional Research Service.

Mann, D. (1986). Can we help dropouts: Thinking about the undoable. *Teachers College Record, 87*(3), 307-323.

National Commission on Excellence in Education. (1983). *A nation at risk.* Washington, DC: Government Printing Office.

Natriello, G., & Dornbusch, S. M. (1984). *Teacher evaluative standards and student efforts.* New York: Longman.

Natriello, G., McDill, E. L., & Pallas, A. M. (1985). School dropouts and potential dropouts. *Educational Leadership, 90.*

Office of Educational Research and Improvement (OERI). (1987). *Dealing with dropouts: The urban superintendents' call for action* (Publication No. 208-912-814/80194). Washington, DC: Government Printing Office.

Ogden, E. H., & Germinario, V. (1988). *The at-risk student.* Lancaster, PA: Technomic.

Orr, M. T. (1987). *Keeping students in school.* San Francisco: Jossey-Bass.

Palaich, R. M., & Mosqueda, P. F. (1987, January). *Review of youth at-risk characteristics.* Paper presented at the meeting of the National Program for Personal Excellence.

Passow, A. H. (1984). Tackling the reform reports of the 1980s. *Phi Delta Kappan, 65* pp. 674-683.

Peng, S. S. (1985). *High school dropouts: A national concern.* Washington, DC: U.S. Department of Education, National Center for Education Statistics.

Phelan, W. T. (1987). Obstacles to high school graduation: The real dropout problem. *Journal of Educational Equity and Leadership, 7*(3), 223-234.

Presseisen, B. Z. (1988). Teaching thinking and at-risk students: Defining a population. In B. Z. Presseisen (Ed.), *At-risk students and thinking: Perspectives from research* (pp. 19-37). Washington, DC: National Education Association and Research for Better Schools.

Ramirez, D., & Robledo, M. R. (1987, April). The economic impact of the dropout problem. *Intercultural Development Research Association Newsletter,* 1-3.

Ramirez, J. D. (1991). *Longitudinal growth in the academic achievement of limited-English-speaking students.* Paper presented at the American Educational Research Association, Chicago.

Researchers find early indicators of students likely to drop out. (1987, August). *Houston Chronicle,* p. 17.

Reynolds, A. (1989). A structural model of first grade outcomes for an urban, low socioeconomic status, minority population. *Journal of Educational Psychology, 81,* 594-603.

Rodriguez, E., & Anderson, S. (1987). *Statewide task forces and commissions* (Publication No. AR-87-S2, 11/87). Denver, CO: Education Commission of the States, Survey of State Initiatives for Youth at Risk.

Rumberger, R. W. (1981, April). *Why kids dropout of school.* Paper presented at the annual meeting of the American Educational Research Association, Los Angeles.

Slavin, R., Leighton, M., & Yampolsky, R. (1991). *Success for All and the language minority student.* Paper presented at the American Educational Research Association, Chicago.

Southwest Education Development Laboratory. (1987). *Parent-involvement update.* Austin, TX: Author.

Staff. (1986, January). Dropouts: Who and why. *Education USA* (National School Public Relations Association Newsletter).

Staff. (1987, August). Hispanic-related dropout studies released. *Texas Education News.*

Staff. (1988, January). Special joint interim committee addressed. *Intercultural Development Research Association Newsletter.*

U.S. General Accounting Office (USGAO). (1986). *School dropouts: The extent and nature of the problem* (GAO/HRD-86-106BR; Briefing Report to Congressional requesters). Washington, DC: Author.

Valverde, S. (1986). *Comparative study of Hispanic LEP and non-LEP high school graduates in an urban public school.* Unpublished doctoral dissertation, University of Houston.

Viadero, D. (1988, January). Study finds "at risk" efforts hindered. *Education Week*, 8.

Wehlage, G. G., Rutter, R. A., Smith, G. A., Lesko, N., & Fernandez, R. R. (1989). *Reducing the risk: Schools as communities of support.* Philadelphia: Falmer.

Williams, S. (1986). *Comparative study of Black dropouts and Black high school graduates in an urban school system.* Unpublished doctoral dissertation, University of Houston.

PART II

Issues Confronting At-Risk Students

JUDITH WALKER DE FELIX, EDITOR

School districts and social scientists designate children "at risk" if they are different than the mainstream students a generation ago. This norm has protected many schools from having to change to meet the new demographic realities. The textbooks, curriculum guides, classroom management practices, and school rules have changed little in spite of dramatic increases in minority-culture student bodies. The many calls for school reform have helped consolidate the notion that one norm for all students is not only acceptable but laudable.

School reformers have tended to highlight the so-called basic skills. For example, the President's Educational Plan calls for a national standardized test, a test that will no doubt focus on facts rather than on problem solving. The rationale for many of the calls for national tests appears to be competition with other countries. The United States may rank low in science test scores, behind less wealthy and powerful countries. A national test could compare school districts around the country to see where students were learning the most (and, obviously, the least).

Similarly, media reporters bombard students with geography, science, and history "tests." In one report on the sad state of U.S. schools, one "education reporter" asked the audience to differentiate between rust and oxidation. It seems to be a matter of national pride that students can spit out facts, as in spelling and geography bees.

Many educators have attempted to point out how short-sighted such pride can be. For example, science educators note that U.S. students do poorer on tests that require rote memorization than on tests that require problem solving. Unlike other countries, in the United States, students have laboratory equipment, math manipulatives, and computers for composition. Students can perform in a wide variety of problem-solving settings. Educators also note that the basic facts change: the capitals of the countries change, new forms of measurement appear, and so on. Students need less memorization of political boundaries and capitals and more understanding of why capital cities arise. They need to know less about how many quarts are in a gallon and more about how to measure various shapes, some of which are too tall to scale and measure directly. Children also need to learn to question what they read and see in the media. And, most of all in the Information Age, they need to know how to conduct research, how to think about "facts," and how to intuit answers to real problems.

At-risk children are different than mainstream children only because they come to schools with differences that schools have generally ignored. Academically, they are no different than mainstream children; they need all the intellectual skills that other children need. In addition, at-risk children usually have to cope with social situations that dominant-culture children and their teachers have never experienced.

Should schools prepare students to solve the problems of their everyday lives: economic deprivation, drug abuse, moving from school to school, or dealing with separated families? If so, how do we prepare them to solve real problems? How do we develop the academic skills that dominant-culture children have before entering school?

Vocal reformers seem to have simplistic answers. Some call for more homework. Yet, at-risk children frequently cannot do homework. Homeless children have no table; children in crowded and noisy homes have no quiet place; children with their own children or smaller siblings to care for have no time for homework. Other reformers call for extended school days. Hungry children, however, cannot pay attention throughout the current school day. Older children work after school to contribute to the family's finances.

Schooling reform needs to take into consideration the social realities of the children. For example, educational researchers have for years known the importance of the background experiences students bring with them to learning settings. Such experiences contribute to the students' cognitive and affective schemata. These experiences also color motivation and opportunities for academic learning. Educators should plan schooling experiences to build on home experiences. According to Cummins (1986), linking school with home experiences empowers students in the academic context.

In Part II, scholars discuss ways of bringing the students' reality into the classroom. The authors describe contextual realities that help put minority students at risk of failing at school. All of these authors underscore that many current schooling experiences, not the cultural or linguistic background experiences, are what put students at risk. These authors give several insights into the differences children bring to the school and ideas for matching schooling experiences with home experiences.

In Chapter 5, Eugene E. Garcia focuses on a group that has faced consistent poor schooling: Spanish-speaking students in the United States. In all definitions of at-risk populations, the following characteristics appear: low socioeconomic status, low parental educational attainment, and poor English skills. It is little wonder that the Chicano/Latino population needs educators' particular attention. No other group fulfills as many of the risk indicators as U.S. Hispanics. In addition, no other group is growing as fast.

Yet there have been numerous examples of so-called at-risk students succeeding in school. Garcia has been responsible for several studies of classroom practices that have been successful with Spanish-speaking children. Here he reviews his own and others' studies to provide a practical guide for practitioners and researchers.

The key ingredients in these programs include the inclusion of the children's home language and culture in the school experiences. One of the successful methods of incorporating the Hispanic culture has been the inclusion of more cooperative, socially meaningful activities.

Richard T. Johnson's chapter presents one method of including socially meaningful activities. He discusses the advantages of a specific context—interactive videodisc environments—for children labeled "at risk". Johnson uses the theoretical framework espoused by John Bransford and his colleagues at the Cognition and Technology Group at Vanderbilt University, that of situated cognition. To these scholars, the context not only provides support for comprehension, it also becomes part of the content that is learned. Videodiscs, with random access capability, can bring varied environments into the poorest classroom.

Technology, even though impressive, is not powerful by itself. Teachers not only need to mediate the acquisition of the content, they are also critical in the presentation of the material. They not only determine the context; they are also part of the context. Johnson discusses programs in which videodiscs were used to evoke problem solving. Many programs for "at-risk" children focus on remedial drill formats. Opportunities for learning higher-level thinking, however, are especially important for students that have economic, social, and personal problems to solve. Such settings also recall the effective classrooms described by Garcia because they are cooperative settings that are socially meaningful.

Olivia N. Saracho and Cynthia Koren Gerstl discuss cognitive style differences among African Americans, Hispanics (particularly Mexican Americans), Native Americans, and Asian Americans. These scholars have conducted a thorough review of the extant literature on these major groups. They caution, however, that such studies should be used to sensitize educators to individual differences and to individualize educational programs, not to stereotype and label children. They point out that within each large ethnic category are cultures of origin that affect the members of the group differentially.

Saracho and Gerstl's review can help educators understand more precisely the nature of individual *differences,* a term that is almost a cliché in schools. Unless they are educational psychologists, however, educators have few definitions of *difference*. In my experience, teachers new to multicultural populations look at external differences such as skin color and language rather than real differences in learning behaviors. Understanding the wide variety of ways students learn should lead to increasing variety in the ways teachers present lessons. This variety can make teaching more interesting to the teacher as well as making the lessons more appealing to the learners.

This part reminds educators that each student comes to school with incredibly complex, diverse background experiences and expectations. What minority children tend to find is a homogenizing institution. When individual differences are recognized and valued, educational programs can be effective. The best way to keep children in school is to assure their learning. The best way to prepare children for a satisfying life is to give them a wide repertoire of techniques for lifelong learning.

U.S. schools have failed too many children over the generations, partly out of ignorance. As these chapters show, we now know a great deal about how to help all children learn. As these scholars also note, however, we need to extend the implementation of these ideas.

Reference

Cummins, J. (1986). Empowering minority students: A framework for intervention. *Harvard Educational Review,* 56(1), 18-36.

• 5 •

Linguistically and Culturally Diverse Children: Effective Instructional Practices and Related Policy Issues

EUGENE E. GARCIA

The United States continues in a trend of ethnic and racial population diversification, particularly among young and school-age children. Moreover, our next generation, in general, and ethnic and racial minority children, in particular, continue to be placed "at risk" in today's social institutions. The future lies in understanding how a diverse population, with many placed in contexts of risk and vulnerability, can achieve *social, educational,* and *employment* competence. Our vulnerable populations must succeed. In them reside the new ideas, energy, and resources for our society's future.

This portrait of vulnerability has been a historical reality for non-English-speaking children in the United States. Although *language minority* is a relatively new educational term, with little appreciation for the diversity among such identified populations, recent educational leaders, such as the former secretary of education, have concluded that such identified populations whose native language is not English and who reside in culturally diverse homes and communities have been perceived by the majority society as linguistically, cognitively, socially, and educationally inferior (Cavasos, 1990). Such a perception has led to a variety of school and educational programs aimed at ridding this population of these "inferior" characteristics (August & Garcia, 1988). Independent of such perceptions and programs, linguistically and culturally diverse populations continue to display a portrait of unrealized success.

Table 5.1 Hispanic Demographic Synthesis

1. **General Demographic Character**
    A. Of the 18.8 million Hispanics in the continental United States, the following characterizes the population's ethnic diversity:

Country/Area of Origin	Number	Percent
Mexico	11.8 million	62.8
Puerto Rico	2.3 million	12.2
Central/South America	2.1 million	11.2
Cuba	1.0 million	5.3
Other	1.6 million	8.5

    B. 82% of this Hispanic population is found in eight states: Arizona (3%), California (31%), Colorado (3%), Florida (6%), Illinois (4%), New Mexico (3%), New York (11%), and Texas (20%).
    C. Average age of this population is 25.1 years (compared with 32.6 years for the general population).
    D. 200,000 Hispanics immigrate legally to the United States yearly (40% of all legal immigrants). An estimated 200,000 Hispanics immigrate illegally.)
    E. The Hispanic population grew by 61% from 1970 to 1980 compared with an 11% growth in the general population.
    F. 11 million Hispanics report speaking Spanish in the home.
    G. 7% of Hispanics live in metropolitan areas; 50% in central cities.

II. **Education**
    A. 40% of Hispanics leave school prior to graduation (40% of these leaving do so by grade 10).
    B. 35% of Hispanics are held back at least one grade.
    C. 47% of Hispanics are overaged at grade 12.
    D. 85% of Hispanic students are in urban districts.
    E. 70% of Hispanic students attend segregated schools (up 56% in 1956).
    F. Hispanics are significantly below national norms on academic achievement tests or reading, math, science, social science, and writing at grades three, seven, and eleven, generally averaging one to two grade levels below the norm. At grade eleven, Hispanics average a grade eight achievement level on these tests.

For example, Table 5.1 summarizes current statistics relevant to the largest population in the United States that fits this category of linguistic and cultural diversity: Hispanics. This table focuses on general demographic indicators as well as on the specific educational characteristics of the population and specific social indices that mark this population as particularly vulnerable to

Table 5.1 Continued

III. Indices of "Vulnerability"

   A. Median family income has fluctuated for Hispanics (1972—$18,880; 1982—$16,227; 1986—$19,995), remaining below non-Hispanics (1972—$26,261; 1982—$23,907; 1986—$30,321).
   B. 29% of Hispanic families live below the poverty line, up from 21% in 1979. (10.2% of White families live below the poverty line.)
   C. 905,000 (23%) of Hispanic families are maintained by female heads of households (up from 17% in 1970); 53% of these households live below the poverty line.
   D. 50% of Hispanic women are in the labor force.
   E. Hispanics are twice as likely to be born to an unmarried, teen mother compared with Whites.
   F. 56% of Hispanics are functionally illiterate compared with 46% for Blacks and 16% for Whites.
   G. 65% of Hispanics hold unskilled and semiskilled jobs compared with 35% of non-Hispanics.

SOURCES: Data from U.S. Bureau of the Census (1984, 1987), American Association of Higher Education (1988), and Appleby, Langer, and Mullis (1988).

U.S. institutions. With regard to the educational situation, the picture painted by these statistics is deplorable: (a) a 40% nongraduation rate, (b) a 35% grade retention rate, (c) a two- to four-grade-level achievement gap, and (d) a school segregation circumstance of 70%, up from 56% in the 1950s. Figure 5.1, although specific to California, documents the dramatic growth of diversity within the school-age populations. By the year 2030, close to 70% of the California school-age population will be non-Anglo. If the goal of U.S. schooling is to advance the educational status of all its populations, then our educational goals are likely to fall significantly short for the majority population.

Recent research has redefined the nature of linguistically and culturally diverse students' vulnerability. It has destroyed both stereotypes and myths and laid a foundation upon which to reconceptualize current educational practices and launch new initiatives. This foundation recognizes the homogeneity/heterogeneity within and between linguistically and culturally diverse populations. It is worthwhile, however, to consider a set of intertwined commonalities that deserve particular attention, such as the bilingual/bicultural, socialization, and instructional circumstances of this population. The

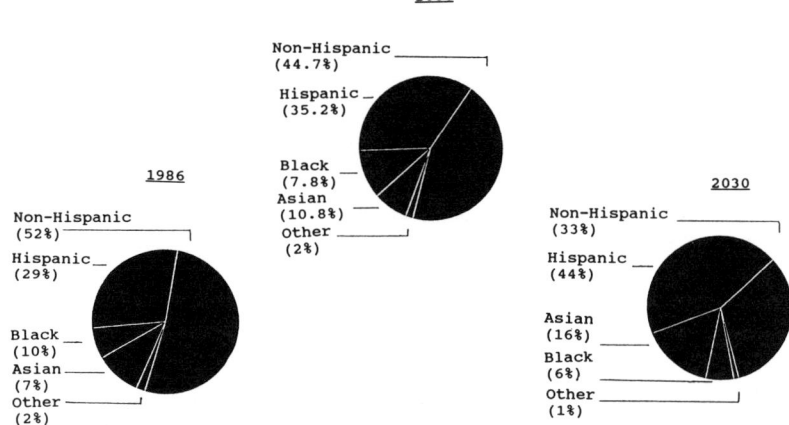

Figure 5.1. California's School Age Population by Race/Ethnicity

following discussion provides a brief overview of these new theoretical contributions with special attention to educational issues of relevance to the growing number of linguistically and culturally diverse children. Particular emphasis is placed on instructional practices that have been identified as "effective" and on how an instructionally responsive stance with regard to these populations can lead to a more productive educational future.

A Theoretical Framework

Before addressing the above questions directly, it seems appropriate to frame this discussion in a broad educationally relevant theoretical continuum. At one end of this continuum, it is argued that addressing a linguistically and culturally diverse population calls for a deeper understanding of the interaction of a students' home culture and the prevailing school culture (Tharp, 1989). This cultural difference position, supported by rich contributions of research, suggests that the educational failure of "diverse" student populations is related to the "culture clash" between home and school. Evidence for such a position comes from Boykin (1986) for African American students; Heath (1983) for poor White students; Weisner, Gallimore, and Jordan (1988) for Hawaiian students; Vogt, Jordan, and Tharp (1987) for

Navaho students; Garcia (1988) and Moll (1988) for Mexican American students; and Rivera-Medina (1984) and Rodriguez (1989) for Puerto Rican students. In essence, these researchers have suggested that lack of consideration for the distinction between home and school culture renders educational endeavors for these culturally distinct students likely to fail. Theoretically, students do not succeed because the difference between school culture and home culture leads to an educational dissonance. Sue and Padilla (1986, p. 62), directly enunciating this position, argue: "The challenge for educators is to identify critical differences between and within ethnic minority groups and to incorporate this information into classrooms practice."

On a large scale, the implementation of bilingual-bicultural education in the United States is an example of a widely implemented educational treatment in concert with this education position for Hispanic populations. This education intervention is based on the notion that using the student's home language coupled with cultural support in school will produce a positive academic effect (August & Garcia, 1988). Whether it does so has been the concern of an ongoing research debate during the last decade (Baker, 1990; Willig, 1987).

At the other extreme of this theoretical continuum lies the position that instructional programs must ensure the implementation of empirically identified "effective" principles of teaching and learning. The academic failure of any student rests on the failure of instructional personnel to implement what we know "works." Walberg (1986) used meta-analysis to identify instructional conditions that have academically significant effects across various conditions and student groups. Other reviews (Baden & Maehr, 1986; Bloom, 1984; Slavin, Karweit, & Madden, 1989) have articulated this same position. In this vein, a number of specific instructional strategies including direct instruction (Rosenshine, 1986), tutoring (Bloom, 1984), frequent evaluation of academic progress (Slavin et al., 1989), and cooperative learning (Slavin et al., 1989) have been particular candidates for the "what works with all students" category. Implied in this *general principle* position is that the educational failure of diverse populations can be eradicated by the systematic and effective implementation of general principles of instruction.

For linguistically and culturally diverse populations, this general principle position has led educators to implement early English development programs. Based on a time-on-task argument, it has been proposed that, the earlier non-English-speaking children are exposed to and required to function academically in English, the more academically successful they will be.

Clearly, the above theoretical positions are somewhat exaggerated. The *cultural compatibility* and *general principles* positions need not be incompatible in any attempt to address the educational circumstances of Hispanic students. It is very likely that both positions have much to offer a more informed perspective with regard to the effective and efficient education of all students. These distinctions are useful only as a starting point in the discussion of instructional practices that might serve to enhance the educational success of a historically unsuccessful student population. The discussion that follows, however, considers as significant the continued failure of past and current schooling practices to serve these students effectively. Moreover, the discussion will address as its major thesis the recognition that teaching/learning issues relevant to a culturally compatible approach are significant with regard to understanding and instructionally addressing the failure and success of diverse student populations, specifically Hispanics. This thesis will be advanced by a systematic review of theoretical and empirical literature cognizant of the linguistic, cognitive, and social contexts of students in concert with "effective" instructional practices.

"Guidelines" for Addressing the Needs of Language-Minority Students

Empirical and theoretical research related to language-minority education and specific educational initiatives has generated several sets of general assumptions that have guided program development and implementation. The California State Department of Education (1984), reflecting a concern for its large Hispanic language-minority population, concluded the following:

1. Under optimal schooling conditions, on the average, students realize the full academic benefits of their bilingualism only after 4 to 11 years of appropriate instructional treatment.
2. Students in bilingual programs, even under the very best conditions, may initially lag behind their monolingually schooled counterparts in some literacy-based skills. After three or four years, however, the bilinguals begin to catch up and, after six or seven years, bilinguals equally and frequently surpass their monolingually-schooled counterparts.
3. When the instructional treatment is adequately designed and appropriately matched to local sociolinguistic realities, native speakers of a majority language may be schooled in a second language for an average of approximately 50% to

75% of the time from kindergarten through grade 12 with no detrimental effects on their academic achievement and native language development. Conversely, it may also be predicted that many language-minority students in the United States could be schooled in their native language for an average of 50% to 70% of the time from kindergarten through grade 12 as an appropriate means of promoting their normal academic achievement, high levels of English language proficiency, adequate psychosocial adjustment, and satisfactory native language development.

4. In formal schooling contexts, additive forms of bilingualism are best achieved through the separate use of two languages. That is, as students are instructed in both their first and their second languages, steps are taken so that students are exposed to each language at different times and for different purposes.
5. To avoid cognitive confusion and greatly increase learning efficiency, program staff should provide initial literacy instruction in bilingual settings in a sequential manner. That is, basic literacy skills should be developed through one language before reading instruction is introduced in the other language.
6. Underachievers and students with learning disabilities seem to experience no detrimental effects from bilingual instruction. When such children receive bilingual schooling, their academic achievement and native language development are similar to those of their counterparts in monolingual programs.
7. Formal second-language instruction, even when provided under optimal conditions, appears to be insufficient to develop all the language skills needed by second-language learners. Some amount of exposure, through natural social interaction, is also required (California State Department of Education, 1984).

Wong-Fillmore and Valadez (1985) generate their own similar but expanded set of assumptions that they suggest currently guide language-minority education in the United States, particularly that of Hispanics:

1. Students who are less than fully proficient in the language used in school will have difficulty deriving academic benefit from their educational experience, because the inability to understand the language in which instruction is given precludes comprehension of the content of the instruction.
2. It takes limited-English-proficient (LEP) students time to acquire the level of proficiency in English needed to participate effectively in all-English classes. During the time that it takes to learn English, they will get little out of their school experience if they are instructed exclusively through English.
3. Instruction in the native language of LEP students allows them to participate in school and to acquire the skills and knowledge covered in the curriculum while learning English. It also allows students to make use of skills, knowledge, and experience they already have and to build on those assets in school.

4. Knowledge and skills are most easily acquired by LEP students in their native language, but computational skills and many literacy skills acquired in the native language can be transferred to the new language once it is mastered. Hence time spent in learning materials in the native language is not time that is lost with respect to the coverage of subject matter in school.
5. Students need adequate exposure to the language of school to acquire it as a second language. This exposure to English is best when it takes place in settings in which the learners' special linguistic needs help to shape the way the language is used. Subject matter instruction given in English can provide the exposure that LEP students need, as long as it is appropriately tailored for them. Subject matter instruction in the school language is an essential component of bilingual education.
6. Formal instruction in English as a second language (ESL) can help students get started learning the language. ESL, whether formal or informal, is an integral part of all U.S. bilingual education programs.
7. The academic potential of all children, including those served by bilingual programs, has the best chance of being realized when students' language skills, social and cultural experience, and knowledge of the world are affirmed in school; these are the foundations of academic development.

These extensive "guidelines" for language-minority program development emphasize features related to prominent home/native language use and development. Conversely, other guidelines emphasizing minimal or no use of the native/home language have also been proposed elsewhere:

1. To the extent possible, all formal instruction should be in English with the home language (L1) used as necessary to clarify instruction;
2. the student should be encouraged to communicate in English as much as possible;
3. instruction should be designed around the immersion model so that English is learned through content-area instruction. Curriculum is presented at a level of understanding commensurate with the student's English development; and
4. more attention should be paid to incorporating into the curriculum remedial programs that focus on subject matter, not language (Baker, 1990; Baker & deKanter, 1983).

As is apparent, the educational debate regarding the identification of the "best" programs for language-minority students has not been totally resolved. Moreover, identification of guidelines from which the "ideal" may be developed does not automatically ensure implementation at the program level.

Effective Educational Practices

Based on the notion that schools, like families, serve to directly or indirectly socialize as much as they formally teach (Spindler, 1955), the development of academic competence is seen to be related to academic socialization (Au & Jordan, 1981; Diaz, Moll, & Mehan, 1986; Duran, 1983; Erickson, 1986; Trueba, 1987). Recent ethnographic studies and case studies (Au & Jordan, 1981; Duran, 1983; Erickson, 1986; Moll, 1988; Tharp & Gallimore, 1988; Trueba, 1988) have reported a significant relationship between cultural congruency in instruction and children's academic success. For example, Gallimore and Tharp (1989) have carefully described the educational program developed for Native Hawaiians. These programs use gender-relevant cooperative education procedures that match this population's gender roles—boys and girls work together in small groups. Similar cooperative education structures differ greatly from those used effectively in Navaho classrooms—boys are grouped together and girls are grouped together (Tharp, 1989). Moll (1988) has also described the use of cooperative techniques in southwestern U.S. schools in which Hispanic students are particularly successful. He concludes that such cooperative social structures directly "match" the type of Hispanic family values and practices. Other sociolinguistic studies have shown that the language of the classroom, or academic discourse, is a highly specialized code that students need to learn and "is not simply a transparent medium through which the academic curriculum is transmitted" (Mehan, 1979, p. 124). From this perspective, schooling not only involves cognitive development and the acquisition of knowledge but socialization as well (Spindler, 1974, 1982).

The implications of this perspective include the understanding that language, culture, and their accompanying values are acquired in the home and community environment (Cummins, 1986; Goldman & Trueba, 1987; Heath, 1981); that children come to school with some knowledge about language, how it works, and its use (Goodman, 1980; Hall, 1987; Smith, 1971); that children learn higher-level metacognitive and metalinguistic skills as they engage in socially meaningful activities (Duran, 1987); and that children's development and learning is best understood as the interaction of linguistic, sociocultural, and cognitive knowledge and experiences (Hakuta & Garcia, 1989; Trueba, 1988). For linguistically and culturally diverse students, however, their attributes and experiences are not those that are celebrated and acknowledged by the schooling enterprise nor are they those upon which school learning and academic socialization are based (Ogbu, 1982; Trueba, 1987). Such a standing serves to foster an inappropriate and negative perception of self as a learner, reader, writer, and speaker. The resulting vulnerability of the Hispanic child is ignored when learning and schooling are not considered within the larger sociocultural context in the classroom and in the larger society (Gutierrez & Garcia, 1989).

A more appropriate perspective, then, recognizes that learning is enhanced when it occurs in contexts that are both socioculturally and linguistically meaningful (Diaz et al., 1986; Heath, 1986; Scribner & Cole, 1981; Wertsch, 1985). Such meaningful events, however, are not generally accessible to Hispanic children. Schooling contributes to the academic vulnerability of this student population. The monolithic culture is transmitted by the schools in the forms of pedagogy, curricula, instruction, classroom configuration, and language (Walker, 1987). Such practices include the systematic exclusion of the students' histories, language, experience, and values from classroom curricula and activities (Giroux & McLaren, 1986; Ogbu, 1982); limited access to academic courses; learning environments that do not foster academic development and socialization (Duran, 1986; Eder, 1982) or perception of self as a competent learner and language user; and limited opportunities to engage in developmentally and culturally appropriate learning that are not limited to the standard teacher-dominated, recitation method of instruction (Garcia, 1988; Tharp & Gallimore, 1988).

The above conclusions can be directly supported by recent research that documents educationally effective practices with linguistically and culturally diverse students in selected school sites around the United States (Tikunoff, 1983) and more specifically in Carpenteria, California (Cummins, 1986), San Diego, California (Carter & Chatfield, 1986), Phoenix, Arizona (Garcia, 1988; Moll, 1988), and Northern California (Lucas, Henze, & Donato, 1990; Pease-Alvarez, Garcia, & Espinosa, 1991). These descriptive studies identified specific schools and classrooms that served non-English students well: Students were particularly academically successful, scoring at or above the national norms on norm-referenced tests of academic achievement. The case study approach adopted by these studies included examination of preschool, elementary, and high school classrooms. Teachers, principals, parents, and students were interviewed, and specific classroom observations were conducted that assessed the "dynamics" of the instructional process.

Tikunoff (1983), in his report on the Significant Bilingual Instructional Features (SBIF) study, ranks as the first to attempt to identify attributes of exemplary approaches. He reports commonalities in organization and instruction in effective language-minority classrooms. The 58 classrooms observed in this study covered six sites and included a variety of non-English languages. All classes were considered "effective" on two criteria: First, teachers were nominated by members of four constituencies—teachers, other school personnel, students, and parents—as being effective. Second, teaching behaviors produced rates of "academic learning time" (a measure of student engagement in academic tasks) as high as or higher than reported in other effective teaching research. The SBIF findings can be divided into two parts: instructional features common to language-minority and majority classrooms and instructional features unique to language-minority classrooms.

An initial set of instructional features identified in the effective classrooms pertain to the delivery and organization of instruction:

1. Successful teachers of limited-English-proficient (LEP) students specify task outcomes and what students must do to accomplish tasks. In addition, teachers communicate high expectations for LEP students in terms of learning and a sense of efficacy in terms of their own ability to teach.

2. Successful teachers of LEP students, not unlike effective teachers in general, exhibit use of "active teaching" behaviors found to be related to increased student performance on academic tests of achievement in reading and mathematics including (a) communicating clearly when giving directions specifying tasks and presenting new information; (b) obtaining and maintaining students' engagement in instructional tasks by pacing instruction appropriately, promoting involvement, and communicating their expectations for students' success in completing instructional tasks; (c) monitoring students' progress; and (d) providing immediate feedback whenever required regarding students' success.

Effective instructional features specific to Hispanic language-minority students included the use of two languages, special activities for teaching a second language, and instructional practices that took advantage of students' cultural background.

According to SBIF reports, across the 58 classrooms, English was used approximately 60% of the time and the native language (L1) or a combination of L1 and the second language (L2) was used the rest of the time, with the percentage of English being used increasing with grade level. An additional significant instructional feature was the particular way in which the two languages were often combined:

1. Successful teachers of LEP students mediated instruction for LEP students by using the students' native language and English for instruction, alternating between the two languages whenever necessary to ensure clarity of instruction. Although this type of language switching occurred, teachers did not translate directly from one language to another.

2. Students learned the language of instruction when engaged in instructional tasks using that language. This integrative approach to developing English language skills during ongoing instruction in the regular classroom contrasts with the more traditional, pullout procedures in which LEP students leave the regular instructional setting to receive special ESL instruction.

Of interest in the above conclusions is the finding that bilingual instruction was characterized by the use of both the native language and English within instructional interaction. This language switching seemed to directly assist in clarifying instructional discourse. Wong-Fillmore and Valadez (1985) have suggested that such switching, particularly if it takes on a translation pattern, may be detrimental to second-language acquisition. Milk (1986), in a study that focused on the use of a concurrent bilingual instructional model, reports that a nontranslation concurrent approach yielded functional language switching discourse patterns similar to those reported for separation instructional models. Students in the study followed a language choice rule ("Speak to the speaker in the language [in which] you are addressed") in a situation that included 45% Spanish use and 55% English use. Such data suggest further that instructional discourse should concentrate on clarity and that such clarity can be enhanced through the use of the students' native language.

The SBIF study also reports that the use of information from the LEP students' home culture can promote engagement in instructional tasks and contribute to a feeling of trust between children and their teachers. The SBIF researchers found three ways in which home and community culture is incorporated into classroom life: (a) Cultural referents in both verbal and nonverbal forms were used to communicate instructional and institutional demands; (b) instruction was organized to build upon rules of discourse from the L1 culture; and (c) values and norms of the L1 culture were respected equally with those of the school.

In recent research that focused on Mexican American elementary school children, Garcia (1988) reported several related instructional strategies used in "effective" schools. These schools were nominated by language-minority colleagues and had students scoring at or above the national average on Spanish and/or English standardized measures of academic achievement. This research characterized instruction in the effective classrooms as follows:

1. Students were instructed primarily in small groups, and academic-related discourse was encouraged between students throughout the day. Teachers rarely used large group instruction or more individualized (e.g., mimeographed work sheets) instructional activities. The most common activity across classes involved small groups of students working on assigned academic tasks with intermittent assistance by the teacher.
2. The teacher tended to provide an instructional initiation often reported in the literature (Mehan, 1979; Morine-Dirshimer, 1985). Teachers elicited student responses but did so at relatively non-higher-order cognitive and linguistic levels.
3. Once a lesson elicitation occurred, students were allowed to take control of the discourse by inviting fellow student interaction, usually at higher-order cognitive and linguistic levels.

Of particular relevance are two intensive case studies of elementary schools (Garcia, 1988; Pease-Alvarez, Garcia, & Espinosa, 1991) and one case study of high schools (Lucas et al., 1990). This recent elementary school research addressed some significant questions regarding effective academic environments for Hispanic students:

1. What role did native language instruction play? These "effective" schools considered native language instruction key in the early grades (kindergarten to grade 3).
2. Was there one best curriculum? No common curriculum was identified. A well-trained instructional staff implementing an integrated "student-centered" curriculum with literacy pervasive in all aspects of instruction, however, was consistently observed across grade levels. Basals were used sparingly and usually as resource material.
3. What instructional strategies were effective? Teachers consistently organized so as to ensure small collaborative academic activities requiring a high degree of heterogeneous grouped student-to-student social (and particularly linguistic) interaction. Individual instructional activity such as work sheets/workbooks was limited as was individual competition as a classroom motivational ingredient.

4. Who were the key players in this effective schooling drama? School administrators and parents played important roles. Teachers, however, were the key players. They achieved the educational confidence of their peers and supervisors. They worked to organize instruction, create new instructional environments, assess effectiveness, and advocate for their students.

In an analysis of specific teacher characteristics, the following conclusions were reached regarding the teachers who served students "effectively":

Knowledge. These "effective" teachers were experienced in working specifically with these students (the average number of years of experience was 6.2). They were able to articulate what they were doing in their classrooms and also substantiate their effects. All were highly competent in the content areas for which they were responsible.

Skills. These "effective" teachers were competent communicators with their students, their teaching colleagues, their administrators, and their students' parents. Early grade teachers were proficient Spanish-English bilinguals. All teachers were biliterate. In their classrooms, these teachers adopted the role of "collaborator," serving more as a coordinator of learning than a dispenser of knowledge. They skillfully implemented collaborative teaching strategies in heterogeneous groups.

Dispositions. These "effective" teachers were both highly confident in their ability and self-critical. They reported being "paradigm flexible," having at different points of their careers adopted distinct beliefs about their teaching role and having changed those beliefs several times. But they never considered themselves eclectic. They had achieved a high degree of autonomy and a high degree of respect from teaching colleagues, administrators, and parents. They were creative, committed, and hardworking: never satisfied that they were doing enough. They looked to teaching colleagues for support and themselves organized and sustained support networks.

Affect. These "effective" teachers were advocates for their students, had high expectations for each student, and displayed pride in students' accomplishments. They were reassuring but demanding and rejected any notion that their students were disadvantaged. In general, their classrooms were managed in the style of the family—they "adopted" these students as if they were children of their own. They were also "adopted" by the students' families.

Lucas et al. (1990, pp. 324-325) report the following to be common features of high schools that promote the achievement of language-minority students:

1. Value is placed on the students' languages and cultures by treating students as individuals, learning about their cultures and languages, hiring bilingual staff, and encouraging students to develop their primary-language skills.
2. High expectations of language-minority students are made concrete by providing minority role models and preparing and supporting language-minority (LM) students for college.
3. School leaders make the education of language-minority students a priority. These leaders maintain high expectations of LM students, are both knowledgeable of and involved in strengthening curriculum for LM students, represent minority groups themselves, and hire bilingual teachers.
4. Staff development is explicitly designed to help teachers and other staff serve language-minority students more effectively. Schools and school districts offer teachers/school staff development programs that include effective instructional approaches for LM students, principles in second-language acquisition, and cross-cultural counseling.
5. A variety of courses and programs for language-minority students are offered. The programs include courses in ESL and primary language instruction, offer advanced and basic courses taught via bilingual and sheltered methods, and establish support programs to help LM students in the transition from ESL to mainstream classes and then to college.
6. A counseling program gives special attention to language-minority students through counselors who share students' language and cultural backgrounds, are well versed in postsecondary educational opportunities for LM students, and believe in the academic success of LM students.
7. Parents of language-minority students are encouraged to become involved in their children's education. Schools can provide and encourage staff who speak the parents' language, hold on-campus ESL classes for parents, and involve parents in planning their children's course schedules.
8. School staff members share a strong commitment to empower language-minority students through education. This commitment is made concrete through staff who devote extra time to LM students, including extracurricular activities; take part in community and political activities in which they act as advocates for minorities; and request training to help LM students to become more effective.

In summary, a responsive curriculum, instructional strategies, and teaching staff recognize that academic learning has its roots in the language experiences and processes of communication. This type of curriculum provides abundant and diverse opportunities for speaking, listening, reading, and writing along with scaffolding to help guide students through the learning process. A focus on congruent home/school processes, both social and cognitive, encourages students to take risks, construct meaning, and seek reinterpretations of knowledge within compatible social contexts. Such an approach recognizes that errors are necessary in experimenting with new ideas, forms, and structures. Within this knowledge-driven curriculum (i.e., academic and cultural knowledge), skills are tools for acquiring knowledge, not a fundamental target of teaching events (Gallimore & Tharp, 1989; Garcia, 1988).

Conclusion

If the discussion of the above-mentioned theoretical conceptualizations and empirical information can be perceived as a new set of "understandings," then the following are specific principles for the increasing number of classrooms where cultural and linguistic diversity is the norm:

- Any curriculum, especially one for "diverse" children, must address all categories of learning goals. We should not expect "less" for this student population.
- The more diverse linguistically and culturally the children we teach, the more the content must be related to each child's own environment and experience.
- The more diverse the children, the more integrated the curriculum should be. Children should have opportunities to study a topic in depth, to apply all kinds of skills they have acquired in a variety of home and school contexts.
- The more diverse the children, the more the curriculum should address learning through active endeavors rather than passive ones, particularly informal social activities such as group projects in which students are allowed flexibility in participating with the teacher and other students in engaging academic material.
- The more diverse the children, the more important it is for the curriculum to offer opportunities to apply what they are learning in a meaningful context (work sheets are not meaningful).
- The more diverse the children, the more likely it is that excessive practice and drill that focuses only on skill development will endanger the disposition to use those skills.
- In general, the more the curriculum emphasizes performance goals rather than learning goals of relevance to the student, the more likely it is that students will distance themselves from the school. Performance goals mean the pressure to get the right answer as opposed to learning goals that emphasize how much one can learn.

References

American Association of Higher Education. (1988, May/June). *Change*. Washington, DC: Author.

Appleby, A. N., Langer, J., & Mullis, I. J. S. (1988). *The nation's report card: NAEP.* Princeton, NJ: Educational Testing Service.

Au, K., & Jordan, C. (1981). Teaching reading to Hawaiian children: Finding a culturally appropriate solution. In H. Trueba, G. Guthrie, & K. Au (Eds.), *Culture and the bilingual classroom: Studies in classroom ethnography* (pp. 139-152). Rowley, MA: Newbury House.

August, D., & Garcia, E. (1988). *Language minority education in the U.S.: Research policy and practice*. Chicago: Thomas.

Baden, B., & Maehr, M. (1986). Conforming culture with culture: A perspective for designing schools for children of diverse sociocultural backgrounds. In R. Feldman (Ed.), *The social psychology of education* (pp. 289-309). New York: Cambridge University Press.

Baker, K. A. (1990). Language minority education: Two decades of research. In A. Barona & E. Garcia (Eds.), *Students at risk: Poverty, minority status, and other issues in educational equity.* (pp. 3-41). Washington, DC: National Association of School Psychologists.

Baker, K. A., & deKanter, A. A. (1983). An answer from research on bilingual education. *American Education, 56,* 157-169.

Barona, A., & Garcia, E. (1990). *Children at risk: Poverty, minority status and other issues in educational equity.* Washington, DC: National Association of School Psychologists.

Bloom, B. (1984). The search for methods of group instruction as effective as one-to-one tutoring. *Educational Leadership, 41*(8), 4-17.

Boykin, A. (1986). The triple quandary and the schooling of Afro-American children. In U. Neisser (Ed.), *The school achievement of minority children* (pp. 57-92). New York: New Perspectives.

Brice-Heath, S. (1986). Sociocultural contexts of language development. In Bilingual Education Office (Eds.), *Beyond language: Social and cultural factors in schooling language minority students* (pp. 197-230). Los Angeles: California State University, Evaluation, Dissemination, and Assessment Center.

California State Department of Education. (1984). *Studies of immersion education.* Sacramento: California State Department of Education.

Cardenas, J. (1986, January). The role of native-language instruction in bilingual education. *Phi Delta Kappan,* pp. 359-363.

Carter, T. P., & Chatfield, M. L. (1986). Effective bilingual schools: Implications for policy and practice. *American Journal of Education, 95*(1), 200-234.

Cavasos, E. (1990, November). *An executive initiative for Hispanic education.* Testimony before U.S. House of Representatives, Committee on Education and Labor.

Cazden, C. (1989). *Classroom discourse*. Cambridge, MA: Harvard University Press.

Cummins, J. (1979). Linguistic interdependence and the educational development of bilingual children. *Review of Educational Research, 19,* 222-251.

Cummins, J. (1981). The role of primary language development in promoting educational success for language minority students. In California State Department of

Education, *Schooling and language minority students: A theoretical framework.* Los Angeles: California State University, Evaluation, Dissemination, and Assessment Center.

Cummins, J. (1984). *Bilingualism and special education.* San Diego, CA: College Hill.

Cummins, J. (1986). Empowering minority students: A framework for intervention. *Harvard Educational Review,* 56(1), 18-35.

Diaz, R. M. (1983). The impact of bilingualism on cognitive development. In E. W. Gordon (Ed.), *Review of research in education* (pp. 23-54). Washington, DC: American Educational Research Association.

Diaz, S., Moll, L., & Mehan, H. (1986). Sociocultural resources in instruction: A context-specific approach. In Bilingual Education Office (Eds.), *Beyond language: Social and cultural factors in schooling language minority students* (pp. 197-230). Los Angeles: California State University, Evaluation, Dissemination, and Assessment Center.

Duran, R. (1983). *Hispanics' education and background: Predictors of college achievement.* New York: College Entrance Examination Board.

Duran, R. (1986). *Improving Hispanics' educational outcomes: Learning and instruction.* Unpublished manuscript, University of California, Santa Barbara, Graduate School of Education.

Duran, R. (1987). Metacognition in second language behavior. In J. A. Langer (Ed.), *Language, literacy, and culture: Issues of society and schooling* (pp. 49-63). Norwood, NJ: Ablex.

Eder, D. (1982). Differences in communicative styles across ability groups. In L. C. Wilkinson (Ed.), *Communicating in the classroom.* Orlando, FL: Academic Press.

Elam, S. (1972). Acculturation and learning problems of Puerto Rican children. In F. Corrdasco & E. Bucchini (Eds.), *The Puerto Rican community and its children on the mainland.* Metuchen, NJ: Scarecrow.

Erickson, F. (1986). Qualitative methods in research on teaching. In M. C. Wittrock (Ed.), *Handbook of research on teaching* (pp. 119-158). New York: Macmillan.

Fishman, J. A., Cooper, R. L., & Ma, R. (1966). *Bilingualism in the barrio.* Bloomington: Indiana University Press.

Galambos, S. J., & Hakuta, K. (1988). Subject-specific and task-specific characteristics of metalinguistic awareness in bilingual children. *Applied Psycholinguistics, 9,* 141-162.

Gallimore, R., & Tharp, R. G. (1989). *Challenging cultural minds.* London: Cambridge University Press.

Garcia, E. (1983a). *Bilingualism in early childhood.* Albuquerque: University of New Mexico Press.

Garcia, E. (1983b). *The Mexican-American child: Language, cognition, and socialization.* Tempe: Arizona State University.

Garcia, E. (1988). Effective schooling for language minority students. In *National clearing house for bilingual education* (New Focus). Arlington, VA: National Clearing House for Bilingual Education.

Giroux, H. A., & McLaren, P. (1986). Teacher education and the politics of engagement: The case for democratic schooling. *Harvard Educational Review, 56,* 213-238.

Goldman, S., & Trueba, H. (1987). *Becoming literate in English as a second language: Advances in research and theory.* Norwood, NJ: Ablex.

Goodman, Y. (1980). The roots of literacy. In M. P. Douglass (Ed.), *Reading: A humanizing experience*. Claremont, CA: Claremont Graduate School.

Gonzalez, G. (1991). *The education of Mexican students during the era of segregation*. Tucson: University of Arizona Press.

Gumperz, J. (1982). *Discourse strategies*. New York: Cambridge University Press.

Gutierrez, K. D., & Garcia, E. E. (1989). Academic literacy in linguistic minority children: The connections between language, cognition and culture. *Early Childhood Development, 51,* 109-126.

Hakuta, K. (1986). *Mirror of language: The debate on bilingualism*. New York: Basic Books.

Hakuta, K., & Garcia, E. (1989). Bilingualism and bilingual education. *American Psychologist, 44*(2), 374-379.

Hall, N. (1987). *The emergence of literacy*. Portsmouth, NH: Heinemann Educational.

Heath, S. B. (1981). Toward an ethnohistory of writing in American education. In M. Farr-Whitman (Ed.), *Variation in writing functional and linguistic-cultural differences: Vol. 1. Writing: The nature, development, and teaching of written communication* (pp. 225-246). Hillsdale, NJ: Lawrence Erlbaum.

Heath, S. B. (1983). *Ways with words: Language, life, and work in communities and classrooms*. Cambridge, England: Cambridge University Press.

Heath, S. B. (1986). Sociocultural contexts of language development. In California Bilingual Education Office (Eds.), *Beyond language: Social and cultural factors in schooling language minority children* (pp. 143-186). Los Angeles: California State University, Evaluation, Dissemination, and Assessment Center.

Hetherington, E. M., & Park, R. D. (1988). *Contemporary reading in child psychology* (3rd ed.). New York: McGraw-Hill.

Hodgkinson, H. (1989, December). Reform? Higher education? Don't be absurd! *Higher Education*, pp. 271-274.

Hudelson, S. (1987). The role of native language literacy in the education of language minority children. *Language Arts, 64*(8), 827-841.

Johnson, D. L., Teigen, K., & Davila, R. (1983). Anxiety and social restriction: A study of children in Mexico, Norway, and the United States. *Journal of Cross-Cultural Psychology, 14,* 439-454.

Kagan, S. (1983). Interpreting Chicano cooperativeness: Methodological and theoretical considerations. In J. L. Martinez & R. H. Mendoza (Eds.), *Chicano psychology* (2nd ed., pp. 289-333). Orlando, FL: Academic Press.

Kagan, S., Knight, G. P., Martinez, S., & Espinoza-Santana, P. (1981). Conflict resolution style among Mexican children: Examination, urbanization and ecology effects. *Journal of Cross-Cultural Psychology, 12,* 222-232.

Keefe, S. E., & Padilla, A. M. (1987). *Chicano ethnicity*. Albuquerque: University of New Mexico Press.

Keefe, S. E., Padilla, A. M., & Carlos, M. (1979). *Mental health issues of significance in Mexican American families* (Hispanic Mental Health Working Papers). Los Angeles: University of California.

Knight, G. P., Bernal, M. E., & Carlos, G. (in press). Socialization and the development of cooperative, competitive, and individualistic behaviors among Mexican American children. In E. Garcia, L. Moll, & A. Barona (Eds.), *The Mexican American child: Language, cognition, and socialization* (Vol. 2). Tempe: Arizona State University.

Knight, G. P., & Kagan, S. (1977a). Development of prosocial and competitive behaviors in Anglo American and Mexican American children. *Child Development, 48,* 1385-1394.

Knight, G. P., & Kagan, S. (1977b). Acculturation of prosocial and competitive behaviors among second and third-generation Mexican American children. *Journal of Cross-Cultural Psychology, 8,* 273-284.

Lucas, T., Henze, R., & Donato, R. (1990). Promoting the success of Latino language minority students: An exploratory study of six high schools. *Harvard Educational Review, 60,* 315-334.

Martinez, J. V. (1976). *Chicano psychology.* New York: Academic Press.

Matute-Bianchi, E. (1990). *A report to the Santa Clara County School District: Hispanics in the schools.* Santa Clara, CA: Santa Clara County School District.

McClintock, C. G. (1972). Social motivation: A set of propositions. *Behavioral Science, 17,* 438-454.

McClintock, C. G. (1974). Development of social motives in Anglo-American and Mexican-American children. *Journal of Personality and Social Psychology, 29,* 348-354.

McClintock, E., Bayard, M. P., & McClintock, C. G. (1983). The socialization of prosocial orientations in Mexican American families. In E. Garcia (Ed.), *The Mexican American child: Language, cognition and social development.* Tempe, AZ: Center for Bilingual Education.

McLaughlin, B. (1987). *Theories of second-language learning.* London: Arnold.

McLaughlin, B. (1990). Development of bilingualism: Myth and reality. In A. Barona & E. Garcia (Eds.), *Children at risk: Poverty, minority status and other issues in educational equality* (pp. 65-76). Washington, DC: National Association of School Psychologists.

Mead, M. (1937). *Cooperation and competition among primitive peoples.* New York: McGraw.

Mehan, H. (1979). *Learning lessons.* Cambridge, MA: Harvard University Press.

Milk, R. D. (1986). The issue of language separation in bilingual methodology. In E. E. Garcia & B. Flores (Eds.), *Language and literacy in bilingual education* (pp. 67-86). Tempe: Arizona State University.

Moll, L. (1988). Educating Latino students. *Language Arts, 64,* 315-324.

Morine-Dirshimer, G. (1985). *Talking, listening and learning in elementary classrooms.* New York: Longman.

Nieto, S. (1979). *Curriculum decision-making: The Puerto Rican family and the bilingual child.* Unpublished doctoral dissertation, University of Massachusetts, Amherst.

Ogbu, J. U. (1982). Cultural discontinuities and schooling. *Anthropology and Education Quarterly, 13*(4), 168-190.

Ogbu, J. U. (1987). Variability in minority school performance: A problem in search of an explanation. *Anthropology and Education Quarterly, 18,* 312-334.

Ortiz, F. I. (1988). Hispanic American children's experience in classrooms. In L. Weis (Ed.), *Class, race, and gender in American education* (pp. 43-62). Albany: State University of New York Press.

Pease-Alvarez, C., Garcia, E. E., & Espinosa, P. (1991). Effective instruction for language minority students: An early childhood case study. *Early Childhood Research Quarterly, 6,* 347-361.

Pedraza, P. (1987). *Language in context: Puerto Rican's in New York.* Unpublished doctoral dissertation, Columbia University.

Ramirez, A. (1985). *Bilingualism through schooling.* Albany: State University of New York Press.

Ramirez, M., & Castaneda, A. (1974). *Cultural democracy, bicognitive development and education.* New York: Academic Press.

Rivera-Medina, E. J. (1984). The Puerto Rican return migrant student: A challenge to educators. *Educational Research Quarterly, 8,* 82-91.

Rodriguez, C. E. (1989). *Puerto Ricans born in the U.S.A.* Winchester, MA: Unwin Hyman.

Rosenshine, B. (1986). Synthesis of research on explicit teaching. *Educational Leadership, 43,* 60-69.

Rossell, C., & Ross, J. M. (1986). *The social evidence on bilingual education.* Boston: Boston University.

Scribner, S., & Cole, M. (1981). Unpackaging literacy. In M. Farr-Whiteman (Ed.), *Variation in writing: Functional and linguistic-cultural differences: Vol. 1. Writing: The nature, development, and teaching of written communications* (pp. 71-88). Hillsdale, NJ: Lawrence Erlbaum.

Slavin, R., Karweit, N., & Madden, N. (1989). *Effective programs for students at risk.* Needham Heights, MA: Allyn & Bacon.

Smith, F. (1923). Bilingualism and mental development. *British Journal of Psychology, 13,* 271-282.

Smith, F. (1971). *Understanding reading.* New York: Holt, Rinehart & Winston.

Snow, C. E. (1987). Beyond conversation: Second language learners' acquisition of description and explanation. In J. P. Lantolf & A. Labarca (Eds.), *Research in second language learning: Focus on the classroom* (pp. 3-16). Norwood, NJ: Ablex.

Spencer, D. (1988). Transitional bilingual education and the socialization of immigrants. *Harvard Educational Review, 58*(2), 133-153.

Spindler, G. (1955). *Anthropology and education.* Stanford, CA: Stanford University Press.

Spindler, G. (1974). *Education and cultural process: Toward an anthropology of education.* New York: Holt, Rinehart & Winston.

Spindler, G. (1982). *Doing the ethnography of schooling: Educational anthropology in action.* New York: Holt, Rinehart & Winston.

Sternberg, R. (1985). *Beyond IQ: A triarchic theory of human intelligence.* New York: Cambridge University Press.

Sue, S., & Padilla, A. (1986). Ethnic minority issues in the United States: Challenges for the educational system. In California Bilingual Education Office (Eds.), *Beyond language: Social and cultural factors in schooling language minority students* (pp. 35-72). Los Angeles: California State University, Evaluation, Dissemination, and Assessment Center.

Tharp, R. G. (1989). Psychocultural variables and k constants: Effects on teaching and learning in schools. *American Psychologist, 44,* 349-359.

Tharp, R. G., & Gallimore, R. (1988). *Rousing minds to life: Teaching, learning, and schooling in social context.* New York: Cambridge University Press.

Thomas, S. V., & Park, B. (1921). *Culture of immigrants.* Cambridge, MA: Newcome.

Thompson, G. G. (1952). *Child psychology.* Boston: Houghton-Mifflin.

Tikunoff, W. J. (1983, September). *Significant Bilingual Instructional Features study.* San Francisco: Far West Educational Laboratory.

Trueba, H. (1987). *Success or failure? Learning and the language minority student.* Cambridge, MA: Newbury House.

Trueba, H. (1988). *Rethinking learning disabilities: Cultural knowledge in literacy acquisition.* Unpublished manuscript, University of California, Santa Barbara, Graduate School of Education, Office for Research on Educational Equity.

U.S. Bureau of the Census. (1984). *Conditions of Hispanics in America today.* Washington, DC: Government Printing Office.

U.S. Bureau of the Census. (1987). *The Hispanic population in the United States: March 1986 and 1987.* Washington, DC: Government Printing Office.

Vogt, L. A., Jordan, C. J., & Tharp, R. G. (1987). Explaining school failure, producing school success: Two cases. *Anthropology and Education Quarterly, 18,* 276-286.

Walberg, H. (1986). Synthesis of research on teaching. In M. Wittrock (Ed.), *Handbook of research on teaching* (3rd ed., pp. 214-229). New York: Macmillan.

Walker, C. L. (1987). Hispanic achievements: Old views and new perspectives. In H. Trueba (Ed.), *Success of failure? Learning and the language minority student* (pp. 15-32). Cambridge, MA: Newbury House.

Walsh, D. (1990, January 21). Californian new students speaking in many languages. *San Francisco Examiner,* pp. B1-B14.

Weis, L. (1988). *Class, race and gender in American education.* Albany: State University of New York Press.

Weisner, T. S., Gallimore, R., & Jordan, C. (1988). Unpackaging cultural effects on classroom learning: Native Hawaiian peer assistance and child-generated activity. *Anthropology and Education Quarterly, 19*(4), 327-353.

Wertsch, J. (1985). *Vygotsky and the social formation of the mind.* Cambridge, MA: Harvard University Press.

Willig, A. (1987). Examining bilingual educational research through meta-analysis and negative review. *Review of Educational Research, 57,* 363-376.

Wong-Fillmore, L., & Valadez, C. (1985). Teaching bilingual learners. In M. S. Wittrock (Ed.), *Handbook on research on teaching.* Washington, DC: AERA.

Zentella, A. C. (1981). Ta bien you could answer me en cualquier idioma: Puerto Rican code-switching in bilingual classrooms. In R. Duran (Ed.), *Latino language and communicative behavior* (pp. 109-132). Norwood, NJ: Ablex.

• 6 •

Learning Technology Contexts for At-Risk Children

RICHARD T. JOHNSON

The past several years have witnessed a renewed focus on at-risk students' opportunities for success in school environments (Boyer, 1990; Clifford, 1990; Knapp, Turnbull, & Shields, 1990; Presseisen, 1988). School districts throughout the United States currently report expanding enrollments of at-risk students (Hodgkinson, 1985; Levin, 1987) and forecast increasingly larger numbers of this population in the coming years (Watson, Northcutt, & Rydell, 1989). While definitions differ from state to state, *at-risk* students are generally defined as those children who are below grade level in mathematics and reading skills, low academic achievers, living in urban poverty or rural isolation, culturally and linguistically different, exhibiting poor attendance at school, and attending schools with large numbers of poor students (Ralph, 1989; Slavin, 1989). Estrom, Goertz, Pollack, and Rock (1987), in a national study, report that the two background characteristics that are most strongly related to dropping out are socioeconomic status and race/ethnicity. Their report verifies that students of lower socioeconomic status have been consistently shown to have higher dropout rates than high socioeconomic status students.

Research illustrates that at-risk children do not perform as well as their classmates, regardless of whether societal variables or the manner in which they are educated contributed most to being disadvantaged (Natriello, McDill, & Pallas, 1990; Sartain, 1989). For instance, in states with large percentages of limited-English-proficient (LEP) children, like Texas (with one of the largest concentrations of at-risk students in the United States), the results from statewide Educational Assessment of Minimal Skills (TEAMS) tests reveal that (a) non-LEP students outperformed LEP students in reading, writing, and math across all grade levels tested, and (b) in third grade mathematics, when tested in English, LEP students trailed non-LEPs by 27 percentage points in 1986, 17 percentage points in 1987, and 14 percentage points in 1988. Even though the scores are higher in Spanish, they do not attain the level of non-LEPs, who scored 88% mastery in 1987 and 92% in 1988. Because the TEAMS is considered a rather low-level, basic test, that some 15%-20% of the children fail to master the test even in their home language is cause for concern. Similar test results are witnessed in other states (like California and Hawaii) that have large populations of immigrant, LEP children entering the school system.

At-Risk Students in the United States

As this population continues to grow, educators are grappling with the notion of how best to educate at-risk students (Alderman, 1990; Clifford, 1990; Levin, 1987). Knapp et al. (1990, p. 4) note that "improving these children's schooling is an increasingly urgent concern. Despite extra resources from the federal government and despite recent educational reforms, these children often leave school ill-equipped for adult life."

Students such as the above mentioned are at risk of not achieving educational success (McPartland & Slavin, 1990). Even if these children choose to actively participate in school, they typically do so at a level different than that of their peers (Slavin & Madden, 1989). For instance, these students often participate in "pullout" programs or are assigned special education resources. Research reveals that these are relatively ineffective programs (Slavin & Madden, 1989). Many of these at-risk students choose not to participate in school, becoming dropouts at a relatively young age (Bennett & LeCompte, 1990; Hahn, 1987; McPartland & Slavin, 1990). Ultimately, many of these students produce families that perpetuate cycles of poverty and underachievement (Baumeister, 1987; Deutsch, 1990).

Several investigators note that poor school performance is a major predictor of dropping out of school and that it is also an *early* predictor. As Willis (1986) notes: "When students in the third and fourth grades are already two years behind their age counterparts, 'catching up' becomes a difficult, if not insurmountable, obstacle." Of course, programs such as Head Start were designed to deal with these types of problems. Data suggest that they were often helpful but not as powerful as one would like (e.g., Willis, 1986).

Yet, a great deal of theoretical and technological progress has been made in the past five years—progress that sets the stage for the design of instructional environments that can have a powerful impact on the development of young students who, without help, will continue to be at risk for school failure (Soled, 1989). This progress involves the classroom implementation of multimedia contexts—instructional technology that proves to be effective for teaching at-risk students. Research on videodisc instruction supports this technology as an effective instructional tool for various types of curricular activities.

Alternate Modes of Classroom Instruction

Videodisc technology has been shown by the Cognition and Technology Group at Vanderbilt University (1990), Johnson (1987, 1990a, 1990b) and others (Pea, 1990; Schwen, Goodrum, Knuth, & Dorsey, 1990; Walker de Felix, Johnson, & Schick, 1990) to provide semantically rich contexts for acquiring knowledge, especially for at-risk populations. The Cognition and Technology Group (1990) argue that the context within which instruction occurs may have important effects on students' abilities to access and use knowledge in the future. They describe the videodisc instructional format as a rich context for teaching real-world problem solving. In these highly effective instructional formats, the presented information allows the learner(s) to perceive problems in a real-world, thematic story sense. The Cognition and Technology Group defines these as *macro contexts* for learning. This term is used because "the context is shared by all students and because the context is sufficiently broad and rich to enable the teacher to integrate instruction across traditional curricular areas (i.e., to teach comprehension, writing, social studies and science using the same materials and in the same time frame)" (Vye, Rowe, Kinzer, & Risko, 1990, p. 2). The instruction therefore allows for what Brown, Collins, and Duiguid (1989) call "authentic" goals for learning designated content. The context invites students to become engaged in the presented information so as to want to solve the problems posed. According to the Cognition and Technology Group (1990), this situated learning is anchored instruction, because the instruction is anchored in multimedia contexts created by the students and teacher.

In ongoing research at the Vanderbilt Learning Technology Center (Bransford, Sherwood, Kinzer, & Hasselbring, 1985; Bransford, Sherwood, Vye, & Rieser, 1986; Bransford, Sherwood, & Hasselbring, 1988; Vye et al., 1989), the scientists select the videodisc medium for several reasons. They (p. 3) express that

> it allows us to teach pattern recognition skills. Students can be taught to recognize significant patterns of information from unorganized arrays. (A major disadvantage of text is that it represents the output of the writer's pattern recognition processes). Second, video allows a more veridical representation of events than text; it is dynamic, visual, and spatial. This is important because the context is used to simulate first-hand experience with particular problem situations. A third reason for using video is that it is assumed that video would initially be more accessible than text for lower functioning students with low knowledge in the domain of interest. This is especially relevant for at-risk learners. A fourth reason for using videodisc technology is that it has random access capabilities. Random-access is advantageous from an instructional viewpoint because it allows the teacher to almost instantly access information for discussion. (Vye et al, 1989)

Researchers at Apple Computer add to Bransford's argument surrounding the power of implementing learning technology in classroom contexts. Rob Semper (1990, p. 54), the director of creative collaboration between Apple Computer and Lucasfilm, Ltd., describes the multimedia teaching/learning context as such: "It allows the integrated access and control of material in multiple modes. These include graphics, text, sound, control of videodiscs, CD-Audio, and computer and film animation. There is something for everybody. This multiple-modality capability is very important for education."

Research on Instructional Applications for At-Risk Students

The primary purpose of effective multimedia contexts, as discussed here, is to focus on questions that seem fundamentally linked to the goals of helping at-risk students develop the competencies necessary to succeed in school. In particular, it is important to help these children develop effective thinking and problem-solving skills that will enable them to make decisions and to learn on their own (Brown, Bransford, Ferrara, & Campione, 1983). To do this, these children must be helped to learn important concepts and to acquire basic thinking and literacy skills related to and necessary for success in school and in later life.

Studies conducted in cognitive laboratories as well as in other settings suggest ways to facilitate people's abilities to spontaneously use relevant knowledge in new contexts (e.g., Bransford, Franks, Vye, & Sherwood, 1986; Brown & Campione, 1987; Brown et al., 1983). In general, these instructional conditions engage students in problem solving and decision making. Such activities help students understand the nature of the problems that various concepts and procedures were designed to solve and hence enable them to understand the functional significance of new information. Under these conditions, when similar problems are encountered in subsequent situations, spontaneous use of relevant concepts and strategies is much more likely to occur. The use of videodisc technology in instructional capacities allows for the applicability of these findings to instruction with children who are at risk for school failure.

A set of studies completed by Johnson (1987) provides an excellent illustration of the importance of thinking about the knowledge presupposed by various attempts to help children learn new information. Johnson worked with 4- and 5-year-old inner-city children who attended a prekindergarten and kindergarten program in the Southeast. Johnson was particularly interested in those children who teachers felt would need extra assistance to be ready for first grade.

As an initial study, Johnson compared the story comprehension and retelling abilities of children who the teachers felt were at risk for school failure with those who they felt were not at risk. The scores of these two groups were almost nonoverlapping, with the at-risk children performing very poorly. The groups also showed very large differences on the Peabody Picture Vocabulary Test. These data suggest that the teachers' assumptions about the need of these children for extra help were warranted.

In a subsequent study, Johnson worked only with learners who the teachers felt were at risk (none of these children had participated in the first study). The goal here was to help the children get a better idea of what it meant to understand a story. A number of researchers (e.g., Stein, 1979; Stein & Glenn, 1979) argue that students must make connections among general story structures (e.g., goals of the protagonist, obstacles to reaching goals) and specific events in a story in order to comprehend.

Half the children in Johnson's study were provided with oral storytelling experiences. The target story was a simplified version of the first part of *Swiss Family Robinson*—the part describing the shipwreck and the attempt to get to shore by building a raft. This story was chosen, in part, because it provides an excellent context for teaching about problem solving. In addition, it was available in a videodisc format. The second half of the children were provided with a videodisc presentation of the identical story.

A verbally presented story such as *Swiss Family*—even a simplified version such as the one used by Johnson—illustrates some of the problems of assessing whether it presupposes too much knowledge for many children. Do they know what a ship is (most indicated they did)? Can they understand a shipwreck, the fact that the family has to break out of their cabin "below deck," the idea of building a raft; the idea of an island; the idea of the vast area of water that makes up an ocean?

Johnson worked individually with children throughout a number of different sessions. First, the children in the story group were read the story and asked to retell it in their own words. Their performance was extremely low. The average number of ideas recalled by the 4-year-olds was 2.07; for the 5-year-olds, it was 6.67. The children's abilities to answer factual and inferential questions about the story were also quite low. In comparison, the videodisc group's mean number of story ideas recalled by 4-year-olds was 6.53; for the 5-year-olds, it was 11.93. The children's abilities to answer factual and inferential questions in the videodisc context were quite high.

For the story recall and comprehension measures, the videodisc group surpassed the verbal group at each testing phase and at each age level. For this particular study, the presentation of story information in videodisc contexts was superior to a strict verbal presentation.

Bransford and his colleagues (in the Cognition and Technology Group at Vanderbilt University, 1990) have investigated the use of videodisc materials with at-risk students. The majority of their empirical findings illustrate that students are better able to comprehend, make inferences, and understand sentences and words when the presentation context is videodisc. At least in part, this seems due to the richness of the environment. These results also speak, however, to the likelihood of success in teaching concept development and problem solving. This is being done within several types of videodisc instructional contexts.

At the Learning Technology Center at Vanderbilt, Bransford created and printed a videodisc: the *Adventure of Jasper*. The video is approximately 15 minutes in length and tells the story of a character named Jasper Woodbury. Jasper takes his small motorboat up river to see a cruiser that he's thinking about purchasing. He and the cruiser's owner, Sal, test run the cruiser. Jasper later decides to buy the boat. With the boat in his possession, Jasper must then consider if he can make it home before dark and if he can do so without running out of gas.

The goal structure of Jasper's problem is somewhat complex. There are 17 subproblems constituting the solution and as many as five levels of problem nesting. All of the number facts relevant to the solution of these problems are embedded in the video. Although the problem is complex, the context of planning for a trip was assumed to be relatively familiar to students. In addition, the problem types constituting the solution are the same found in elementary and middle school curricula.

Results of a recent study reveal that using the Jasper disc for presenting problem-solving information and testing comprehension within that context are advantageous for teaching in a number of different content areas like mathematics and social studies (Johnson, 1990b). Other videodiscs have been "repurposed" and used to deliver various types of content-area subject matter. In fact, the Cognition and Technology Group have instructionally implemented Hollywood-quality videodisc movies, such as the *Young Sherlock Holmes*, in several elementary classroom research studies (see Kinzer, Hasselbring, Schmidt, & Meltzer, 1990; Rowe, Goodman, Moore, & McLarty, 1990; Vye, Rowe, Kinzer, & Risko, 1990). Results of their work reveal that macro-context instruction in videodisc settings enhances problem-solving abilities, improves understanding of story grammar and comprehension, and improves writing.

Theoretical Background

The research reviewed here is theoretically embedded in a framework that focuses on the active construction of knowledge. Constructive approaches to comprehension and learning have a long history in developmental psychology (e.g., Piaget, 1952). Recent research has tested and refined constructive views and found them important for understanding areas such as language comprehension (Bransford, Barclay, & Franks, 1972; Bransford & Johnson, 1972), reading (e.g., Beck & Carpenter, 1986; Bransford, 1984), science education (e.g., Carey, 1986; Linn, 1986; Sherwood, Kinzer, Bransford, &

Franks, 1987), and mathematical thinking (e.g., Bransford, Hasselbring, Barron, Littlefield, & Goin, 1987; Brown & Campione, 1987). At a general level, proficiency in these areas helps people become literate adults (e.g., Rowe, 1986).

Constructive approaches to knowledge acquisition are especially important for understanding the plight of at-risk children because these approaches emphasize how the learner must provide active contributions to the teaching/learning context for comprehension to occur (e.g., Bransford & Johnson, 1972; Schwen et al., 1990). If the learner does not have the knowledge necessary to make such contributions, or if the teacher and student do not share the necessary knowledge, comprehension and learning will be impaired.

People who lack the knowledge presupposed by various messages and events are at a distinct disadvantage. Teachers and parents often attempt to help students activate knowledge that is relevant to understanding (e.g., Bransford & Haldemeyer, 1983) yet find themselves at a loss when they are unfamiliar with the knowledge available to individual children. This is particularly true with LEP families, many of whom are either illiterate in English or unfamiliar with U.S. texts and schooling. One of the major goals of effective multimedia instructional applications is to provide rich sets of background knowledge that teachers, students, and parents can share. Cummins (1981) labels these "cultural knowns."

Cummins (1981) argues that the process of becoming educationally at risk stems from the usual break between prior experience in the home and expectations in the school environment. He provides evidence that, simply by valuing the language-minority children's culture(s) and beginning instruction with cultural knowns, schools could provide a basis for future success by building self-efficacy among students. Because of the semantically rich aspects of videodisc technology, cultural knowns are even more evident and immediately relevant.

Combining Knowledge Acquisition With Problem Solving

As noted above, the goal of much of the experimental research on educational applications of videodisc technology is to study ways that video technology and instruction in problem solving can be combined to develop useful sets of knowledge and skills that will enable young children to think for themselves and function effectively in traditional academic settings (Kinzer et al., 1990; Risko, Kinzer, Vye, & Rowe, 1990; Rowe et al., 1990; Vye et al., 1990).

Research on thinking suggests strongly that, to achieve the goal of helping students learn to think for themselves, we must focus simultaneously on general "metacognitive" processes of problem solving (e.g., Brown, 1986) and on well-organized knowledge structures that provide conceptual tools for thinking (e.g., Bransford & Stein, 1984; Bransford et al., 1986). Many educational programs focus either on the acquisition of specific sets of conceptual or procedural knowledge or on general strategies for problem solving.

The discussion below describes a videodisc-contextualized knowledge acquisition task that is extremely common—namely, a task involving picture naming. Gradually this task is transformed into one that should also teach problem solving plus fundamental information for math literacy. The major focus of this sample videodisc teaching task is to assess the "value added" as the lessons move from simple to more elaborate teaching formats.

Sample Videodisc Teaching Formats

Teaching Format 1: Knowledge Acquisition Through Picture Naming

An extremely important part of any attempt to prepare at-risk children to succeed in school involves an emphasis on vocabulary. Students who do not have verbal labels for many objects and events will have a very difficult time in school (e.g., Feuerstein, Rand, Hoffman, & Miller, 1980). As noted earlier, in Johnson's work with at-risk students, there were large differences on the Peabody Picture Vocabulary test between 5-year-old students who teachers felt were prepared to go to school and those they felt were at risk.

A common and entirely reasonable approach to vocabulary instruction is to encourage children to identify and name pictures. Because some types of information no doubt can be better communicated dynamically rather than statistically (e.g., plant or animal growth, the force of a storm involving dynamic information, uses of writing to remember important information), an exemplary videodisc could include hundreds of short scenes and still pictures that teachers could use for instruction. The disc would be much better than a tape because the teacher could easily and flexibly access images as various needs arise. Nevertheless, even though picture naming is important, it fails to develop important components of knowledge.

Format 2: Picture Naming Plus an Emphasis on Function

Picture naming lessons are often supplemented with questions and information about the functions of the objects in the pictures. Children may be asked not only to name an object (e.g., a coat) but also to state when one is useful ("when the weather is very cold"). Research conducted by the Cognition and Technology Group at Vanderbilt University shows quite clearly that information about function or uses can be very important—especially for transfer. For example, in one study, they discuss data from students who knew what logarithms were yet had no idea about why they were useful; they therefore failed to consider them as possibilities when trying to solve problems for which they would help a great deal (Bransford et al., 1985). Similarly, data in metacognitive literature has shown that, when students do not know the conditions under which procedural knowledge such as counting or other strategies are useful, the information is not used in new tasks (e.g., Brown et al., 1983).

Format 3: Knowledge Acquisition in the Context of Decision Making

Lessons that involve the naming of objects plus elaborating their functions can become even more powerful if they are embedded in the context of decision making. The latter can be cast in the form of an adventure that various protagonists undertake.

It should be noted that many developers of computer software and other curricula often talk about teaching decision making in the context of adventures yet do not allow *informed* decision making. For example, a frequently used computer program called *Oregon Trail* asks students to make a number of decisions yet provides them with no advanced knowledge that makes some decisions more reasonable than others. Instead of teaching "trial and error" decision making as with the computer program, the focus in this videodisc format is on the act of finding information necessary to make informed decisions.

Bransford and Johnson (1988) worked informally with a videodisc-based adventure involving two protagonists who want to rescue a friend. Instead of simply starting out to rescue the friend, they first realize they need to find out about where they are going so they can plan ahead. Mathematics-related problem-solving episodes are embedded in the story.

By looking at pictures (characters and the pictures are available on an experimental videodisc), the protagonists in the initial story discover that they have a three-day trip ahead of them. On the first day, they must go through a dense forest. On the second day, they must cross a very large body of water. On the third day, they must climb to the top of a mountain where their friend is being held. Students can see pictures of each of these types of terrain so that they can develop a better mental model of the problems that they will eventually face (for example, they can see that the mountain is snowcapped).

Adventure formats such as this one provide a context for making decisions related to math problem solving. For example, the protagonists try to decide how many types of shoes they should bring (tennis shoes, snow boots, or other types). They realize that they cannot take all types because of lack of space. One decides to take tennis shoes because "they will be great at the beach" (our character therefore completely forgets about the snow-covered mountains). Children are encouraged to make their own arguments for what to take and to imagine that these decisions affect the protagonists.

Other decisions include whether to carry drinking water (and, if so, how much) or drink from the lake, whether to wear shorts or long pants ("the shorts are great for swimming" is what our character decides), whether to take candy instead of sandwiches, whether to swim across the water (distance/measurement) or to bring an inflatable boat, whether to write down important information or rehearse it several times to remember it, whether to look in the yellow pages or a dictionary to find the phone number for a store that sells camping gear, and so on. For each decision, the instructor can ask for reasons and also provide additional information to help students evaluate their arguments. For example, our experimental videodisc includes close-up scenes of snow-covered mountains plus scenes of other people hiking in cold mountains. This helps clarify why snow boots and long pants should be worn.

*Format 4: Integrating the Innovative Format
Into the Broader Teaching Context*

Even the adventure format described above is not optimal unless it is integrated appropriately into the broader teaching context. For example, an adventure involving decisions could be linked to a set of "hands-on" teaching activities that build upon and refer back to the adventure. A major goal of initial descriptive research has been to assess the "value added" when video-based adventures are integrated into the larger, everyday context of the classroom.

Applications in the Classroom

Overall, these four sample formats for teaching suggest a set of progressive elaborations that should increase the quality of children's learning. Based on previous experiences, the first two formats are used quite frequently in preschool and elementary settings; the second two are not. Formats such as those described in Formats 3 and 4 should have a number of potential advantages over the more common format of naming pictures and talking about functions of objects. The instruction will, of course, focus on the names of objects and on their functions, but the innovative videodisc teaching formats should help students develop additional competencies as well. These are competencies that should help them problem-solve more successfully in all content areas.

First, *the teaching formats provide information about planning and problem solving.* Because they emphasize events such as writing and use different sources of information such as the yellow pages versus dictionaries, and so on, they will provide important information about literacy.

Second, *the teaching formats help students learn to make decisions* relative to an activated mental model of the problem situation in which they are trying to find solutions. For example, consider the previously discussed problem involving a trip through the forest on the first day, across a lake on the second day, and into snow-covered mountains on the third day. Initially, we expect many children to accept arguments such as "I'll take the tennis shoes rather than the snow boots because the tennis shoes will be great for the beach" because they forgot about the other constraints on their problem (i.e., the forest and the cold mountains). We do not feel that these children will have the necessary background knowledge to make initial decisions about these types of problem. With practice and with analogical examples that are contextually relevant to them, however, they should become proficient at this task.

Third, *students should learn to make and evaluate arguments.* It is assumed that these arguments will become relatively sophisticated; for example, you would eventually expect to hear arguments such as "I'll give you two reasons why they should not take that large TV set to the mountains—it's too heavy and you can't plug it in." "The dictionary won't help us find the address for a store that sells tents."

Fourth, *the integrated formats should make it much easier to remember what was talked about in the lessons* because it provides cues for retrieval (data are already available on these benefits for middle school students and college students; e.g., Bransford et al., 1985). In addition, students should learn more from sets of hands-on activities if these are linked to a video-based adventure than if they are not. Data with 3-year-old children recently collected by Gray and Fivush (1987) lend strong support to this prediction.

Finally, because *the teaching formats are analogous to many story formats, they should help students develop story schemas that can facilitate subsequent understanding* (e.g., Stein & Glenn, 1979). As noted earlier, however, instruction that actively encourages decision making should be much more effective than instruction that focuses on the retelling of stories where the main characters in the story make decisions and the students simply watch them doing this. Eventually, the students can use images from the videodisc to create their own decision-making adventures, and they should learn to make links spontaneously between hands-on activities and adventures based on the videodisc.

As noted earlier, an experimental videodisc has been created that allows us to conduct studies about the relative advantages of various adventure formats. The disc has been developed so that we can use it with considerable flexibility. For example, we have a number of scenes of protagonists, possible villains, and so on that are approximately 10 seconds each. Also, scenes are programmed showing various emotional reactions to these people (happy, sad, confused) and scenes where they provide feedback to the students ("great idea, thanks"). A number of still scenes are on the disc that can be used to show terrains and to show various objects that can be used for decision making. These 10-second moving scenes show mouth movements and emotions, but, for most of them, there is no story line on the disc—this is supplied by the teacher or the researcher. Thanks to the rapid, random access capabilities of the videodisc, the teacher can access any scene that seems appropriate (the teacher has a menu of scenes and frame numbers). Literally hundreds of adventures can be created in this way.

Overall Significance of the Technology

Overall, the classroom instructional use of video-based technologies has the potential to have a powerful impact on at-risk students' learning. Initial data collected by the Cognition and Technology Group (1990) and Johnson (1987) provide support for this claim. The cumulative impact of these experiences throughout the course of one or two years could be a tremendous boost for children who are at risk for school failure (Bransford et al., 1988; Clifford, 1990; Cuban, 1989; Lehr & Harris, 1988).

Despite the tremendous potential of video technology, it also seems clear that the mere availability of images on a disc or tape are not powerful in and of themselves. They need to be incorporated into teaching formats that help students develop powerful sets of knowledge and skills. More empirical research is warranted that allows researchers (teachers and scientists alike) to assess the "value added" of systematically elaborating various teaching situations in ways that encourage children to think for themselves and to understand the value of literacy for their own problem solving. By working with teachers plus designing important experimental tests, we can provide information that can have a powerful impact on the development of children who are at risk for school failure. With the acquisition of this knowledge and the communication of it to teachers, parents, and others, at-risk children will benefit greatly from exposure to and participation in these highly contextualized, effective learning settings.

References

Alderman, M. K. (1990). Motivation for at-risk students. *Educational Leadership, 48,* 27-30.

Baumeister, A. A. (1987, February). *Effective planning strategies to prevent mental retardation among socially disadvantaged populations.* Paper presented at the National Conference on State Planning for the Prevention of Mental Retardation and Related Disabilities, Washington, DC.

Beck, I. L., & Carpenter, P. A. (1986). Cognitive approaches to understanding reading: Implications for instructional practice. *American Psychologist, 41,* 1098-1105.
Bennett, K. P., & LeCompte, M. D. (1990). *How schools work.* New York: Longman.
Boyer, J. B. (1990). Teacher education that enhances equity. In H. P. Baptiste, Jr., H. C. Waxman, J. Walker de Felix, & J. E. Anderson (Eds.), *Leadership, equity, and school effectiveness* (pp. 244-258). Newbury Park, CA: Sage.
Bransford, J. D. (1984). Schema activation versus schema acquisition. In R. C. Anderson, J. Osborn, & R. Tierney (Eds.), *Learning to read in American schools: Basal readers and content texts* (pp. 259-272). Hillsdale, NJ: Lawrence Erlbaum.
Bransford, J. D., Barclay, J. R., & Franks, J. J. (1972). Sentence memory: A construction vs. interpretive approach. *Cognitive Psychology, 3,* 193-209.
Bransford, J. D., Franks, J. J., Vye, N. J., & Sherwood, R. D. (1986). *New approaches to instruction: Because wisdom can't be told.* Paper presented at the Illinois Conference on Similarity and Analogy.
Bransford, J. D., & Haldemeyer, K. (1983). Learning from children learning. In J. Bisanz, G. Bisanz, & R. Kail (Eds.), *Learning in children: Progress in cognitive development research.* New York: Springer-Verlag.
Bransford, J. D., Hasselbring, T., Barron, B., Littlefield, J., & Goin, L. (1987, January). *The use of macro-contexts to facilitate mathematical thinking.* Paper presented at the Advances in Mathematics Education Conference, San Diego, CA.
Bransford, J. D., & Johnson, M. K. (1972). Contextual prerequisites for understanding: Some investigations of comprehension and recall. *Journal of Verbal Learning and Verbal Behavior, 11,* 717-726.
Bransford, J. D., & Johnson, R. T. (1988). *New approaches for teaching at-risk children mathematics.* Unpublished manuscript.
Bransford, J. D., Sherwood, R., & Hasselbring, T. (1988). The video revolution and its effects on development: Some initial thoughts. In G. Foreman & P. Pufall (Eds.), *Constructivism in the computer age* (pp. 173-201). Hillsdale, NJ: Lawrence Erlbaum.
Bransford, J. D., Sherwood, R., Kinzer, C., & Hasselbring, T. (1985). *Havens for learning: Toward a framework for developing effective uses of technology* (Technical Report No. 85.1.1). Nashville, TN: Vanderbilt University, Learning Technology Center.
Bransford, J. D., Sherwood, R., Vye, N. J., & Rieser, J. (1986). Teaching thinking and problem solving: Suggestions from research. *American Psychologist, 41,* 1078-1089.
Bransford, J. D., & Stein, B. S. (1984). *The IDEAL problem solver.* New York: Freeman.
Brown, A. (1986, November). *Facilitating transfer in young children.* Paper presented at the Illinois Conference on Similarity and Analogy, Champaign, IL.
Brown, A. L., Bransford, J. D., Ferrara, R. A., & Campione, J. C. (1983). Learning, remembering, and understanding. In J. H. Flavell & E. M. Markman (Eds.), *Carmichael's manual of child psychology* (Vol. 1). New York: John Wiley.
Brown, A., & Campione, J. (1987, January). *The importance of understanding what you are doing.* Paper presented at the Advances in Mathematic Education Conference, San Diego, CA.
Brown, J., Collins, A., & Duiguid, P. (1989). Situated cognition and the culture of learning. *Educational Researcher, 18,* 32-42.

Carey, S. (1986). Cognitive science and science education. *American Psychologist, 41,* 1123-1130.
Clifford, M. M. (1990). Students need challenge, not easy success. *Educational Leadership, 48,* 22-26.
The Cognition and Technology Group at Vanderbilt. (1990). Anchored instruction and its relationship to situated cognition. *Educational Researcher, 19,* 2-10.
Cuban, L. A. (1989). At-risk students: What teachers and principals do. *Educational Leadership, 46,* 29-31.
Cummins, J. (1981). The role of primary language developing in promoting educational success for language minority students. In *Schooling and language minority students: A theoretical framework.* Los Angeles: California State University, Evaluation, Dissemination, and Assessment Center.
Deutsch, M. (1990). The disadvantaged child and the learning process. In K. J. Dougherty & F. M. Hammack (Eds.), *Education and society.* Florida: Harcourt Brace Jovanovich.
Donaldson, M. (1978). *Children's minds.* New York: Norton.
Estrom, R. B., Goertz, M. E., Pollack, J. M., & Rock, D. A. (1987). Who drops out of high school and why? Findings from a national study. In G. Natriello (Ed.), *School dropouts, patterns and policies* (pp. 52-69). New York: Teachers College Press.
Feuerstein, R., Rand, Y., Hoffman, M. B., & Miller, R. (1980). *Instrumental enrichment.* Baltimore, MD: University Park Press.
Gray, J., & Fivush, R. (1987). *Young children's memory.* Prepublication manuscript, Emory University, Atlanta, GA.
Hahn, A. (1987). Reaching out to America's dropouts: What to do? *Phi Delta Kappan, 69,* 256-263.
Hodgkinson, H. L. (1985). *All one system: Demographics of education—kindergarten through graduate school.* Washington, DC: Institute for Educational Leadership.
Johnson, R. T. (1987). *Uses of video technology to facilitate children's learning.* Unpublished doctoral dissertation, George Peabody College at Vanderbilt University, Nashville, TN.
Johnson, R. T. (1990a). The video-based setting as a context for learning story information. *Childhood Education, 66,* 168-171.
Johnson, R. T. (1990b). Supporting gifted student's acquisition of relevant knowledge for solving math problems. *Early Child Development and Care.*
Kinzer, C., Hasselbring, T. S., Schmidt, C. A., & Meltzer, L. (1990, April). *Effects of multimedia to enhance writing ability.* Paper presented at the annual meeting of the American Educational Research Association, Boston.
Knapp, M. S., Turnbull, B. J., & Shields, P. M. (1990). New directions for educating the children of poverty. *Educational Leadership, 48,* 4-8.
Lehr, J. B., & Harris, H. W. (1988). *At-risk, low-achieving students in the classroom.* Washington, DC: National Education Association.
Levin, H. M. (1987). Accelerated schools for disadvantaged students. *Educational Leadership, 44,* 19-21.
Linn, M. C. (1986). *Establishing a research base for science education: Challenges, trends, and recommendations* (Report of a National Science Foundation national conference). Berkeley: University of California.

McPartland, J. M., & Slavin, R. E. (1990). *Policy perspectives: Increasing achievement of at-risk students at each grade level* (OERI No. 433J47900838). Washington, DC: Government Printing Office.

Natriello, G., McDill, E. L., & Pallas, A. M. (1990). *Schooling disadvantaged children: Racing against catastrophe.* New York: Teachers College Press.

Pea, R. (1990, April). *Integrative media in education: Progress and prospects.* Paper presented at the annual meeting of the American Educational Research Association, Boston.

Piaget, J. (1952). *The origins of intelligence in children* (M. Cook, Trans.). New York: International Universities Press.

Presseisen, B. Z. (1988). *At-risk students and thinking: Perspectives from research.* Washington, DC: National Education Association.

Ralph, J. (1989). Improving education for the disadvantaged: Do we know whom to help. *Phi Delta Kappan, 70,* 395-401.

Risko, V. J., Kinzer, C., Vye, N., & Rowe, D. (1990, April). *Effects of videodisc macrocontexts on comprehension and composition of causally-coherent stories.* Paper presented at the annual meeting of the American Educational Research Association, Boston.

Rowe, D. (1986). *Literacy in the child's world: Young children's explorations of alternate communication systems.* Unpublished doctoral dissertation, Indiana University, Bloomington.

Rowe, D. (1987). *Preschoolers as authors: Literacy learning in the social world of the classroom.* Prepublication manuscript, Vanderbilt University, Nashville, TN.

Rowe, D., Goodman, J., Moore, P., & McLarty, K. (1990, April). *Effects of videodisc macrocontexts on classroom interaction and student questioning during literacy lessons.* Paper presented at the annual meeting of the American Educational Research Association, Boston.

Sartain, H. W. (1989). *Nonachieving students at risk: School, family, and community intervention.* Washington, DC: National Education Association.

Schwen, T. M., Goodrum, D. A., Knuth, R. A., & Dorsey, L. T. (1990, April). *Enriched learning and information environments.* Paper presented at the annual meeting of the American Educational Research Association, Boston.

Semper, R. (1990). Hypercard and education: Reflections on the Hyperboom. In K. Hooper & S. Ambron (Eds.), *Learning with interactive multimedia* (pp. 52-67). Cupertino, CA: Microsoft Press.

Sherwood, R. D., Kinzer, C. K., Bransford, J. D., & Franks, J. J. (1987). Some benefits of creating macro-contexts for science instruction: Initial findings. *Journal of Research in Science Teaching, 24,* 417-435.

Slavin, R. (1989). Students at risk for school failure: The problem and its dimensions. In R. E. Slavin, N. L. Karweit, & N. A. Madden (Eds.), *Effective programs for students at risk.* Needham Heights, MA: Allyn & Bacon.

Slavin, R. E., & Madden, N. A. (1989). What works for students at risk: A research synthesis. *Educational Leadership, 46,* 4-13.

Soled, S. W. (1989). Higher level thinking: Educational opportunity or educational necessity? In J. M. Lakebrink (Ed.), *Children at risk* (pp. 264-276). Springfield, IL: Charles C Thomas.

Stein, N. L. (1979). How children understand stories: A developmental analysis. In L. Katz (Ed.), *Current topic in early childhood education* (Vol. 2, pp. 261-290). Hillsdale, NJ: Ablex.

Stein, N. L., & Glenn, C. G. (1979). An analysis of story comprehension in elementary school children. In R. Freedle (Ed.), *New directions in discourse processing* (Vol. 2, pp. 53-120). Hillsdale, NJ: Ablex.

Vye, N. J., Bransford, J., Furman, L., Barron, B., Montavon, E., Young, M., Van Haneghan, J., & Barron, L. (1989, March). *An analysis of students' mathematical problem solving in real-world settings*. Paper presented at the annual meeting of the American Educational Research Association, San Francisco.

Vye, N. J., Rowe, D., Kinzer, C., & Risko, V. J. (1990, April). *The effects of anchored instruction for teaching social studies: Enhancing comprehension of setting information*. Paper presented at the annual meeting of the American Educational Research Association, Boston.

Walker de Felix, J., Johnson, R. T., & Schick, J. E. (1990). Socio- and psycholinguistic considerations in interactive video instruction for limited English proficient students. *Computers in the Schools, 7,* 173-190.

Watson, D. L., Northcutt, L., & Rydell, L. (1989). Teaching bilingual students successfully. *Educational Leadership, 46,* 59-62.

Willis, H. D. (1986). *Students at-risk: A review of conditions, circumstances, indicators, and educational implications* (Technical Report). Elmhurst, IL: North Central Regional Educational Laboratory.

• 7 •

Learning Differences Among At-Risk Minority Students

OLIVIA N. SARACHO
CYNTHIA KOREN GERSTL

Educators and researchers have become increasingly concerned with the academic performance of at-risk students. The term *at risk* emerged from the medicine and public health field (Slavin, 1989). Risk groups in the United States were first identified more than 400 years ago. According to Laosa (1984, p. 1), "There is remarkable historical continuity in Anglo-American social welfare policies toward children; in every era over the past 400 or more years, certain groups of children have been considered as being 'at risk,' and hence at social concern and responsibility." These groups include students with handicaps and serious diseases, orphans, indigent children, and neglected, abused, and delinquent students. Recently, specific ethnic, racial, and language groups have been added as "risk" categories, becoming a major focus of social concern and public responsibility (Laosa, 1984).

Minorities represent a sizable and growing proportion of the population in the United States. By 1990, ethnic and racial minorities will constitute more than 65% of the student population in the metropolitan schools of this country (Bruno, 1987-1988). The increase in the proportion of African Americans, Hispanic Americans, and Asian Americans in our schools during the past few years is expected to continue. It has become a major concern of educators and social prognosticators because many of these individuals lack the ability to meet the schools' academic, behavioral, and intellectual expectations, become frustrated, and drop out of school. Minority students in the United

States have a proportionately higher "dropout" rate from school and achieve lower scores on standardized intelligence tests and achievement measures (Baca & Cervantes, 1989; Hale, 1982; Howard, 1987; Ogbu, 1978; Swisher & Deyhle, 1987).

This country's future will heavily depend on the productive skills of today's youth, of which one third will represent minority groups. It is essential that strategies be employed to cultivate the educational performance of this growing population, which includes African Americans, Mexican Americans, Native Americans, and Asian Americans.

African Americans

In 1986, more than 6.5 million African American school children in the United States represented 16.1% of the total school-age population (U.S. Department of Education, 1986). African Americans were and continue to be the largest minority group in the United States. This population is not homogeneous, however. More than a decade earlier, Valentine's (1971) study on poverty and African American culture noted the existence of at least 14 distinct African American subcultures in one local community. These people represent subgroups with backgrounds in different languages, national origins, and types of environments. They have diverse patterns of behavior, beliefs, family structures, value systems (Howard, 1987; Olstad, Juarez, Davenport, & Maury, 1981; Valentine, 1971), and degrees of assimilation with mainstream society. The dropout rate fluctuated during the period of 1970 to 1986 between 10% and 21.1% for this population, with an initial increase followed by some decrease (Bruno, 1987-1988).

Mexican Americans

The Mexican American population is one of the fastest growing ethnocultural groups in the United States. It currently encompasses 8% of the American people, with most of them residing in California, Arizona, New Mexico, Colorado, Texas, and New York (Trueba, 1988). Mexican Americans view themselves as America's forgotten minority and are playing an important role in the industrial, agricultural, artistic, intellectual, and political life of the country (Saracho & Hancock, 1983). In 1986, the U.S. census showed 44.7% of high school graduates were from the Mexican American community (Díaz, 1989). The dropout rate for this group ranged from 12.2% to 15.2% for the period 1975-1986 (Bruno, 1987-1988). Thus a sizable number of Mexican American students fail to succeed in the U.S. school system.

Native Americans

American Indians and Alaskan Natives have a higher dropout rate than any other ethnic group in U.S. schools (Kleinfeld, McDiarmid, & Hagstrom, 1989). Estimates of the dropout rate vary considerably, however, ranging from a low of 38% to a high of 87% (Ogbu, 1978). In the 1980 census, less than 50% of adults living on the 10 largest reservations had high school diplomas (U.S. Bureau of the Census, 1980b). There is a 29% dropout rate for American Indian and Alaska Native high school sophomores (Kleinfeld et al., 1989). Native American students in one urban setting had a four-year average dropout rate of 29% (Eberhard, 1989). Between 1984 and 1986, Crawford (1986) found that, in 96 schools in Arizona, New Mexico, and Utah, 32% of Navajo children dropout each year, 10% of the students never returned to school, and a 90% cumulative dropout rate for this population was projected if the trend continues. A fairly high and steady rate of dropping out exists across the elementary years, beginning in kindergarten. The dropout rate for kindergarten through grade 6 averaged 26% and for grades 7 to 13, 32%. Native American officials have been greatly concerned about this high dropout rate (Crawford, 1986).

Obviously, these findings need to be challenged for two main reasons: (a) the lack of consistent a definition for the term *dropout* (Morrow, 1986) and (b) the lack of a consistent set of procedures and safeguards for determining the data (Hammack, 1986; Morrow, 1986).

Asian Americans

Asian Americans are the fastest growing ethnic group in the United States (Divorky, 1988), with about 3.5 million people in 1980 (U.S. Bureau of the Census, 1980a). Individuals of Asian and Pacific Island descent constitute a significant minority ("Preliminary 1980 Census Results," 1982). People of

Chinese, Filipino, Japanese, Korean, Vietnamese, Hawaiian, and Samoan ancestry totaled more than 3 million, at least doubling the population figure from the 1970 census (Kitano, 1983). This is a very diverse population, with different customs, languages, and religions (Mizokawa & Morishima, 1979). The 1980 census shows more than 20 different Asian and Pacific islander groups, with the close to 300,000 Pacific Islanders composed of Polynesians, Micronesians, and Melanesians (U.S. Bureau of the Census, 1980a). The largest groups in the United States in 1980 were Chinese, Filipinos, Japanese, Asian Indians, Koreans, Vietnamese, Laotian, Cambodian, Pakistani, Indonesian, and Hmong.

Asian Americans have achieved a high rate of academic success (Divorky, 1988; Kitano, 1983). Chinese Americans and Japanese Americans have been shown to be equal or to surpass Anglo-Americans in mathematics and reasoning skills (Edward, Graham, & Funaki, 1981; Stodolsky & Lesser, 1967). Asian American students have also surpassed Mexican Americans, African Americans, Puerto Ricans, and Native Americans in tests of reading, math, and verbal ability (Ogbu, 1987). The stereotype of Asian Americans as members of a successful "model minority" may have been generalized to school performance (Kitano, 1983). But this stereotype overlooks the large numbers of students who are not successful and constitute a sizable at-risk population, including immigrants, Pacific Islanders, more recent refugees, and inner-city youth (Mizokawa & Morishima, 1979). More than one quarter of Asian Americans students drop out of school in New York City, and Pacific Islanders have a dropout rate of 17.1% in San Diego, California (Divorky, 1988).

Culturally Induced Cognitive Style

Recent literature indicates the possibility that ethnic minority students' academic performance may be affected by their learning style, which is greatly influenced by their culturally induced cognitive style. The construct of cognitive style denotes dimensions of individual differences in thinking, communicating, interacting, and perceiving that are important to knowledge acquisition. The U.S. educational system has failed ethnic minority students with its lack of sensitivity for predominant minority cognitive styles (Ramírez, 1982). One of the contributing factors in the lack of success of minority students is incompatibility of the minority students' cognitive style with the instructional demands in the majority of U.S. schools. The purpose of this chapter is to provide a selective review of the literature for educators, sociologists, and researchers who seek to better understand how culturally induced cognitive styles influence the academic performance of those at-risk students who are members of a minority group. There are several minority groups. Because at least one in five Americans today is an African American, Mexican American, Native American, or Asian American (Kasarda, cited in Fernandez & Velez, 1985), however, this chapter will focus on the cognitive style of students in those groups.

Field Dependence/Independence

Cognitive style refers to the way in which people perceive, process, and remember information. Cognitive styles characterize a person's mode of understanding, thinking, remembering, judging, and solving problems (Witkin, Moore, Goodenough, & Cox, 1977). These stylistic characteristics are apparent in an individual's experience (Anastasi, 1988), such as perceptual styles, personality, intelligence, and social behavior. Individuals reconstruct incoming information, organize new knowledge, and merge it within the memory structure. This mechanism strengthens the individuals' intellectual development, extending his or her repertoire of cognitive skills that have been accumulated throughout life. Cognitive styles influence the students' intellectual and academic achievements. Field dependence/independence (FDI) is the dimension of cognitive style that has been most widely studied (Cazden & Leggett, 1981; Kogan, 1987).

The FDI dimension of cognitive style distinguishes between the approaches field-dependent (FD) and field-independent (FI) individuals use to cognitively manage complex and confusing incidents in different situations. Saracho and Spodek (1981, p. 154) describe the characteristics of FD and FI individuals:

Field-dependent individuals:
   rely on the surrounding perceptual field;
   experience their environment in a relatively global fashion by conforming to the effects of the prevailing field or context;
   are dependent on authority;
   search for facial cues in those around them as a source of information;

are strongly interested in people;

get closer to the person with whom they are interacting;

have a sensitivity to others which helps them to acquire social skills;

prefer occupations which require involvement with others.

In contrast, field-independent individuals:

perceive objects as separate from the field;

can abstract an item from the surrounding field;

solve problems that are presented and reorganized in different contexts;

experience an independence from authority which leads them to depend on their own standards and values;

are oriented towards active striving;

appear to be cold and distant;

are socially detached but have analytic skills;

prefer occupations that allow them to work by themselves.

These extreme behaviors actually occur along a continuum and are assumed to be value free. Thus most individuals possess to some degree the characteristics of both FD and FI cognitive styles. These characteristics are remarkably pervasive and congruent, influencing the students' learning.

Students' Learning

Learning styles reflect the cognitive and social characteristics of individuals. FD and FI students differ in their ability to use divergent types of information (Saracho, 1989a), therefore they receive and process information differently (Shade, 1989b). Although there is no difference in learning ability and memory (Witkin et al., 1977), the students' cognitive styles affect their ability to assimilate information and solve problems (Cohen, 1969). Students with cognitive styles different than the style generally used in their schools and classrooms are likely to have difficulty succeeding, regardless of their level of native intelligence (Cohen, 1969). Although the success of a particular approach is often context dependent, FI students have an advantage as their strategies are more compatible with instructional methodologies. Numerous studies comparing the achievement of FD and FI students in U.S. schools have found FI students outperforming their FD peers (Davis, 1987; Davis & Cochran, 1989; Ramírez & Castañeda, 1974). Success in school

Table 7.1 Characteristics Field-Independent and Field-Dependent Students Need to Succeed

Field Independent	Field Dependent
Success in school requires a number of field-independent skills and behaviors: —structure and organize their environment (Saracho, 1989a; Witkin, 1978); —extract information from distractions; —adhere to organized time schedules; —spend extended periods of time doing seat work; —learn individually (Hale, 1982; Ramírez and Castañeda, 1974); —attend to learning tasks without social interaction; —use analytical thinking (Cohen, 1969); —have a relatively long attention span; —work well with charts and graphs where factual details are highlighted (Holtzman et al., 1979); —use trial and error methodology; —learn from verbal or written instructions; —use hypothesis testing techniques (Witkin et al., 1977); —attempt unfamiliar tasks (Witkin et al., 1977); —respond well to feedback, even if negative (Holtzman et al., 1979).	In contrast, field-dependent students: —need structure and organization (Holtzman, Goldsmith, & Barrera, 1979; Witkin, 1978); —need clearly defined goals and objectives (Laosa, 1977; Saracho, 1989a); —prefer social interaction in the learning process (Witkin, 1978; Witkin, Moore, Goodenough, & Cox, 1977); —learn material in a social context; —enjoy fantasy and humor (Holtzman et al., 1979); —retain more information when taught using concrete, visual examples rather than verbal instructions; —prefer using a "spectator" or observer approach to learning (Witkin et al., 1977); —react well to praise and very poorly to negative feedback (Holtzman et al., 1979); —learn best in a cooperative, humanistic setting, where guidance and example are readily available (Shade, 1981a)

requires a number of FI characteristics and behaviors. Table 7.1 describes the characteristics that both FD and FI students need to succeed in the school environment.

As subject matter becomes more sophisticated in the upper grades, there is a greater dependence on analytical reasoning and a need for a larger information base (Cohen, 1969). Analytic skills help FI students succeed in such subjects as science, mathematics, and reading (Davis, 1987; Davis & Cochran, 1989; Witkin, 1978). Their lack of analytic skills may help explain the high dropout rate of minorities from science and mathematics in the upper grades (Olstad et al., 1981) and the lower grades on standardized measures (Cohen, 1969).

At-Risk Students

Researchers studying at-risk students have determined that school environments generally favor the analytic or FI learner (Hale, 1982; Hilliard, 1989; Ramírez, 1989; Ramírez & Castañeda, 1974; Saracho, 1989a). It has been suggested that many at-risk and minority students have FD cognitive styles (Howard, 1987; Ramírez & Castañeda, 1974), with the various ethnic groups having diverse perceptual abilities (Hsi & Lim, 1977). Consequently, instructional and environmental incompatibilities develop that hinder successful learning.

Studies comparing achievement of FD and FI students in U.S. schools have found FI students outperforming their FD peers (Davis, 1987; Davis & Cochran, 1989; Ramírez & Castañeda, 1974). The successful student needs FI skills that include the ability to attend to learning tasks without social interaction, extract information from distractions, and use analytical thinking (Cohen, 1969). The student must have a relatively long attention span and also be able to adhere to organized time schedules, spend extended periods of time doing seat work, and learn individually (Hale, 1982; Ramírez & Castañeda, 1974). This may explain the high dropout rate of minorities from science and math in the upper grades (Cohen, 1969; Olstad et al., 1981).

Standardized intelligence and achievement measures (Davis & Cochran, 1989; Ramírez & Castañeda, 1974) assess the understanding of concepts and cumulative general information via logic, which depends on analytic abilities (Cohen, 1969) and a reflective response style (Shade, 1981b). Nonanalytic assessment measures are generally not available in U.S. schools (Cohen, 1969). Therefore FD students usually have poorer scores.

Standardized assessment measures have also been accused of containing elements of cultural bias (Baca & Cervantes, 1989) and cognitive style bias (e.g., abstract thinking). Several nonverbal, culture-free standardized measures have been created as a response to criticisms of cultural bias in assessment (Baca & Cervantes, 1989). These tests may be even more culturally biased, however, in their dependence on analytical-logical reasoning (Cohen, 1969) and reflective response styles (Shade, 1981b). The most intelligent nonanalytic students, regardless of ethnicity, will receive the poorest grades because of their greater reliance on relational strategies and their inability to use the analytic processes (Cohen, 1969) and abstract thinking.

Culturally Diverse Cognitive Styles

The rhetoric of the 1960s characterizes culturally different students who do not do well in school and depict poor learning styles as "culturally disadvantaged." In the 1980s, these children were characterized as "children at risk." These students possess performance deficits that are attributed to the family and its socialization practices as well as family structures. In addition to this sociological explanation, ethnicity is also considered a contributing influence. Such students possess a distinctive inclination for learning modalities and manner of presentation, information organization, and evaluation that deviates from the academically successful student (Shade, 1989a).

Differences in socialization and child-rearing practices in a culture affect the development of cognitive styles by favoring a specific value system and set of behaviors (Witkin, 1978). Consequently, members of an ethnic or racial culture learn to focus on specific types of salient cues in their environment. Cultural conflicts develop when the salient cues provided are incompatible with the cues found relevant in the individual's background and training (Cohen, 1969).

Diverse Communities

The range of value systems and behaviors within ethnic/racial groups are influenced by the level of individual and group acculturation within the majority society. Ramírez, Castañeda, and Herold (1974) found that, the more acculturated a group is within U.S. society, the more FI are its members. Ramírez and Castañeda (1974) characterize three types of communities: traditional, dualistic, and atraditional.

In **traditional** groups, roles are less defined and members of the community share important functions such as child rearing (Cohen, 1969), and cooperation and group interdependence are important values (Witkin, 1978). Members from this type of community perceive their environment more globally, are more context sensitive (TenHouten, 1989), and more FD

(Ramírez & Castañeda, 1974). Conversely, in more *atraditional* and assimilated societies, there is more formal role responsibility (Cohen, 1969). Individualism and competition are important values and people are more FI (Ramírez & Castañeda, 1974). A varied combination of **traditional** and **atraditional** socialization and child-rearing practices exist in communities that are dualistic in nature (Ramírez & Castañeda, 1974).

African Americans

Several researchers have suggested that there is a unique African American perceptual pattern. This assertion is supported by studies of ethnic group patterns that find performance patterns to be essentially the same in all classes within an ethnic group (Stodolsky & Lesser, 1967). These similarities are attributed to shared African roots, the U.S. "Black" experience, and current African American concerns and political movements. The American Black living in a bicultural environment derives behavior patterns from both African American ethnic behavior and mainstream Euro-American culture. For example, Hale (1983) suggests that the emotion-charged, people-oriented quality of Black expression is a part of the African heritage. Additional research can help determine whether intergroup commonalities exist (Valentine, 1971).

African Americans may be relatively homogeneous due to "the recognition that 'color' affects the environmental responses of all African-Americans, regardless of social class" (Shade, 1984, p. 1). Currently, history continues to be a viable social-cultural system transmitting both the African American worldview and the cognitive behavioral patterns to all levels of the community. Wade Nobles (cited in Hale, 1982) describes African American child-rearing practices as mediating between the Black African and the mainstream U.S. cultures. Nobles depicts an African cultural worldview as emphasizing cooperation, interdependence, and collective responsibility, whereas Euro-American cultural values include competition, individualism, and independence.

African Americans generally do not process visual information as the dominant culture does (Shade, 1984). Compared with other ethnic minorities, African American students have difficulty interpreting pictorial representations (Stodolsky & Lesser, 1967). Recognizing and interpreting abstract visual forms is an essential prerequisite to learning to read (Shade & Edwards, 1987). Apparently, the perceptual style of African Americans differs from other cultural groups in several ways. The preferred learning modality for African Americans is kinesthetic and tactile rather than visual (Shade, 1984). Therefore they learn more efficiently when they are able to create movement and with hands-on experiences. The African American culture places a high value on oral and nonverbal communication. Students usually learn by listening and demonstrate understanding by speaking. African American students are more successful when they can present their work orally. Their verbal communication style uses dramatic talking with rhythm, word order, and nonverbal mannerisms (Gilbert & Gay, 1985).

Conversely, African Americans are generally better able to recognize people and to understand and interpret facial expressions and nonverbal reactions (Shade & Edwards, 1987). Research with African American children shows them to be more people oriented. Most African American children are raised in large families where they have a great deal of human interaction (Hale, 1983). Several studies have shown that this perceptual orientation may affect gazing behaviors, interrupting or impeding communication between African American students and their teachers (Feldman, 1985; LaFrance & Mayo, 1976). Gazing behaviors that can cause cultural misunderstandings include averting the eyes when listening intently (Byers & Byers, 1972; Howard, 1987). The averting of eyes may be a remnant of respectful behaviors toward higher-status people in Africa or perhaps learned behaviors from slave days (Byers & Byers, 1972). The listener may attempt to ignore nonverbal messages and concentrate solely on comprehending what is being said (Shade, 1989b).

African American students may use a different timing pattern and sequence when gazing at someone and attempting to get his or her attention. Byers and Byers (1972) analyzed a film taken at a nursery school in New York City. Two of the children were middle-class White, two children were Black, and the teacher was White. Initially, when the researchers analyzed the teacher-student contact time, they assumed that the White teacher was paying less attention to the Black students. On further investigation, the researchers realized that there was a different pattern in the staring behaviors of the children. The White students watched the teacher carefully and timed the moments of eye contact to coincide with when the teacher would notice. The Black students, however, did not time the gazes to the teacher's gaze pattern. When they finally made eye contact, the Black students rarely maintained it. Consequently, their gazing pattern interfered with their communication with the teacher.

African American children are usually trained to focus on animate rather than inanimate objects (Damico, 1985). According to Young (1970, pp. 279-280), "There are always eyes on the baby and idle hands to take away the forbidden objects and then distract the frustrated baby. The personal is thus often substituted for the impersonal." As babies reach to grasp an object or feel a surface, they are usually redirected to feeling the holder's face or involved in a game of rubbing faces as a substitute (Young, 1970). Consequently, African Americans frequently relate more to people and events and have less affective attachment to objects. A study of photographs of a school environment taken by Black and White students showed distinct differences in the content and tenor of the photos. White students included photos of their school building, inanimate objects in the school, and their teachers in relaxed poses. On the other hand, the Black students concentrated on photos of people. They included photos of their teachers but in professional "teacher postures" (Damico, 1985).

Students learn more effectively in a people-oriented, socially interactive, and cooperative environment (Howard, 1987) in which they work closely together with their teachers to achieve common goals (Gilbert & Gay, 1985; Hale, 1982). This affective orientation is an essential component that is overlooked in traditional educational settings. Rapport with the teacher is important to the African American students' academic performance (Hale, 1983).

Most of African Americans' learning styles have characteristics of FD cognitive styles such as cooperation, interdependence, tactile learning, hands-on experiences, nonverbal reactions, facial expressions, and their relationship to people and events. The specific research on cognitive styles supports this assumption, although it is limited and is mainly found in unpublished dissertations. In these few studies, African Americans tend to be FD. For example, Perney (1976) found racial differences with a group of 40 sixth graders. African Americans were more FD than Anglo-Americans. Ramírez and Price-Williams (1974) also found a group of fourth-grade African Americans to be more FD. Shade (1981b) found racial differences with college students at the beginning of their freshman year. African Americans were more FD. Racial differences seem to disappear when socioeconomic class is controlled (e.g., Battle & Rotter, 1963; Schratz,

1976). Obviously, some inconsistencies exist in the research on the cognitive style of African Americans. Regardless of the inconsistencies, a pattern seems to emerge suggesting that African Americans have an FD cognitive style (Shade, 1982). Jones (1978) supports this assumption.

Dimensions of the African American cognitive style include the need to have an overall, global, or holistic picture for a learning task (Howard, 1987) and to use intuitive rather than deductive or inductive reasoning (Shade, 1981b). The characteristics described above suggest that the learning style of African Americans may be relatively FD (Shade, 1981b) and relational (Hale, 1982).

Mexican Americans

Children who differ from the majority culture in the school often behave in a manner incompatible with the accepted majority societal norms. Traditional Mexican American cultural characteristics are FD in nature, such as the tendency to be less competitive, less comfortable in trial and error situations, and less interested in the finer details of concepts or nonsocial activities (Ramírez, 1989; Ramírez & Castañeda, 1974). Additionally, Mexican American students have also been characterized as preferring cooperative instruction and social interaction (Ramírez & Castañeda, 1974).

Differences in parental patterns of communication that affect learning behaviors have been noted. In a study examining verbal cues used by mothers in Anglo-American and Mexican American families, the total number of teaching behaviors were similar, but the nature of the behaviors differed. Hispanic mothers were found to extensively use more nonverbal cues and far fewer questions than Anglo mothers (Laosa, 1977).

Ramírez et al. (1974) concluded that the traditional parents from the Mexican American community focus on social conformity, influencing children to be more FD. Children from less acculturated and more traditional families have been shown to be significantly more FD than those from more acculturated families (Ramírez & Price-Williams, 1974; Ramírez et al., 1974).

Mexican American students also have been found to be more FD and perform more poorly on mathematics and reading than the Anglo-American students. The effect of field dependence was greater on mathematics than on reading (Kagan & Zahn, 1975; Olstad et al., 1981).

A comparison of low economic Hispanic, Anglo-, and African American teenagers indicate African Americans are more FD than the Mexican American and Central or South American students. There is great diversity in achievement within the Hispanic communities. Hispanics from Central and South America have been found to outperform Mexican Americans and mainland Puerto Ricans (Suarez-Orozco, 1987). Several studies have shown that Mexican Americans born in Mexico do better in school than those born in the United States (Valverde, cited in Ogbu, 1987). Cognitive styles of Mexican American students may be age specific (Figueroa, 1980).

Research on cognitive style with Mexican Americans shows that they are more FD than Anglo-Americans (Kagan & Zahn, 1975; Ramírez & Castañeda, 1974; Ramírez & Price-Williams, 1974; Sanders, Scholz, & Kagan, 1976), which is attributed to the traditional child-rearing practices of the Mexican American families that promote close family ties (Saracho & Hancock, 1983). According to Ramírez et al. (1974), individuals from traditional communities with Mexican cultural values and social practices have FD characteristics. Mexican American parents emphasize social integrative values; thus their children are more socially oriented. In contrast, middle-class Anglo-Americans' child-rearing practices emphasize assertiveness, autonomy, and a more individualistic sense of self-identity.

Many have assumed that a generally FD prosocial orientation endures in Mexican American children, although a number of studies (e.g., Holtzman, Díaz-Guerrero, & Swartz, 1975; Sanders et al., 1976) have failed to sustain this assumption. In these studies, the child-rearing practices of Mexican American parents failed to reflect such assumptions. Also, studies of young Mexican American children's cognitive style also failed to support these assumptions (e.g., Saracho, 1983a, 1983c). It is interesting that a study of young Mexican American children found 5-year-olds who were FI (Saracho, 1983b). Thus she believes that individual variation may exist within the Mexican American culture. These results are supported by another study by Saracho (1983c). This confirmation disputes the results of earlier studies by other researchers (e.g., Kagan & Zahn, 1975; Ramírez & Price-Williams, 1974; Sanders et al., 1976) and suggests that generalizing about the Mexican American children's social orientation and their cognitive style is not appropriate. Individual differences need to be taken into account when evaluating the interaction of cognitive style and ethnic groups (Saracho, 1989b). *FDI* is a relative term instead of an absolute term. Extensive data must be collected and analyzed before generalizing that all Mexican American students are FD.

Native Americans

High dropout rates and school failure among Native American students are pressing educational reform to objectively assess educational approaches. The challenge of providing a more effective education for Native American students has raised educators' and researchers' interest in examining closely the concept of cognitive styles. In light of educational reform in Native American schools, methods and materials of instruction can be adapted to better suit the learning styles of Native American students. Effective teaching leads to effective learning, which leads to success in school (Kaulback, 1984).

Research and teacher observations suggest important differences in the learning style of Native American students and their non-Native American counterparts (Karlebach, 1986; More, 1984; Williams, 1986). The differences are consistent enough to warrant careful attention (More, 1987a).

Research on contemporary Native American culture and cognitive styles is limited (Osborne, 1985; Tafoya, 1983). Considerable attention has been devoted in the past few years to cognitive processes, such as FDI (Cullanine, 1985) and global/analytic processing (More, 1984). Studies on cognitive style show inconclusive and unsubstantiated results. Native American culture generally has a generalistic orientation, where tribal members are interested in both people and things (Shade, 1984). The Native American cognitive style is composed of many components, which vary from tribe to tribe. Native American experiences in America, living conditions both on and off the reservation, relative segregation from mainstream society, and language differences influence cognitive style.

Assumptions that Native Americans are FD, based on traditional socialization and child-rearing patterns, have not been substantiated (Swisher & Deyhle, 1987). More (1987b) found that many Native American students use primarily a global (FD) strategy in reading in the primary grades. Teacher interviews suggest that Native American students learn more effectively using concrete instead of abstract processing (More, 1984), although empirical research has not been conducted to support these teachers' opinions. It may be that these concrete materials used in the learning tasks were more culturally relevant. Therefore concrete/abstract differences of Native American students can be attributed more to irrelevance/relevance than to cognitive style differences. Pepper and Henry (1986) also believe that Native American students learn more rapidly when the teaching style uses concrete strategies at first and then moves to the abstract. According to Leith and Slentz (1984), elementary students prefer strategies that require problem solving rather than individual assignments. Both concrete processing and group interaction are characteristics of an FD cognitive style. On the other hand, Vernon (1969) demonstrated that the most highly developed abilities for Canadian Inuit and northern Indian students were perceptual and spatial abilities.

In Kaulback's (1984) review of studies on the Native American students' performance on visual, auditory, and kinesthetic perceptual tasks, he found that Native American children are most successful at processing visual information, which is a characteristic of FI cognitive style. Cullanine's (1985) study shows that non-Native American elementary students are slightly more FI than Native American students from two relatively isolated Indian villages. Some studies, however, show Native Americans to be FI with traditional Native Americans more FI than Anglo-Americans (Dinges & Hollenbeck, 1978). Canadian Eskimos and northern Indians, as representatives of hunting-gathering societies, were found to be more FI. As a result of their living style and child-rearing practices, they had the ability to impose a structure on a field when it needed organization (e.g., unmapped territory; MacArthur, 1968). Weitz (1971) examined two Native American cultural groups (Algonkian and Athapaskan). Within these groups, she created several categories: urban/transitional and traditional, male/female, and older/younger. The results indicated that the overall group scored very high on FI, and the more traditional people were more FI than the urban Native American people. In addition, FI increased with age, and females were more FI than males. More (1984, 1987b) also found that FI increased with age for school-age Native American children. Thus Native American children became more FI as they matured (More, 1987a).

The predominant mode of learning for Native Americans is visual (Brewer, 1977; John, 1972; Rhodes, 1988; Swisher & Deyhle, 1987, 1989; Tafoya, 1989), which helps them achieve FI scores in tests of cognitive style. The Native American student generally prefers to learn by observing others (Brewer, 1977; Tafoya, 1989). The emphasis on visual learning may assist Native American students to develop excellent skills in visual perception and discrimination. They learn to classify and categorize early in life. Rural or reservation students are able to differentiate between various types of animals, to distinguish between the numerous brands used on the animals, and to determine types of cloud formations (Brewer, 1977). Regardless of the specific nature of their cognitive style, the traditional Native American population seems to use a thought process very different than that of the mainstream population (Rhodes, 1988; Swisher & Deyhle, 1989).

The uniqueness of this thought process is exemplified by the symbolism of the circle, which is very important in Native American philosophy. The circle is a symbol of harmony, a state all are trying to achieve. Tafoya (1989) describes a typical Native American extended family genealogical chart with several concentric circles. Three circles represent levels of family relationships and responsibilities.

The main circle centralizes all siblings, including cousins who are referred to as "brother" and "sister." The next level includes grandparents—not parents, as in the Anglo-European chart. This level also includes other relations on the same generational level as the grandparents, such as grandaunt or godparents. The people on this level represent the caregivers and teachers of discipline. The outer and final circle includes the biological parents and their siblings, the aunts and uncles of the children in the central circle. Tafoya (1989) relates that, in some tribes, an uncle or aunt may have primary responsibility for the children. In that case, the biological parents would then be responsible for their own nieces and nephews.

The circle also plays an important part in storytelling and descriptions. A holistic and nonlinear approach is commonly used in which the entire story is important (More, 1987b). The manner of storytelling instills certain cultural values and concepts. Teachers need to understand the meaning of storytelling for Native Americans, who have long understood the power of words and images. The strategy of storytelling reaffirms and re-creates reality in their actions. Teachers may lose this understanding of their students when they lecture (Tafoya, 1983). Details are as important as are the feelings of the individuals involved and the context of the situation being described. It is through storytelling that many complex concepts are taught to the students (Tafoya, 1989). Main ideas and chronology are deemphasized. When the speaker remembers a detail, it is told, even if out of sequence. Therefore summarizing and determining main points can be extremely difficult for the Native American student (Rhodes, 1988).

Native American students are frequently able to learn tasks without verbal instructions. They observe older peers (Brewer, 1977; Rhodes, 1988) as well as grandparents and other elders (More, 1987a; Tafoya, 1983). Deyhle (1983) noted that Navajo children came to school with the cultural knowledge of the way to observe a task and then master it privately.

Traditionally, the Native American learns a task well before demonstrating that knowledge to anyone else. Contrary to practices in mainstream education, public learning is not valued (Brewer, 1977). It is common for other children to ridicule clumsy or inept actions (Swisher & Deyhle, 1987). Therefore the Native American students practice privately and are not forced to show what they know (Brewer, 1977; Rhodes, 1988; Swisher & Deyhle, 1987). Once the task is learned, Native American students receive help to improve the quality of their performance (Rhodes, 1988).

Native American students also use manipulation and experimentation, developing into strong haptic learners (Rohner, 1965). They usually need to have new material presented globally (More, 1987a). The Native American student views the whole as more important than its parts. Therefore, to instruct in the parts, the teacher must relate them to the overall concept (Rhodes, 1988).

Cooperation and an avoidance of competition are cultural behaviors of many of the Native American tribes. Brown (1980) ascribes the cooperative behavior of the Cherokee people to their pre-Columbian heritage. In that type of society, based on an ecology of hunting, cooperation is needed for survival.

Cherokee children have a need for harmony. Competition interferes with the harmonious relationship of the group and is therefore avoided. Students often pace themselves in a group so as not to outdistance a slower student. They will work cooperatively, helping each other complete the task (Wolcott, 1967). Thus a high degree of cooperation hinders academic achievement by preventing Native American students from actively participating in the lessons and responding in class. Those who volunteer answers, or respond when other students are unable to, are not cooperating with the wishes of their peers. Therefore Native American students keep a low profile in class (Brown, 1980; Philips, 1983) and blend in with the group rather than be singled out by praise or criticism (Brewer, 1977).

Native American students may be reluctant to participate when called on by the teacher but willing to participate in small group work and student-initiated endeavors. Philips (1983) found that Native American first graders talk more with their classmates, even while the teacher is speaking. They persist in social interaction longer than their peers who are not Native

American. Often, they attend more to what their friends are doing than to their teacher. In play activity, if the game involves a leader, they are reluctant to assume the role. If left to their own devices, however, the Native American children become involved in team competition to a greater degree than peers who are not Native American (Philips, 1983). Although individual competition is not valued, team endeavors are encouraged. Competition can exist, but it must be a group effort in competing with another group (Brewer, 1977).

Native American students were also found to be high kinesthetic learners with visual and tactile skills. They learn better through activities involving movement, touch, and observation. Yakima Native Americans of Washington State were found to be have higher spatial than sequential skills and higher sequential than verbal skills (Diessner & Walker, 1989).

Male Crow and Cheyenne adolescents personalize their learning by drawing relationships between previous knowledge and new knowledge. They then used new information in discussion to increase learning. Thus cooperative learning, small group work, and personal interpretations are factors in learning (Walker, 1989).

The Native American students' mode of learning has both FD and FI characteristics. FD characteristics are found when Native American students

1. have a need to have new material presented globally
2. cooperate and avoid competition
3. participate in small group work and student-initiated endeavors
4. persist in social interaction
5. are reluctant to assume a leadership role
6. are peer oriented

FI characteristics are found when Native American students

1. consider details to be important
2. use manipulation and experimentation

Obviously, Native American students generally possess more FD than FI characteristics. Differences in FDI cognitive style carry far-reaching implications for the teacher.

Asian Americans

In spite of the successful image in terms of income, mental health, and education, instructional practices more appropriate to the Asian American students must be identified. Studies of cognitive style with Asian Americans living in the United States have been limited (Hsi & Lim, 1977). Hsia (1981) reviewed studies of cognitive style and Asian Americans and made inferences from aptitude and performance test scores from field-career choices. Typical Asian American individuals tend to be more FI. The evidence is weak, however, in assuming that Asian Americans are more FI because they do better in tasks requiring restructuring ability rather than social sensitivity. Harvey, Graham, and Funaki (1981) found that Samoans favored working independently—an FI characteristic. This outcome might be attributed to a greater difficulty in assimilating into the dominant culture, however, than has been the case with other South Pacific Islanders. Chan, Takanishi, and Kitano (1975) examined the learning characteristics of preschool Asian American children to determine similarities and differences in Asian American children's cognitive styles. They found broad differences within each group. Chinese, Japanese, Korean, and Hawaiian children's FI scores were similar across groups to their Anglo-American counterparts. Asian American children from these ethnic groups may be entering school with a well-formulated FI perceptual style. Hansen's (1984) study demonstrated that South Pacific males are significantly more FI than females and that Hawaiian Americans achieved higher FI scores than the other South Pacific Islanders.

Chan et al. (1975) investigated concept development in mathematics and discovered that Asian American school-age children achieve an average or better level of development in mathematical concepts—an FI characteristic. Hsi and Lim (1977) insist that Asian Americans are equal to or surpass Anglo-Americans in mathematics and reasoning skills, which relate to an FI cognitive style. Kitano (1983) concluded that Asian American students enter school with a good understanding of visual discrimination skills and quantitative concepts that are essential for school readiness, although Filipino American children have less visual discrimination skills than the other groups.

Asian Americans possess different learning styles characterized by a visual perceptual response, favoring visual images or graphic representations to promote learning; analytic skill or the ability to identify figures embedded in a complex background field; and spatial reasoning ability (Griggs & Dunn, 1989). Some have difficulty with analytic processes because of Chinese socialization patterns (Yao, 1985) and child-rearing practices, which relate experiences and knowledge to personal experiences and past knowledge (Chiu, 1972). Young Chinese Americans generally perceive the world as a network of relationships and interdependence. They usually need highly concrete information in learning and lack imaginative and inferential skills (Chiu, 1972). The relationship between socialization practices and FDI of four ethnic groups shows that Hong Kong Chinese Americans are more FI than other Asian American groups (Dawson, Young, & Choi, 1974). Urban Korean environments reflect both traditional and more Western values. Apparently, urban environments may generate a more FI cognitive style than traditional rural communities (Park & Gallimore, 1975). Conflicting evidence has been found, however, relating to Asian Americans' FDI (Hsi & Lim, 1977).

Conflicting results have been found in research on Asian American students. Hsi and Lim (1977) found that not all Asian Americans are FI. Mathematical and reasoning abilities only provide an incomplete representation of the cognitive style of Asian American students. A study by Harvey et al. (1981) indicated that Polynesians are more FD, with the exception of the Samoan group, who preferred to work independently.

Cognitive styles from an Asian American Education Project suggest Filipino American preschoolers may be more FD than other Asian American children. In addition, Chinese American children may enter school with a highly reflective response style, taking a relatively long time to answer questions (Kitano, 1983). Although research similar to that of Ramírez and Castañeda (1974), which is based on Mexican American students, has not been conducted with Asian American students' cognitive style and cultural values, differences do exist. Tong (1978) comments that FDI cognitive style is interesting and valid for Asian Americans, but it lacks the power to justify other historical and cultural complexities of the Asian American experience.

A characteristic of research with Asian Americans is that it discloses early developmental differences among the Asian American cultural groups and implies that teachers at all levels must be aware of such differences. Teachers need to be aware that differences exist between Asian American groups in learning strategies. A repertoire of instructional techniques are necessary to provide the best match between a student's cognitive style and the instructional strategy. Teachers must understand that students need methods appropriate to their dominant cognitive style. For example, FD children might be sensitive to social cues and be more susceptible to incidental learning and contextual elements. On the other hand, FI Chinese American children may need extra time to reflect on and respond to questions (Kitano, 1983).

The small number of studies on cognitive style differences in Asian Americans that have been conducted have had conflicting results, which imply that caution must be used in interpreting the learning characteristics concerning Asian Americans' cognitive style or their socialization practices because of the diversity that has been found among the subgroups. Although group differences insinuate that cultural differences affect cognitive style, it is essential to accept that cognitive styles are unique for each individual instead of accepting stereotypical group styles. Within any group, the variation is greater than the between-group differences. Asian Americans as a group, as compared with other cultural groups, prefer learning through visual modality. Many Asian Americans favor an auditory, tactual, or kinesthetic learning modality instead of a visual one (Griggs & Dunn, 1989). Teachers must assess each Asian American student individually to determine his or her cognitive style preferences to plan instructional strategies.

Patterns related to culture do exist. The characteristics of successful Asian American pupils indicate their high success in mathematics as compared with certain other groups (Hilliard, 1990). A combination of factors may be responsible for the academic success of Asian American students such as (a) a preference for group study, (b) responsibility for each other's progress, (c) and a conviction that none of the students in the group is going to do poorly. Higher grade point averages (GPAs) of the San Diego, California, Asian population correlate with traditional values, ethnic pride, and close social and cultural ties with members of the same ethnic group (Divorky, 1988). Hamilton, Blumenfeld, Akoh, and Miura (1989) support these findings using Asian Japanese students. They attribute part of Japanese success in school to the need to please authority figures like parents or teachers. Thus these students achieve for the sake of their families.

Traditional Asian ethnic communities value education (Divorky, 1988; Pitler, 1977; U.S. Bureau of the Census, 1980a) and stress conformity and discipline. A great deal of respect exists for parental authority and a mutual dependence in the family (Park & Gallimore, 1975; Pitler, 1977). Pitler (1977) relates a discussion with a bilingual high school teacher who commented on the strictness in the traditional Korean home. The family is usually an extended family, with the father head of household.

Immigration to the United States and the exigencies created by newly formed life-styles have caused changes in some of these relationships (Yao, 1985). Both parents may need to work and are not able to give their children as much guidance and attention (Pitler, 1977). Children may be more vocal, adopting the habits of their U.S.-born peers (Yao, 1985). They may have difficulties adjusting to a society where male and female children are equally valued and sibling authority is not dependent on the age of the child (Yao, 1985). These changes have created difficulties for many of the Asian American children whose families still demand high grades, success (Divorky, 1988), and family responsibility (Yao, 1985).

Differences exist between expectations of the Asian American student and family and the realities of the U.S. educational system. Asian American students from traditional backgrounds are accustomed to passive learning and find critical thinking foreign (Yao, 1985). They may perform well in rote memorization but have difficulty in tasks that involve creative writing or problem solving (Pitler, 1977).

Teachers are highly respected in Asia, and the student-teacher relationship is very formal (Pitler, 1977). In traditional Asian classrooms, the teacher is at the front of the room. Usually the teacher lectures and students are called on to recite for memory. Therefore recent immigrant Asian parents may have unrealistic expectations of U.S. teachers and the educational system. The immigrant parents expect to perpetuate traditional values, creating conflicts within the school and at home.

Conclusion

Through the early 1960s, student learning differences received comparatively little attention in the professional literature. Even when learning style was discussed, it was largely an academic exercise that rarely resulted in program development. During the last few years, a concern with retaining at-risk minority students has appeared in the academic literature and in institutions because minority students represent an important resource. The concern with retention demands that institutions implement special programs to provide minority students with the kind of support necessary for their academic survival.

All components of a culture are built upon some pattern of beliefs and values that define a way of life and the work in which people act, judge, decide, and solve problems. In each culture, reality is distinctively conceptualized in implicit and explicit premises and derivative generalizations that together form a coherent system.

The conceptual system becomes embedded in a particular network and is transmitted to members through a complex matrix of socialization practices. The socialization process merely transmits choreographed patterns of behavior that a person learns to copy. Each person learns in a particular way. Different cultures produce different learning styles and aspects of perception and cognition behavior as well. Different ethnic groups with different cultural histories, different adaptive approaches to reality, and different socialization practices will differ concerning their respective cognitive style.

Because the social, cultural, and environmental milieus of ethnic groups differ, these differences reflect their cultural/cognitive styles. Whereas it was once fashionable to deny the existence of cultural assets and variations among minority groups, social researchers now recognize that such traditional approaches have become anachronistic. The failure of retention programs, the ineffectiveness of service delivery to multiethnic populations, and the inability to produce effective communication between majority and minority members demonstrate that new models and approaches must evolve that not only deal with debilitating misconceptions about minorities but, more important, operate within a framework of equal respect and appreciation for the similarities and differences among groups.

A different set of understandings about the way diverse populations communicate, behave, and think need to be developed. Until this occurs, education will continue to stagnate in the dark ages and educators will provide lip service instead of action to the egalitarian values associated with pluralism and multiculturalism. Minority researchers have begun to affirm the value and viability of their cultural strengths and will expect institutions to reciprocate. As professional educators, we must settle for nothing less. It is vital that the process of acculturation and formal education be considered in the development of psychological differentiation. Witkin and Berry (1975) concluded that this differentiation affects acculturation, which influences the behavior of many cultural groups. The question of the operative variables, such as proficiency in the second language, is still open.

The study of learning styles is one aspect of the study of individual differences. As educators and researchers tried to understand the range and dimensions of individual differences between children, they began to look for the sources of these differences. One significant source is cultural differences. People who share a common cultural background also share, to a certain extent, common patterns of intellectual abilities, thinking styles, and interests. Ethnic groups, independent of socioeconomic status, display characteristic patterns of thinking styles that are strikingly different than one another.

This is not to deny the importance of individual differences. It is to say that cultural differences are one important component of individual differences.

There are dangers in characterizing the learning styles of cultural groups. Emphasis on learning style may lead to new forms of inaccurate labeling and stereotyping of students from a different culture. Or, worse, learning style differences may be attributed to genetic differences. The most effective use of research on learning styles lies in more effective individualization of instruction, not labeling. The research strongly suggests that differences in the learning styles of students from diverse cultures are related to different background experiences, not to racial or genetic differences.

It is our responsibility as educators to prepare our students to be able to cope in various situations. All students have skills in other cognitive styles, and these need to be encouraged to keep us from locking our students into a certain mold. There is a need to remain flexible in our approach. We can prepare students for success in living in a bicultural world with bicultural success (Pepper & Henry, 1986).

When learning style differences are understood and accepted, the classroom changes to a place where individual differences among students become an incentive for teachers to provide a rich variety of lessons, teaching strategies, learning activities, and testing challenges. This variety not only enhances the equity of the instructional setting but enriches the thought processes and behavior learning styles of all students (Pepper & Henry, 1986).

Educators may assist students to succeed. Teachers can adapt their instructional strategies to the needs of different learning styles (Ramírez & Castañeda, 1974; Witkin et al., 1977). Educators can also help students develop a greater repertoire of techniques by using the strengths of the individual student to gradually introduce the learner to techniques not consistent with his or her dominant cognitive style (Ramírez, 1989; Saracho & Spodek, 1981). The more successful student is one who is able to use a more differentiated approach, employing the strengths of both FD and FI cognitive styles as needed in the particular context (Ramírez, 1989; Shade, 1981a).

References

Anastasi, A. (1988). *Psychological testing.* New York: Macmillan.
Baca, L. M., & Cervantes, H. T. (1989). *The bilingual special education interface.* Columbus, OH: Charles E. Merrill.
Battle, E. S., & Rotter, J. (1963). Children's feelings of personal control as related to social class and ethnic group. *Journal of Personality, 31,* 482-490.
Brewer, A. (1977). On Indian education. *Integrated Education, 15*(1), 21-23.
Brown, A. D. (1980). Cherokee culture and school achievement. *American Indian Culture and Research Journal, 4*(3), 55-74.
Bruno, R. R. (1987-1988). School enrollments—social and economic characteristics of students: October 1987-1988. *Current population reports* (Series P-20, No. 443). Washington, DC: U.S. Department of Commerce, Bureau of the Census.
Byers, P., & Byers, H. (1972). Nonverbal communication and the education of children. In C. B. Cazden, V. P. John, & D. Hymes (Eds.), *Functions of language in the classroom* (pp. 3-31). New York: Academic Press.
Cazden, C. B., & Leggett, E. L. (1981). Culturally responsive education: Recommendations for achieving Lau remedies II. In H. Trueba, G. Guthrie, & K. Au (Eds.), *Cultural and the bilingual classroom* (pp. 69-86). Rowley, MA: Newbury House.
Chan, K. S., Takanishi, R., & Kitano, M. K. (1975). *An inquiry into Asian American preschool children and families in Los Angeles.* Los Angeles: University of California. (ERIC Document Reproduction Service No. ED 117 251)
Chiu, L. (1972). Cross-cultural comparison of cognitive styles in Chinese and American children. *International Journal of Psychology, 7*(4), 235-242.
Cohen, R. A. (1969). Conceptual styles, culture conflict, and nonverbal tests of intelligence. *American Anthropologist, 7,* 828-856.
Crawford, J. (1986, December 3). One-third of Navajos drop out annually, new study finds. *Education Week,* pp. 1, 14.
Cullanine, D. (1985). *A cognitive style study of Native Indian children.* Unpublished master's thesis, University of British Columbia.
Damico, S. B. (1985). The two worlds of school: Differences in the photographs of Black and White adolescents. *The Urban Review, 17*(3), 210-222.
Davis, J. K. (1987). The field independent-dependent style and beginning reading. *Early Child Development and Care, 29,* 119-132.
Davis, J. K., & Cochran, K. F. (1989). An information processing view of field dependence-independence. *Early Child Development and Care, 43,* 129-145.
Dawson, J. L., Young, B. M., & Choi, P. P. C. (1974). Developmental influence in pictorial depth perception among Hong Kong Chinese children. *Journal of Cross Cultural Psychology, 5*(1), 3-22.
Deyhle, D. (1983). Measuring success and failure in the classroom: Teacher communication and tests and the understandings of young Navajo students. *Peabody Journal of Education, 61*(1), 67-85.
Díaz, C. (1989). Hispanic cultures and cognitive styles: Implications for teachers. *Multicultural Leader, 2*(4), 1-4.
Diessner, R., & Walker, J. L. (1989, August). A cognitive pattern of the Yakima Indian students. *Journal of American Indian Education,* pp. 84-88.
Dinges, N. G., & Hollenbeck, A. R. (1978). Field dependence-independence in Navajo children. *International Journal of Psychology, 13,* 215-220.

Divorky, K. (1988, November). The model minority goes to school. *Phi Delta Kappan, 70*(3), 219-222.

Eberhard, D. R. (1989, October). American Indian education: A study of drop outs, 1980-1987. *Journal of American Indian Education*, pp. 32-40.

Edward, H. T., Graham, M. A., & Funaki, I. F. (1981). *An investigation of cross-cultural cognitive styles among traditional and assimilated communities of Polynesians and Asian-Americans.* Paper presented at the annual convention of the National Association for Asian and Pacific American Education, Honolulu.

Feldman, R. S. (1985). Nonverbal behavior, race and the classroom teacher. *Theory into Practice, 24,* 45-49.

Fernandez, R. P., & Velez, W. (1985). Race, color, and language in the changing public school. In L. Maldonado & J. Moore (Eds.), *Urban ethnicity in the United States* (pp. 123-144). Beverly Hills, CA: Sage.

Figueroa, R. A. (1980). Field dependence, ethnicity, and cognitive styles. *Hispanic Journal of Behavioral Sciences, 2*(1), 33-42.

Gilbert, S. E., II, & Gay, G. (1985). Improving the success in school of poor Black children. *Phi Delta Kappan, 67*(2), 133-137.

Griggs, S. A., & Dunn, R. (1989). The learning styles of multicultural groups and counseling implications. *Journal of Multicultural Counseling and Development, 17,* 146-155.

Hale, J. (1982). *Black children: Their roots, culture, and learning styles.* Provo, UT: Brigham Young University.

Hale, J. (1983). Black children: Their roots, culture, and learning styles. In O. N. Saracho & B. Spodek (Eds.), *Understanding the multicultural experience in early childhood education* (pp. 17-34). Washington, DC: National Association for the Education of Young Children.

Hamilton, V. L., Blumenfeld, P. C., Akoh, H., & Miura, K. (1989). Japanese and American children's reasons for the things they do in school. *American Educational Research Journal, 26*(4), 545-571.

Hammack, F. M. (1986). Large school systems' dropout reports: An analysis of definitions, procedures, and findings. *Teachers College Record, 87*(3), 324-341.

Hansen, L. (1984). Field dependence-independence and language testing evidence from six Pacific Island cultures. *TESOL Quarterly, 18*(2), 311-324.

Harvey, E., Graham, M., & Funaki, I. (1981, April). *An investigation of cross-cultural cognitive styles among traditional, assimilated communities of Polynesians, Asian-Americans.* Paper presented at the annual conference of the National Association for Asians and Pacific American Education, Honolulu. (ERIC Document Reproduction Service No. ED 206 705)

Hilliard, A. G. (1989). Teachers and cultural styles in a pluralistic society. *NEA Today, 7*(6), 65-69.

Hilliard, A. G. (1990, August). *Changing attitudes.* Keynote address presented at the Multicultural Education Workshop of Prince George's County Public Schools, Greenbelt, MD.

Holtzman, W. H., Díaz-Guerrero, R., & Swartz, J. D. (1975). *Personality in two cultures.* Austin: University of Texas Press.

Holtzman, E. H., Goldsmith, R. P., & Barrera, C. (1979). *Field dependence/field independence: Educational implications for bilingual education.* Austin, TX: Dissemination and Assessment Center for Bilingual Education.

Howard, B. C. (1987). *Learning to persist/persisting to learn.* Washington, DC: American University.

Hsi, V., & Lim, V. (1977). *A summary of selected research on cognitive and perceptual variables.* Berkeley, CA: Berkeley Unified School System, Asian-American Bilingual Center.

Hsia, J. (1981). *Cognitive assessment of Asian Americans.* Los Alamitos, CA: National Center for Bilingual Research. (ERIC Document Reproduction Service No. ED 222 1628)

John, V. P. (1972). Styles of learning-styles of teaching: Reflections on the education of Navajo children. In C. Cazden, D. Hymes, & V. P. John (Eds.), *Functions of language in the classroom* (pp. 331-343). New York: Teachers College Press.

Jones, E. E. (1978). Black-White personality differences: Another look. *Journal of Personality Assessment, 42,* 244-252.

Kagan, S., & Zahn, G. L. (1975). Field dependence and the school achievement gap between Anglo-American and Mexican-American children. *Journal of Educational Psychology, 67*(5), 643-650.

Karlebach, D. (1986). *A cognitive framework for deriving and interpreting learning style differences among a group of intermediate grade native and nonnative pupils.* Unpublished doctoral dissertation, University of British Columbia, Vancouver.

Kaulback, B. (1984). Styles of learning among native children: A review of the research. *Canadian Journal of Native Education, 11,* 27-37.

Kitano, M. K. (1983). Early education for Asian-American children. In O. N. Saracho & B. Spodek (Eds.), *Understanding the multicultural experience in early childhood education* (pp. 45-66). Washington, DC: National Association for the Education of Young Children.

Kleinfeld, J., McDiarmid, G. W., & Hagstrom, D. (1989, May). Small local high schools decrease Alaska Native drop-out rates. *Journal of American Indian Education, 28*(3), 24-30.

Kogan, N. (1987). Some behavioral implications of cognitive styles in childhood. *Early Child Development and Care, 29*(2), 95-117.

LaFrance, M., & Mayo, C. (1976). Racial differences in gaze behavior during conversation. *Journal of Personality and Social Psychology, 33,* 547-552.

Laosa, L. M. (1977). Multicultural education: How psychology can continue. *Journal of Teacher Education, 27*(3), 26-30.

Laosa, L. M. (1984). Social policies toward children of diverse ethnic, racial, and language groups in the United States. In H. W. Stevenson & A. E. Siegel (Eds.), *Child development research and social policy* (pp. 1-109). Chicago: University of Chicago Press.

Leith, S., & Slentz, K. (1984). Successful teaching strategies in selected Northern Manitoba schools. *Canadian Journal of Native Education, 11,* 38-49.

MacArthur, R. (1968). Ecology, culture and cognitive development: Canadian Native youth. In L. Drieger (Ed.), *The Canadian ethnic mosaic* (pp. 133-146). Toronto: McClelland & Stewart.

Mizokawa, T., & Morishima, J. K. (1979, Summer). The education for, by, and of Asian/Pacific Americans. *Research Review of Equal Education, 3,* 1-33.

More, A. (1984). *Okanagan/Nicola Indian quality of education study.* Penticton, Canada: Okanagan Indian Learning Institute.

More, A. J. (1987a, October). Native Indian learning styles: A review for researchers and teachers. *Journal of American Indian Education,* pp. 17-28.

More, A. J. (1987b). Native Indian students and their learning styles: Research results and classroom applications. *British Columbia Journal of Special Education, 11,* 23-37.

Morrow, G. (1986). Standardizing practice in the analysis of school dropouts. *Teachers College Record, 87*(3), 342-355.

Ogbu, J. U. (1978). *Minority education and caste: The American system in cross cultural perspective.* New York: Academic Press.

Ogbu, J. U. (1987). Variability in minority student performance: A problem in search of an explanation. *Anthropology and Education Quarterly, 18,* 312-334.

Olstad, R. G., Juarez, J. R., Davenport, L. J., & Maury, D. L. (1981). *Inhibitors to achievement in science and mathematics by ethnic minorities.* Seattle: University of Washington.

Osborne, B. (1985). Research into Native North American's cognition: 1973-1982. *Journal of American Indian Education, 24*(3), 9-25.

Park, J., & Gallimore, R. (1975). Cognitive style in urban and rural Korea. *Journal of Cross-Cultural Psychology, 6*(2), 227-237.

Pepper, F. C., & Henry, S. (1986). Social and cultural effects on Indian learning style: Classrooms implications. *Canadian Journal of Native Education, 13,* 54-61.

Perney, V. H. (1976). Effects of race and sex of field dependence-independence on children. *Perceptual and Motor Skills, 42,* 975-980.

Philips, S. (1983). *The invisible culture: Communication in classroom and community on the Warm Springs Indian Reservation.* New York: Longman.

Pitler, B. (1977). Chicago's Korean American community. *Integrateducation, 15*(4), 44-47.

Preliminary 1980 census results. (1982). *Pacific/Asian American Mental Health Research Center Research Review, 1*(1), 9.

Ramírez, M. (1982, March). *Cognitive style and cultural diversity.* Paper presented at the annual meeting of the American Educational Research Association, New York.

Ramírez, M. (1989). A biocognitive-multicultural model for a pluralistic education. *Child Development and Care, 51,* 129-136.

Ramírez, M., & Castañeda, A. (1974). *Cultural democracy, bicognitive development, and education.* New York: Academic Press.

Ramírez, M., Castañeda, A., & Herold, P. L. (1974). The relationship of acculturation to cognitive style among Mexican Americans. *Journal of Cross-Cultural Psychology, 5*(4), 424-433.

Ramírez, M., & Price-Williams, D. R. (1974). Cognitive styles of children of three ethnic groups in the United States. *Journal of Cross-Cultural Psychology, 5,* 212-219.

Rhodes, R. W. (1988). Holistic teaching/learning for Native American students. *Journal of American Indian Education, 27*(2), 21-29.

Rohner, R. P. (1965). Factors influencing the academic performance of Kwakiutl children in Canada. *Comparative Education Review, 9,* 331-340.

Sanders, M., Scholz, J. P., & Kagan, S. (1976). Three social motives and field independence-dependence in Anglo-American and Mexican American children. *Journal of Cross-Cultural Psychology, 7*(4), 451-462.

Saracho, O. N. (1983a). Cognitive style and Mexican American children's perceptions of reading. In T. Escobedo (Ed.), *Early childhood education: A bilingual perspective* (pp. 201-212). New York: Teachers College Press.

Saracho, O. N. (1983b). Cultural differences in the cognitive style of Mexican American students. *International Journal of the Association for the Study of Perception, 18*(1), 3-10.

Saracho, O. N. (1983c). The relationship of teachers' cognitive styles and ethnicity to predictions of academic success and achievement of Mexican-American and Anglo-American students. In E. García & M. Sam-Vargas (Eds.), *The Mexican American child: Language, cognitive and social development* (pp. 107-122). New York: Teachers College Press.

Saracho, O. N. (1989a). Cognitive styles and classroom factors. *Early Childhood Development and Care, 47,* 149-157.

Saracho, O. N. (1989b). Cognitive style: Individual differences. *Early Childhood Development and Care, 53,* 75-81.

Saracho, O. N., & Hancock, F. M. (1983). Mexican-American culture. In O. N. Saracho & B. Spodek (Eds.), *Understanding the multicultural experiences in early childhood education* (pp. 3-15). Washington, DC: National Association for the Education of Young Children.

Saracho, O. N., & Spodek, B. (1981). Teachers' cognitive styles: Educational implications. *The Educational Forum, 45,* 153-159.

Suarez-Orozco, M. (1987). Becoming somebody: Central American immigrants in U. S. inner city schools. *Anthropology and Education Quarterly, 18,* 287-299.

Schratz, M. A. (1976). *Developmental investigation of sex differences in perceptual differentiation and mathematic reasoning in two ethnic groups.* Unpublished doctoral dissertation, Fordham University.

Shade, B. J. (1981a). *Afro-American cognitive style: A variable in school success?* Madison, WI: Research and Development Center for Individualized Schooling.

Shade, B. J. (1981b). Racial variation in perceptual differentiation. *Perceptual and Motor Skills, 52,* 243-248.

Shade, B. J. (1982). Afro-American cognitive style: A variable in school success? *Review of Educational Research, 52*(2), 219-244.

Shade, B. J. (1984, August). *The perceptual process in teaching and learning: Cross-ethnic comparisons.* Paper presented at the annual meeting of the American Psychological Association, Toronto, Canada.

Shade, B. J. (1989a). Creating a culturally compatible classroom. In B. J. Shade (Ed.), *Culture, style and the educative process* (pp. 189-196). Springfield, IL: Charles C Thomas.

Shade, B. J. (1989b). The influence of perceptual development on cognitive style: Cross ethnic comparisons. *Early Child Development and Care, 51,* 137-155.

Shade, B. J., & Edwards, P. A. (1987). Ecological correlates of the educative style of Afro-American children. *Journal of Negro Education, 56*(1), 88-99.

Slavin, R. E. (1989, March). *Disadvantages vs. at-risk: Does the difference matter in practice?* Paper presented at the annual meeting of the American Educational Research Association, San Francisco.

Stodolsky, S. S., & Lesser, G. S. (1967). Learning patterns in the disadvantaged. *Harvard Educational Review, 37*(4), 546-593.

Swisher, K., & Deyhle, D. (1987). Styles of learning and learning of styles: Educational conflicts for American Indian/Alaskan Native youth. *Journal of Multilingual and Multicultural Development, 8*(4), 345-360.

Swisher, K., & Deyhle, D. (1989, August). The styles of learning are different, but the teaching is just the same: Suggestions for teachers of American Indian youth. *Journal of American Indian Education,* pp. 1-13.

Tafoya, T. (1983). Coyote in the classroom: The use of American-Indian oral tradition with young children. In O. N. Saracho & B. Spodek (Eds.), *Understanding the multicultural experience in early childhood education* (pp. 35-44). Washington, DC: National Association for the Education of Young Children.

Tafoya, T. (1989, August). Coyotes eyes: Native cognition styles. *Journal of American Indian Education,* pp. 29-42.

TenHouten, W. D. (1989). Application of dual brain theory to cross-cultural studies of cognitive development and education. *Sociological Perspectives, 32*(2), 153-167.

Tong, B. (1978). Warriors and victims: Chinese-American sensibility and learning styles. In L. Morris, G. Sather, & S. Scull (Eds.), *Learning styles from social/cultural diversity: A study of five American minorities* (Southwest Teacher Corps Network). Washington, DC: U.S. Department of Health, Education and Welfare.

Trueba, H. (1988). English literacy acquisition: From cultural trauma to learning disabilities in minority students. *Linguistics and Education, 1,* 125-152.

U.S. Bureau of the Census. (1980a). *We, the Asian and Pacific Islander Americans.* Washington, DC: Author.

U.S. Bureau of the Census. (1980b). *We, the first Americans.* Washington, DC: Author.

U.S. Department of Education, Office of Civil Rights. (1986). *School enrollment.* Washington, DC: Author.

Valentine, C. A. (1971). Deficit, difference, and bicultural models of Afro-American behavior. *Harvard Educational Review, 41*(2), 137-156.

Vernon, P. (1969). *Intelligence and cultural environment.* London: Methuen.

Walker, B. J. (1989, August). Learning preferences of capable American Indians of two tribes. *Journal of American Indian Education,* pp. 63-71.

Weitz, J. (1971). *Cultural change and field dependence in two native Canadian linguistic families.* Unpublished doctoral dissertation, University of Ottawa.

Williams, D. (1986). *Simultaneous and sequential processing, reading, and neurological maturation of Native Indian (Tsimshian) children.* Unpublished doctoral dissertation, University of British Columbia, Vancouver.

Witkin, H. A. (1978). *Cognitive styles in personal and cultural adaptation.* Worcester, MA: Clark University Press.

Witkin, H. A., & Berry, J. W. (1975). Psychological differentiation in cross-cultural perspective. *Journal of Cross-Cultural Psychology, 6,* 4-87.

Witkin, H., Moore, C., Goodenough, D., & Cox, P. (1977). Field dependent and field-independent cognitive styles and their educational implications. *Review of Educational Research, 47*(1), 1-64.

Wolcott, H. F. (1967). *A Kwakiutl village and school.* New York: Holt, Rinehart & Winston.

Yao, E. L. (1985). Adjustment needs of Asian immigrant children. *Elementary School Guidance and Counseling, 19*(3), 222-227.

Young, V. H. (1970). Family and childhood in a southern Georgia community. *American Anthropologist, 72,* 269-288.

PART III

Leadership and Training Programs for Educational Improvement

JAMES E. ANDERSON, EDITOR

Historically, the social and educational institutions of U.S. society have been molded and shaped by assimilation ideologies and monocultural perspectives. The principal theories and elements of these ideologies have been Anglo-conformity, varying forms of social and economic middle-classism, and the perennialism of the melting pot philosophy (Gordon, 1964). While the historical origins of these elements have traditionally been described as Western and Northern Euro-centric, the social and political nature, in fact, has been monocultural and undemocratic.

From a broad institutional perspective, this cultural hegemony of Anglo-conformity, middle-classism, and melting pot theory have formed both institutional screens and ethnically and culturally norming policies and practices that historically "sifted out" and "procedurally eliminated" substantive institutional diversity and truly democratic processes. The presence and operation of these phenomena have been readily observable in all kinds of social institutions in our society over the years whether in the preference for certain Anglo-cultural orientations in speech and dialect patterns in the "public arena," the treatment of the "poor" in public health care and hospitals, or the paucity of female and racial minorities in leadership positions in corporate America.

The resulting condition has been that, in virtually all social institutions in the United States, the "dynamics of inclusion," referring to access, meaningful involvement, and beneficial results based on institutional priorities, practices, and programs, have always been controlled by the "politics of exclusion." This condition has been true in terms of institutional priorities, practices, and programs as well as in the development of leadership and training because of the institutionalization of assimilative theories and accompanying paradigms that rejected and often "blamed the victims" themselves for not fitting in. Thus historically and systematically, there have always been individuals and groups who were "sorted out" and relegated to various statuses of disfavor and dysfunctionalism. In the eyes of society, those groups have always been people of color, the poor, people with limited English proficiency, and groups whose cultural politics ran contrary to the politics of assimilation. If you will, people "at risk" in the "hegemonic eyes" of our social systems.

In education, and schooling, the preponderance of these assimilative theories and their accompanying educationally reflective paradigms of deficiency, deprivation, and disadvantage, which were fashionable in the 1960s and 1970s, have reincarnated themselves in the "risk" paradigms in the 1990s. As our society has grown in cultural and ethnic diversity, and become more socially and politically complex, the need for the development of multicultural educational environments that reflect equity in learning opportunities has become critical. There is a need to create educational enterprises that "include" rather than "exclude" people. In a society based on democratic ideals, education must place children "at promise" rather than "at risk."

While the history of a cultural hegemony based on assimilative theories and paradigms is well documented in terms of its linkage to the current educational malady known as "at-riskness," what remains problematic and elusive are how this perpetual cycle of "out-groupness" can be broken as well as the way to develop and prepare educational leaders and practitioners in the future to avoid repeating these failures of the past and extending the "cycle." Nearly all analyses of current educational dialogues and reviews of literature on the problems of education indicate that the terms *reform, restructure,* and *retrain* are the most frequently used descriptors in identifying strategies and approaches to educational improvement. It may well be that the concepts of reform, restructure, and retrain, as we have seen them related to "risk" issues in the past, have been too confining, limiting, and restrictive in the sense that both past and current efforts directed toward solving these problems are still based on assimilation theories and old paradigms. The result is that problems are never resolved, only "recast" and "retitled."

The authors in this part have taken the position that most of our educational institutions and schools have been formulated from theories and paradigms that have created and maintained a cultural hegemony that inherently disqualifies ideas and individuals that are not reflective of assimilative theory. And so, as long as you "work with" or "fidget with," *re*-structure or *re*-form or *re*-train within the established theoretical and paradigmatic structures that are the cultural basis of our schools, the values and perspectives within these paradigms will continue to control and structure our institutions inequitably. These formulations will continue to block new thinking and the type of behavior needed for the development of effective leadership and teacher training in a multicultural society. Popkewitz (1984) sheds light on this proposition in his discussion of the relationships of educational research to social theory. He points out that underlying most theory development is a social context embedded with assumptions, values, and worldviews that refer to particular viewpoints about social groups, social control, order, and responsibility. He further implores us to remember that they are not neutral or value free.

Thus it is the opinion of the authors in the part that the kind of paradigm development needed—which reflects new constellations of data, asks penetrating questions, poses new directions, and uses multiculturalism and equity as foundational contexts—can never be constructed and applied if leaders, teachers, and researchers are locked, consciously or unconsciously, into old paradigms based on assimilative theories. They wholeheartedly advance the position that we need new theories and paradigms generated by individuals who do not see their own identities, statuses, positions, or themselves at risk. Equally, if not more, important is their appraisal that the institution of public schooling as the basic foundation for a democratic society may be what really is at risk.

Eugene E. Eubanks and Ralph Parish, in their chapter, suggest that leadership must become a catalytic force prompting instability in educational institutions if there is to be any hope for "at-risk" students. The authors ground their argument in the basic premise that traditional "how-to" approaches in the training of administrators maintain the types of "stability," or "sameness," in school systems that reinforces organizational cultures based on assimilative hegemony. These organizational climates and practices in the minds of these writers create and maintain barriers to learning for students who are often described as being at risk.

Parish and Eubanks plead for fresh approaches and new paradigm development that also recognize schools as synergistic learning systems. In relation to this point, they encourage us to replace the current concept of "training people" with the idea of "helping people" develop as leaders in schools.

Correspondingly, this point is further explored by their intriguing viewpoint that there are no lockstep sets of sequentially ordered courses or "steps," only "paths" of real experiences that have the power to move individuals through levels of leadership development. In their view, training that reflects prescribed sets of experiences limited in place, time, situation, and complexity is inadequate. Leadership and its paths of development, in their eyes, must be real world oriented.

Throughout the chapter, the authors demonstrate a strong commitment to the proposition that "learning" ought to be the key focal point of all theoretical and practical dimensions of change and restructuring. They propose new questions, they challenge us to use new methodologies, and they ask us for new commitment for solving old problems.

A. Reynaldo Contreras, in his work, focuses on the challenge of developing leaders in an era where they are asked to achieve "equity and excellence" in schools that are serving increasingly large numbers of students who are characterized as being at risk. In response to this challenge, he presents a thought-provoking discussion relating to the emerging nature of "cultural politics" and its impact on schools, as well as educational leadership and its relationship to cultural politics and "at-risk" students, and presents several recommendations for preparing educational leaders of "at-risk" schools.

Early in his chapter, Contreras points out that, given the increasing cultural diversity and social complexity in today's school environments, leaders must be prepared to negotiate the "cultural politics" of schools. In his presentation, he draws upon various educational writers and their ideas and succinctly identifies several crucial points that must be considered if leaders and administrators are going to be effective. At the center of his rationale is the concept referred to as "cultural politics," or the relationship of conflict between what cultural knowledge a person or group has and the interactional life circumstances in which they find themselves.

He further makes and elaborates on a powerful distinction between "politics" and "policy" in education. In this discussion, he notes that essentially they are different ways of distributing power. Therefore, in school districts, when different cultural factions or groups are seeking change, traditional leadership seeks to have issues of conflict defined as policy issues, thus allowing only individuals "certified" by office or training to make decisions on them. As a result, school districts and boards can continually stifle or hold at bay cultural group politics in education that may be contrary to their controlling mind-sets and philosophies.

In today's climate of educational reform, issues related to "diversity" are defined as matters of policy on which administrators and reformers tell at-risk youth and their parents what is good for them and they are expected to acquiesce to these pronouncements. He further goes on to point out that, if these issues are defined as political or "politics," then there is an opportunity for alternative and diverse input by the different groups or publics that are affected. His point is that traditionally we have kept at-risk groups out of participation in the problem-solving process and we continue to perpetuate school systems that do not serve them well.

In his description of leadership and its relationship to cultural politics, Contreras's examination of this relationship vividly describes the cultural and political nature of schools. He clearly illuminates the point that, by its nature, this political context has a great effect on whether students are "cloned" in the culture of someone else or whether people struggle to shape a culture to their needs. His analysis reflects and concludes that successful educational leadership with at-risk students occurs when there are successful efforts in shaping and linking school and learning with meaningful values and experiences in their lives. Contreras finishes by recommending several ideas for preparing leaders to build successful schooling cultures, specifically in the areas of political behavior involving analysis, judgment, and advocacy.

Marilynne Boyle-Baise and Carl A. Grant's contribution centers on the need to develop new multicultural paradigms for education, schools, and teacher training programs. They begin their discussion with a serious concern about the nature of the term *at risk* and then proceed to use the term as a focal point and "lens" to historically examine its usage and application.

As they describe the genesis of the term, they begin with the national "risk" reports and commission studies. They adroitly points out that *at risk* originally stood for paradigms consisting of sets of explanations and descriptions of mediocrity in the schooling processes. The "mediocrity paradigm," as they refer to it, was seen primarily as decreasing test scores, the need to improve content particularly in math and science scores, the call for higher test scores, and, in general, more "quality assurance." Their analysis clearly illustrates that schools, teachers, and the educational programs, themselves, were the focus of the accusations originally.

In contrast to the "mediocrity paradigm," they propose the multicultural education paradigm as being an appropriate philosophical instrument that offers promise for students who have not been well served because of their color and culture. Throughout the discussion of the multicultural paradigm, the authors pose significant questions about the viability and nature of teacher education programs.

Summarily, Boyle-Baise and Grant's dialogue concludes that teachers and educators must develop "multicultural literacy," a concept they describe as being built on attitudes related to awareness and comfortability with many types of diversity. In accord with this notion, they offer a number of suggestions for in-service and teacher training and encourage us not to see students from at-risk perspectives but to view them in at-promise postures.

The authors in this section collectively and strongly call for "new responses" to what has been characterized as the concept of "at-riskness." For them, this task begins with new analysis, interpretations, and definitions of the problem in hopes of providing effective solutions. Seeking to accomplish this task, they have provided a number of exciting and stimulating ideas.

References

Gordon, M. M. (1964). *Assimilation in American life: The role of race, religion and national origins.* New York: Oxford University Press.

Popkewitz, T. S. (1984). *Paradigms and ideologies in educational research.* London: Falmer.

• 8 •

Leadership That Promotes Instability: A Hope for At-Risk Students

EUGENE E. EUBANKS
RALPH PARISH

This chapter's purpose is to discuss a fundamental issue in education, "at-risk" students, and educational leadership in relation to that issue. In many cases, what happens in a chapter of this sort is a very technical analysis of the elements of an issue and a logical-technical-simplistic linear list of things for leaders to do to solve a problem(s) or "to be trained." The solution list or training list is usually based upon different research that has been done, will already be generally known in the literature, at least to many, and will be presented as new findings. It too often is old wine in a new bottle. It is our intent in this chapter to avoid that trap. What is needed is new wine for new bottles. We do not feel constrained therefore to stay within in existing paradigms (organizational cultures) of either accepted or common notions regarding leadership, leadership development, or instruction in urban settings.

The search for such research-developed lists, in the culture of schooling and education, produces school improvement efforts that maintain the status quo. We mean that within the culture of teacher preparation institutions and schooling in America are covenants, worldviews, customs, traditions, and legends that assure their own continuation and the continuation of current schooling outcomes. It is continuation of a schooling that sorts children to replace their parents in the social/economic order.

The historical cultural belief in America and other Western cultures is that people are born with different levels of ability. Their station in life is essentially a function of their innate ability, and this is fixed at birth. Those children who come from families high in the social order come from parents of high ability and therefore will most likely have high ability themselves, and so on down through the hierarchy. In the language of schooling, "it is the way things are." It is not what Americans say schooling is, but it is U.S. schooling practice. Because this old history is embedded in the culture, it blocks reformers and those who seek fundamental change from making a new history. Naturally, if research and change are conducted within old paradigms, the clues to new paradigms get ignored.

We would like to add that educators, in universities and practitioners alike, are not consciously aware of these cultural covenants and the effect they have on children—but we must be. The outcomes of schooling in the United States are too clear. We cannot say we do not know the history of schooling in the United States. We should not be allowed to get away with saying, "That's not my intention. I'm just doing my job. It's not my fault." One of the strongest of these school covenants allows educators to blame the victims of discriminatory and inequitable schooling for their own plight. The victims are not the ones who structure, organize, and deliver schooling. Educational leaders and policymakers have not looked with tough enough minds into our schooling practices. They continue to advocate policies and programs that flow from the existing schooling culture and thus only tinker with "what is" in an effort to maintain the same historical/social schooling outcomes.

Therefore it must be understood that all that we say in this chapter is grounded in a basic premise: "How-to" approaches to organizational practice form an approach to "training" administrators that promotes stability, maintains a system of schooling that sorts children, and establishes organizational practices that do not work well. The substantive changes that we propose are ones that recognize that organizations are living, changing organisms. Therefore organizations must establish structures that are in a constant state of development. That means organizations become learning systems. Learning organizations require leaders and managers who understand that helping the organization (the people in it) to develop is their consummate role. Therefore they themselves are also in a constant state of development. "Training" must be replaced with a "helping people to develop" concept for leaders and others. There are no steps, only a path(s). Yet, *expecting schools of education or existing school organizations to be these places of development may be more than is reasonable to expect.*

What tough-minded questions must those who seek reform ask in order to provide a quality schooling for 80% or more of America's children? (a) It must be understood that the purpose of culture in any social system is the survival of the social system. Schooling is a cultural enterprise therefore designed to teach the young to replenish and continue the same culture that spawned them. Schooling in the United States primarily works to maintain the same historical social class hierarchy that evolved to support a privileged class, mercantilism, and industrial/capitalism. This outcome must change if for no other reason than it no longer meets the need of a twenty-first-century, culturally diverse, global culture. (b) It depends upon the ability to educate at-risk children with the same quality and care now reserved for the privileged. They must be provided real opportunities to enrich themselves, to be in control of their lives, and to become productive participating members of society. (c) The twenty-first century will require a better quality education than any now receive. Such schooling compels U.S. society to make substantive changes that restructure and replace the current system of schooling. (d) Tinkering (improving what is) will not do it. It requires the introduction of instability and ambiguity into the schooling culture to promote change. (e) It requires leadership that can design and manage unstable and ambivalent organizational cultures. (f) It may be more of a substantive change than is possible to accomplish by members of current schooling cultures.

New outcomes from schooling with equity and efficacy must be defined as a survival issue for the society. U.S. society will expect those involved in restructuring schooling to educate persons for new roles demanded by the twenty-first century. Such an expectation requires educators to be able to imagine and then develop a schooling outside their experiences: to invent the unknown. It is also very clear that, when 80% or more of a society are well educated, they will not think only about their work and careers. They will think about their lives. A very different, culturally diverse society will emerge. Therefore a more appropriate way to describe the schooling issues confronting the United States may be in terms of the future at risk rather than children at risk. Imagination and development are the essential qualities of a twenty-first-century leader.

Why Is Change a Survival Issue?

History is replete with examples of societies that have gone down clinging to no longer viable cultural beliefs, covenants, ruling classes, and structures. The current U.S. romance with a conservative past in politics, national purpose, and education may be a passing fancy or the last-ditch battle of a ruling class clinging to its power. Capitalism may in fact supersede democracy and freedom (Shapiro, 1990), in which case educational reform that maintains the status quo and even promotes refinements that more effectively sort the young will continue to dominate public policy as it has during the decade of the 1980s. In such an event, the United States will not be able to develop and provide the quality of citizens needed for twenty-first-century success. This has been the ongoing U.S. political battle since Jefferson and Hamilton.

The children who are at risk in this nation's current traditional schooling are those children who are not now receiving, and have not historically received, an education that allowed them full or meaningful participation in an industrial/capitalistic society—let alone an informational/technical culture of the twenty-first century. This nation puts itself in peril if it continues to provide a Third World education and schooling to its inner-city and poverty rural children, particularly children of color. Thus far, there is little evidence even to suggest that the United States as a society realizes that cultural survival is at risk and that educating all of its young well is the key to survival.

Without such a new societal demand, the rest becomes academic. Schooling will continue to provide the same outcomes today's educational leaders and teachers have been educated and trained to provide. There is already serious consideration among policymakers that twenty-first-century education need not necessarily include public schools or education for all. Some policymakers are already advocating that a system of private schooling at public expense is an ideal restructuring model. Schools of choice, for example, are viewed by many as schooling that assures a high correlation between quality of schooling and social/economic/racial factors. The point is that, within U.S. society, there are still many who believe in and argue for maintaining the historical sorting of students according to the ethnicity, race, and class of their families. This historical cultural view still appears to be a dominant policy view.

If current schooling outcomes are continued, the effect on future U.S. culture and political life will be dramatic. It certainly means that the U.S. Constitution could no longer be the basis for public and social institutions. In a culture where some are educated well and most remain relatively uneducated, notions of democracy, voting on issues and leaders, equity and equality, liberty, property, and thus life itself all become too inefficient and unnecessary for the uneducated to be allowed to participate as equals. The uneducated will not take their assignment as "have-nots" peaceably. Economically, such a society will not be able to perform at a world-class level. It will lack the educated work force necessary for maintaining a high level of global social/economic relationships and structures. It is a high price to pay to preserve a historical-social hierarchy based upon class and racial and ethnic prejudice.

Lest our words confuse, because many will declare that educating everyone well is and has been historically a cultural mission for schooling in America, we need to explain. Such a purpose is at times a prominent part of national, state, and local political rhetoric. But what this political rhetoric says is not now, nor has it ever been, what schooling actually does in the United States. U.S. policymakers and educators understand this very well. What schooling actually does is what we must be concerned about if restructuring is to occur. What schooling in America has done since Colonial days is to provide children from different social backgrounds that degree of education necessary to maintain them in their social/economic strata. It takes Herculean efforts for a person to escape this cultural condition, and relatively few are allowed out.

Thus, to us, *at-risk students* refers to those students who have been historically excluded from meaningful participation in the industrial/capitalistic social order and, unless fundamental restructuring occurs, will continue to be excluded from the information/capitalistic social order of the twenty-first century. Currently, in the national dialogue over this issue, we hear few words and see no actions advocating fundamental change in schooling. Those education and schooling policies currently being recommended as "reforms" appear to be political policies rather than educational ones. They promote and maintain the same historical schooling outcomes that put and keep these young people at risk. The changing demographics of U.S. society make it clear that there will be increasing numbers of these children of color and poverty that constitute the population of America.

Who Are the Children at Risk?

Culture is the glue that holds a society together. Schooling carries a primary responsibility for transmitting a society's cultural schemata from generation to generation (social reproduction). In the United States, by the late seventeenth century, a social/economic hierarchy existed throughout each of the colonies that was brought with them from their Albion seed

(Fischer, 1989). Uniformly at the bottom were African Americans, Native Indians, Hispanics, Asians, and other persons of color. By the late nineteenth century, the Industrial Revolution and mercantilism had transformed the United States from an agrarian to an industrial/capitalistic social system. The historical social hierarchy remained in place.

It is not surprising then to find that the children we now refer to as "at risk" are disproportionately non-Euro-ethnic children of color and other children of the poor, mostly in urban centers and in historically poor rural areas. This in large measure explains why urban schools and poverty rural areas appear to have such difficulty in educating their clients well. They have the young people who are to be educated to fill the lower level(s) of the hierarchy. Schooling, combined with other social conditions, continues to do its assigned cultural role well. It prepares these children to become what McDermott (1974) describes as the "pariahs" of the culture.

An examination of current educational outcomes from U.S. schooling provides a clear picture. The permanent national dropout level is slightly in excess of 25%. Among Hispanic, African, and a number of other American populations of color, however, the permanent dropout rate is slightly more than 50% (American Council on Education, Education Commission of the States, 1989). Asian populations have a rate less than 35%. During the last decade, the percentage of White Euro-ethnic high school graduates who continued on to postsecondary education increased by a little more than 12%. During the same period, African American, Hispanic American, and other Americans of color with the exception of Asian Americans had a decline of more than 10% of high school graduates who pursued postsecondary education. Three hundred years ago, children from these same social levels in the hierarchy were denied education entirely or were limited to two or three years of elementary education, which is what they needed then to maintain themselves at their social level. In today's social context, while everyone receives more schooling, it is still in the amount that will keep these young people at the lower level of the hierarchy (Apple & Weis, 1977; Giroux, 1981, 1988; National Center for Educational Statistics, 1988; Shore, 1986). Such a lesson makes clear the meaning of "the basics." We need only to understand that what is considered to be traditional-basic U.S. schooling/education is a major cultural structure for maintaining the stability of this social hierarchy.

As we understand more about learning and how the brain works, the racial and class sorting outcomes from traditional schooling become understandable. We are beginning to understand how culture works to program the brain.

Success in traditional schooling depends more upon what cultural (social/economic) schemata a student brings to school than upon what a conventional teacher does in the classroom. We discuss this in more detail below.

If reform is to change these historical outcomes of schooling then, fine-tuning and trying to "improve" traditional schooling will not do it. Making traditional schooling more effective (as in most current school reform efforts) will continue to have, as a major outcome, more effective sorting of children according to the historical social hierarchy. Similarly, better preparation ("training") of leaders for traditional schooling will not develop leaders for schools that can provide quality outcomes for at-risk students. It requires fundamental structural (cultural) change in schooling to change these outcomes.

The nature and process of cultural change requires *instability* in a social system. Cultural change needs ambiguity and structures that are in a state of flux. The more substantial the changes needed, the higher the need for destabilizing a system. Hard scientists have known this for ages regarding the natural world. Social scientists are coming slowly to understand this same cultural condition of social change. Instability profoundly scares the members of social systems, particularly those who are highly vested in a culture. It is a critical problem for America and other twentieth-century societies that are endeavoring to transform into twenty-first-century information/technological societies.

Is It Even Possible to Educate All With Quality?

Before we can comfortably talk about substantive change, it is important to know and agree about what can be changed. If we do not know how to educate all the children so that at least 80% can achieve a college degree of quality, then developing leadership for such schools seems pointless. There is sufficient knowledge available about learning for humans and about building ambiguous learning-based organizations. There is no need to be timid—only a need to be reflective, creative, and developmental.

It is not uncommon to find that educators often talk about parts of things: a new technique, an effective strategy, lists of steps to follow for making someone effective, and so on. This is true whether the issue involved is teacher work, administrator work, curriculum and instruction work, staff development work, or school climate/culture efforts. Practitioners are presented "training" menus of supposedly effective parts from which to choose for improvement efforts. It is the scientific method applied to social research. Even if a new part offers promise, implementing it in traditional schooling cultures guarantees that success and any substantive change will be illusive (Fullan, 1988; Goodlad, 1990; Haberman, 1988; Huberman & Miles, 1984; McLaughlin, 1987; Miles, 1983). Parts get culturally "adapted" to fit what is.

Restructured schools must be structured around learning outcomes as opposed to curriculum and teaching inputs. It is a substantive cultural shift in schooling. Four interactive learning paradigms will be used below to illustrate the point. They are paradigms that have the effect of significantly improving schooling for at-risk students. A second set of paradigms relating to leadership needs for such schooling follows the learning paradigms. Such schooling requires those in schools to ask different questions concerning "what is going on here" and to decide "how we will change (develop) ourselves."

Learning as the Basis of Restructuring

Learning is essentially a schema-development process. From the beginning of sentient activity, the brain, with the biological responsibility for survival, develops schemata that organize and store survival information (Piaget, 1926, 1927/1930, 1932/1952, 1937/1954; Restak, 1984; and hosts of others). There are different types of schemata in different locations in the brain that store information and provide the structure for recalling and using information, skills, or processes. Any child who can use a human language by the age of 3 or 4 has the intellectual capacity to learn anything required for a bachelor's degree (i.e., to become smart; Brainin, 1985; Stigler & Barnes, 1988; and others).

Schema development is almost always experiential. In the later teens and beyond, some also learn by developing schemata that allow for intellectual or cognitive schema manipulation (Gardner, 1982; Piaget, 1934/1954). Thus learning starts where a learner is schematically. Schemata are consequently highly culture driven and culture related: What experiences do you have? Teaching and curriculum can and often do start somewhere else: where a curriculum or school structure wants certain parts taught and the language used in presenting the parts. Such placements often reflect a particular cultural, ethnic, or class bias. As information or experiential data enter the brain, there is a search to find existing schemata with which to link and thus be quickly available for use (learned; Gardner, 1982; Minsky, 1988; Restak, 1984).

When a teacher encounters a learning situation where something is not learned, it does not usually mean a lack of intelligence or ability to learn; it most often means that an appropriate schema for connecting the information is lacking, or the skill, information, or process did not find the right cognitive home. In such cases, experiential approaches involving active learning, cooperative learning, model building, hands-on manipulatives, or computer manipulatives can be employed if desired learning (schema connection) is to occur (Bossert, 1988; Flanagan, 1984; Piaget, 1964; and others). Traditional instruction (repetitive practice, drill, reading, and telling) in such cases where experience has not provided an existing schema almost guarantees that little or no significant learning will occur.

Learning is not sequential. Traditional curriculum development for schools assumes that, in the skill development and academic discipline areas, there are natural sequences or hierarchies. Such an assumption is generally unsupported in cognitive or educational research and generally conflicts with what is known about learning. Curriculum and subject matter experts in academic disciplines often prescribe an aligned local curriculum. Such curriculum alignments carry with them requirements for certain schemata or experiences to be present in the learner. Such alignments are often cultural or class-related schemata (Apple & Weis, 1977; Shore, 1986; and others). The reality of schooling is that children bring different schemata based upon their experiences of race, ethnicity, and class. There is no convincing data to support an assumption of a natural order in either skill or content. It is learning that must be developmental rather than an artificially created curriculum sequence.

Certain approaches can assist with developing a learning approach that provides urban teachers and teachers in isolated rural poverty areas a way to mediate against such rigid curricula. Such approaches allow for the use of learner experiences as the basis for learning development. What a learner brings is used rather than expecting that a learner bring certain schemata. Logic would suggest that in fact this is what a teacher has to work with in any event. Such a holistic approach offers a chance for high achievement for at-risk students, particularly if modern interactive technology and media are used to assist the learning. Student Team Learning and similar approaches that make use of learner schemata through cooperative teams are often most effective to promote skill and recall-type learning. For the higher levels of intellectual development, cooperative group learning, small group projects, active learning approaches, and personalized learning offer teachers and students a chance at success, providing that the teacher understands how to structure and manage these more complex learning processes. Clearly, varied uses of time, varied learning approaches, and supportive learning cultures require different and more flexible structures than those in current practice (Flavell, 1976, 1977, 1978; Knapp & Turnbull, 1990).

Learning has style and modality. Learning is developed through the use of the human senses. Most urban students and many students from isolated rural poverty areas come from racial, ethnic, and/or class backgrounds that provide them with certain preferred modal learning preferences (Pai, 1990). For example, the culture of many non Euro-centric learners makes use of oral learning, group rather than individual relationships, and particular cultural patterns of speaking and thinking. Some with working-class backgrounds come with cultural experiences that do not value "school learning" but do value "practical" knowledge. Many children of color come from a cultural environment that values working in groups or "families."

It is true that ultimately making use of all the senses and developing a multimodal learning style is desirable for mature learners. Research would seem to indicate, however, that using a learner's preferred learning modality(ies) to initiate new learning and using secondary modalities for applied practice is a particularly powerful learning approach with most learners. Thus teachers must make use of *multimodal* and participatory learning experiences. Learning centers, interactive computer programs, interactive video, small group activities as well as some individual learning experiences thus constitute a well-designed and effective at-risk classroom environment and ethos.

Each of us also has a cognitive style that appears to be structured into our schema process. Some of us are deductive or holistic: There is a need to see a whole picture or starting point and then work backward to understand the various parts. Some of us are inductive or concretely sequential: There is a need to identify all the parts and then proceed to determine how the parts go together. While each of us may be able to be both deductive and inductive at times, it is clear that each of us also has a preference, particularly when new conditions confront us.

Classrooms and schools that include style and mode become much more active, productive, and lively. Schools of education or school districts do not as yet generally prepare teachers or school leaders for developing such schools and such learning environments. Some very few school leaders and teachers, almost on their own, develop these "learning" leadership skills. Such teachers and leaders are exceptions and are often viewed and treated as mavericks. Such mavericks tend to have effective schools (Levine & Lezotte, 1989).

A common school cultural belief is that urban and poverty students in general need rigid structure and directive control accompanied by repetitive drill and practice. Such beliefs guarantee that most, if not all, culturally diverse urban and poverty children will not be able to achieve intellectually or in school. Which is, as we have said, the expected reproductive outcome of U.S. schooling.

Learning is connected. This schema may seem to be a part of the other three and, of course, it is. It also requires special discussion. Traditional teaching is so often composed of unconnected parts "that just have to be learned." Curriculum and instructional approaches are usually connected in the minds of curriculum developers, university professors, and teachers. But the question is this: Are the information, processes, or skills to be learned being connected in the mind of a learner? As explained above, if learning cannot be connected to a schema in a learner's mind, it will not stick and will be discarded. Most teachers have had this experience: "When they left here yesterday, they all knew that, and today you would think we had never studied it." Such a problem is not in the students but in the instruction as well as the curriculum.

Teachers cannot assume that what is being taught today is "logically" connected to what we learned yesterday or last week. Teaching may be logically connected as a curriculum or as logical content steps or as specific strategies, which may have little or no connection within a learner. The logic changes when learning (our purpose) is the issue rather than teaching (our work). Schools must be restructured around the purpose. Teachers must continually provide *structure* in classrooms that connects new schemata and other things to be learned to previous schemata. Approaches such as integrating instruction across a curriculum, infusing instruction from different content areas, doing projects that require application from several disciplines, providing higher-order thinking opportunities at the same time as lower-order thinking provide such connections (Knapp & Turnbull, 1990).

A learner may come from experiences that have developed analytical or synthesis ability at a higher level than the ability to recall or make direct application. It is possible to take the high road to get to the low road in a thinking taxonomy (Bloom, 1984). Creativity and imagination, for example, are intellectual abilities that most urban learners have and are powerful learning tools. The imagination and creativity that gets many children in difficulty in many traditional urban at-risk classrooms can be directed toward learning and will transform a classroom into a productive and successful place.

A Learning Organization

If the learning paradigms discussed here are to be implemented in schools that possess large numbers of at-risk students, then it must take place, we suggest, in school contexts that support and promote such paradigms. Such schools will have substantively and even radically different classroom and schooling structures than those found in traditional schooling. In some cases, we must picture schools in our minds that have not been experienced yet. Thus we must keep their structures fluid, somewhat unstructured, and ambiguous. These new schooling cultures and structures must be unstable organizations in which students are free to learn: What many are coming to call the "Learning Organization."

If one looks at some of the available research regarding effective school structures that promote renewing and substantial restructuring of schooling, a picture of a particular cultural ethos emerges. This research comes from the work of Argyris (1982), Edmonds (1979), Levine and Lezotte (1989), Miles (1983), Sarason (1977, 1990), Schmuck and Runkel (1989), and many others. This research suggests that certain restructured organizations produce highly effective and productive outcomes. We can also describe such structures as developmental organizational learning cultures. Such restructured schools will have the following:

1. There must be a double loop communication and information sharing process in the school structure. A persistent effort is maintained to collect accurate information concerning the performance of the school for students, administration, and staff. These data are known by all and inform shared decision making and planning.

2. There must be a problem-solving focus in basic organizational structures: Problems and issues are identified and confronted, understanding and meaning are sought, and decisions are made through collaboration and cooperative work by those who are responsible for implementing decisions.
3. There is an ethos in the school of a cohesive family that works together and supports one another, thus providing a safe, nonthreatening climate. There is a close connection and active relationship between the school family and the home family, whatever it is.
4. Hard work, persistence, and determination characterize the level of effort for all in the school. These efforts are focused upon learning through instructional arrangements that are flexible and varied. Outcomes are valued more than inputs.
5. There is a collective and shared vision of what the purpose of the school is, and this vision drives the day-to-day efforts as well as the planning for everyone in the school.
6. Processes of learning and thinking are emphasized as are the organizing structure for instruction, particularly including the higher-order thinking and learning processes. There is no established schedule for everyone to do the same things at the same times. Curriculum content, skills, and subject matter are the tools and "stuff" used to develop the processes of learning and thinking, and they are selected to match the culture and schema of the particular learners involved. Whole group instruction is a seldom-used mode of teaching.
7. There is active learning going on all the time among the staff in regard to changing and altering time, instruction, and school structure. Nothing is ever closed or beyond or above consideration for change. The school structure and climate are in a constant state of evolving, investigating, and learning. *Unconventional* and *maverick* describe qualities revered in the school.

Leadership Development, Not Training

There is considerable research literature that describes such organizational settings and culture. There is very little available research or knowledge that informs us concerning how to develop leaders for such schools, particularly if such leaders must come from existing school structures. Leadership development is a path and direction. There is never a time when one is "developed," let alone "trained." Even an attempt to describe "steps to follow" or to think of such leadership development as "training" blocks the development. Development also means that there is a place in the path where a person is ready and needs to continue development by "being in the practice." People will arrive at such a place differently and in different time.

Places that develop such leaders must also have such structures. There is no place, for example, for courses of set length with finite limits.

Overcoming the stability of existing schooling cultures appears to be a task that few if any have successfully accomplished, except temporarily. Sarason (1990) describes this as systems control rather than as cultural covenants as we do, but we are discussing the same phenomenon. Research (Miles, 1983; and others) clearly indicates that approaches involving incremental change and mandated policy changes have thus far produced the same result: a continuation of the same traditional schooling with the same historical sorting outcomes for children. How do we convince leaders to put their jobs at risk by creating unstable school cultures? Do we even have the right to require that bravery and maverickism be the essential qualities of leaders for reformed and restructured schools? Dare we suggest that divisions of educational administration become places to prepare their clients for such roles?

Summary

It seems clear that, while there is still much to be learned about how to create quality schooling for all, there is no need to wait. There is still more to discover about how the brain works and the effect that culture and social settings have upon learning. There is still more to learn about creating school settings that in fact do educate all in culturally diverse environments. There is still more to learn about how to develop leaders for substantively reformed schools. By developing "Learning Organizations," we will learn these things by doing them and then being thoughtful and reflective about the outcomes. By becoming active learners in our work and by developing through our experiences new schemata that connect with what we know, a new paradigm or two may be waiting out there for us to discover. Thus we need unstructured, flexible, and ambiguous organizational settings. For these are the ones that will allow for growth and promote intelligent searches for a path (may the Force be with us).

Finally, such restructured school settings require substantive and fundamental change. At-risk students have no chance in historically traditional schooling. Schooling for all requires organizational cultures that are in a constant state of evolvement and development. In other words, organizational settings that are not stable; organizational settings that are full of ambiguity, are dynamic and synergistic; organizational settings where changes in schedules, policies, and practices can be changed daily or even hourly; organizational settings where learning and development are part of what the adults in them do as well.

The changes we have discussed here cannot be implemented incrementally, cannot be done without pain, cannot be done without considerable havoc to existing school cultures. It is not that today's educators cannot learn but that the school cultures within which most work do not allow them to do so. Being smart, being brave, and being able to risk mark the qualities of restructuring leadership—qualities that can be learned and developed by anyone who spoke a human language by the age of 3 or 4 and who is willing to be determined and work hard.

Organizations of this type are the model for the twenty-first century and are beginning to emerge in today's modern organizational structures. The type of human educator needed in such organizational settings is dramatically different than the type of educator being prepared today, let alone those who have been prepared during the past two decades. Rather than seeking order and control, these leaders must learn to manage disorder and be comfortable with shared power and decision making. Leaders must be comfortable with the idea that nothing is ever known for sure and promote this idea as a basic good and part of the school ethos. Leaders must promote the understanding that, in the postmodern world, the one constant is change. Change must be embraced and developed as a friend. It cannot be resisted.

References

American Council on Education, Education Commission of the States. (1988, May). *One-third of a nation* (A report on Minority Participation in Education and American Life). Washington, D. C.

Apple, M., & Weis, L. (1977). *Ideology and practice in schooling.* Philadelphia: Temple University Press.

Argyris, C. (1982). *Reasoning learning and action: Individual and organizational.* San Francisco: Jossey-Bass.

Bloom, B. S. (1984). The 2 sigma problem: The search for methods of group instruction as effective as a one-to-one tutoring. *Educational Researcher, 13* 4-16.

Bossert, S. T. (1988). Cooperative activities in the classroom. In E. Z. Rothkopf (Ed.), *Review of research in education* (Vol. 15). Washington, DC: American Educational Research Association.

Brainin, S. S. (1985). Mediating learning: Pedagogic issues in the improvement of cognitive functioning. In E. W. Gordon (Ed.), *Review of research in education* (Vol. 12). Washington, DC: American Educational Research Association.

Edmonds, R. R. (1979, October). Effective schools for the urban poor. *Educational Leadership*, pp. 15-27.
Fischer, D. H. (1989). *Albion's seed: Four British folkways in America.* Oxford: Oxford University Press.
Flanagan, O. (1984). *The science of the mind.* Cambridge: MIT Press, Bradford Books.
Flavell, J. (1976). Metacognitive aspects of problem solving. In L. B. Resnick (Ed.), *The nature of human intelligence.* Hillsdale, NJ: Lawrence Erlbaum.
Flavell, J. (1977). *Cognitive development.* Englewood Cliffs, NJ: Prentice-Hall.
Flavell, J. (1978). Metacognitive development. In J. M. Sandura & C. J. Brainerd (Eds.), *Structural/process theories of complex human behavior.* New Amsterdam, The Netherlands: Sijthoff and Noordoff.
Fullan, M. (1988). *Change process in secondary schools: Towards a more fundamental agenda.* Toronto: University of Toronto.
Gardner, H. (1982). *Art, mind and brain: A cognitive approach to creativity.* New York: Basic Books.
Giroux, H. (1981). *Ideology, culture and the process of schooling.* Philadelphia: Temple University Press.
Giroux, H. (1988). *Schooling and the struggle for public life: Critical pedagogy in the modern age.* Minneapolis: University of Minnesota Press.
Goodlad, J. I. (1990). *Teachers for our nation's schools.* San Francisco: Jossey-Bass.
Guilford, J. P. (1988). *The analysis of intelligence.* New York: McGraw-Hill.
Haberman, M. (1988). *Preparing teachers for urban schools.* Bloomington, IN: Phi Delta Kappa Foundation.
Huberman, M., & Miles, M. (1984). *Innovations up close.* New York: Plenum.
Knapp, M., & Turnbull, B. (1990, January). *Better schooling for the children of poverty: Alternatives to conventional wisdom* (Written under Contract No. LC88054001 by SRI International, Menlo Park, CA and Policy Studies Association, Washington, DC). Washington, DC: U.S. Department of Education.
Levine, D. U., & Lezotte, L. W. (1989). *Unusually effective schools: A review and analysis of research and practice.* Madison: Wisconsin Center for Education Research, National Center for Effective Schools.
McDermott, R. P. (1974). Achieving school failure: An anthropological approach to illiteracy and social stratification. In G. Spindler (Ed.), *Education and cultural process: Toward an anthropology of education.* New York: Holt, Rinehart & Winston.
McLaughlin, M. (1987). Learning from experience: Lessons from policy implementation. *Educational Evaluation and Policy Analysis, 9,* 171-178.
Miles, M. (1974). *Social architecture in education.* New York: Center of Policy Research.
Miles, M. (1983). Unraveling the mystery of institutionalization. *Educational Leadership, 4,* 14-19.
Minsky, M. (1988). *The society of mind.* New York: Simon & Schuster, Touchstone Books.
National Center for Educational Statistics. (1988). *The conditions of education: Post secondary education* (Vol. 2). Washington, DC: U.S. Department of Education, Office of Educational Research and Improvement.
Pai, Y. (1990). *Cultural foundations of education.* Columbus, OH: Charles E. Merrill.

Piaget, J. (1926). *The child's conception of the world* (J. and A. Yomlinson, Trans.; original work in French). New York: Harcourt, Brace, & World.

Piaget, J. (1930). *The child's conception of physical causality* (M. Worden, Trans.). New York: Harcourt, Brace, & World. (Original French edition published 1927)

Piaget, J. (1952). *The origins of intelligence in children* (M. Cook, Trans.). New York: International Universities Press. (Original French edition published 1932)

Piaget, J. (1953). How children form mathematical concepts. *Scientific American, 189*(5), 74-79.

Piaget, J. (1954). *The construction of reality in the child* (M. Cook, Trans.). New York: International Universities Press. (Original French edition published 1937)

Piaget, J. (1964). Development and learning. *Journal of Research in Science Teaching, 2*, 176-186.

Restak, R. (1984). *The brain.* New York: Bantam.

Rose, A. M. (1980). *Information processing abilities.* In R. E. Snow, P. A. Frederico, & W. E. Montague (Eds.), *Aptitude, learning and instruction: Cognitive process analyses of aptitude* (Vol. 1). Hillsdale, NJ: Lawrence Erlbaum.

Rose, S. (1976). *The conscious brain.* New York: Vintage.

Sarason, S. (1977). *Creation of settings and future societies.* San Francisco: Jossey-Bass.

Sarason, S. (1990). *The predictable failure of educational reform: Can we change course before it's too late?* San Francisco: Jossey-Bass.

Schein, E. (1985). *Organizational culture and leadership.* San Francisco: Jossey-Bass.

Schmuck, R., & Runkel, P. (1989). *The handbook of organizational development in schools* (3rd ed.). Prospect Heights, IL: Waveland.

Shapiro, S. (1990). *Between capitalism and democracy.* New York: Bergin and Garvey.

Shore, I. (1986, November). Equality is excellence: Transforming teacher education and the learning process. *Harvard Educational Review, 56*(4), 406-426.

Stigler, I., & Barnes, R. (1988). Culture and mathematics learning. In E. Z. Rothkopf (Ed.), *Review of research in education* (Vol. 15). Washington, DC: American Educational Research Association.

• 9 •

Thinking Differently About Leadership Development in a Culturally Plural Society

A. REYNALDO CONTRERAS

> The meat of an administrator's work is not the technical aspect of management; rather, it involves the establishment of community and a culture within an organization and the development of an organization's self-reflective ability to analyze its purpose and goals.
>
> W. Foster

Cultural diversity in the United States has deepened considerably during the last two decades. The aging of the mainstream population (Dychtwald & Flower, 1989) and the influx of immigrants from new corners of the world to the United States since the Immigration Reform Act of 1965 (Plesser, Siegel, & Foster, 1987) have resulted in a rapid rise in the proportions of different ethnic, linguistic, racial, and religious minorities in the nation's public schools. The civil rights movement of the 1960s and 1970s and the resulting legislation have increased the diversity of micro cultures (Gollnick & Chinn, 1986) within the schools and have challenged educators to become more sensitive and more responsive to the particular educational needs of girls, the disabled, gifted, poor, non-English speakers, non-Caucasian, and non-Christians, who in the reform movement of the 1980s have been considered "at-risk" students—students who lack the resources to benefit from conventional schools.

At the same time, training and development of leaders for the education of at-risk students has come to need refocusing to mediate the new diversity that is characteristic of our at-risk schools. Administrators who are now pressed to pursue "equity" and "excellence" in leading schools into the twenty-first century must be prepared to negotiate the politics of schools serving large numbers of at-risk youth. Leadership for excellence in education, Sergiovanni (1984) argues, encompasses leadership forces brought to bear by administrators and teachers on the schooling process "to bring about changes needed to improve schooling." These forces include (a) technical, (b) human, (c) educational, (d) symbolic, and (e) cultural forces. Sergiovanni (1984, p. 6) asserts that these leadership forces are related in a hierarchical order with the cultural being the most fundamental force necessary for providing excellence in schooling. Sergiovanni's argument suggests that, as a school culture is accepted and internalized, the school is better able to move toward ideals it holds and objectives it wishes to pursue.

While the notion of "cultural building" assumes that a culture has been accepted, Bates (1987) notes that it fails, as do discussions of leadership for effective schools and associated administrative theories, to consider "cultural politics" as an essential element in cultural building for excellent schools. Giroux and Simon (1984) point out that "cultural politics" is essential to revealing the forms of conflict that characterize a cultural building process. Thus, in failing to consider the cultural politics of leadership for excellence, educators misread the importance of the implications of education as a cultural building enterprise and the schools as cultural sites (Bates, 1987).

In shedding light on this shortcoming of contemporary discussions of educational leadership for excellence in schooling, this chapter (a) explores the concept of cultural politics, (b) examines the role of educational leaders in the culture politics of the school, and (c) provides several recommendations for preparing educational leaders for at-risk schools.

Cultural Politics

Erickson (1987) notes that, within the concept of "culture politics," school structure and culture are seen as interwoven, identifying differences in patterns of sharing of cultural knowledge. Culture evolves through conflicts resulting in differing groups becoming progressively different. From this perspective, the central interest is not the nature of cultural knowledge itself but the relationship between the content of cultural knowledge and the life situation of the person or group in which knowledge is held. Culture is defined within this perspective by Erickson (1987, p. 14) as follows:

Cultural knowledge—whether in small information bits or larger conceptual structures—is being created continually in daily social life. This new culture is accepted, learned, and remembered or rejected, ignored and forgotten, depending upon where one sits in the social order.

Erickson's definition highlights two dimensions of culture: (a) the systematic nature of variation in cultural knowledge within a society and (b) social conflict as a fundamental process by which the variation is organized (Giroux, 1981; McDermott & Goldman, 1983; Willis, 1977). This definition of culture accounts not only for transmission of traditions but also for cultural learning and change within a single generation and across generations. Conflict is viewed as a fundamental social process from which arises the regularity that can be seen in society.

When we speak of *cultural politics*, the term sounds strange to our ears. Nevertheless, when we speak of *politics* regarding education, we need to assume, in the same context, *policies*. What is the distinction between *politics* and *policies*? Kjolseth (1983) notes that a matter of politics is one that is socially defined as decisions wherein all those directly affected by the outcomes are granted rights to influence the decision directly. Policy, on the other hand, involves decisions wherein only those certified (by training or office) are granted the right to directly influence a decision.

Politics and policies as defined by Kjolseth legitimate two very different ways of distributing power. On the one hand, politics becomes a window of opportunity for participation by a wide range of actors and interests, thereby producing the circumstances for a less rapid and less predictable outcome. Policy, on the other hand, withdraws the matter to a narrow range of legitimate and predictable actors, thereby facilitating quicker and more predictable outcomes.

When an issue arises in the community, the first action is to define it as "politics" or "policy." With this action, the rules of the game and legitimate players are set. Politics is played by the rules of democracy while policy is played by technocratic rules. Thus there are two ways of defining power relations.

A key property of policy decisions is that they exclude from power those most directly affected by the exercise of power. The important question here then is this: Why do we use the term *policy* so much? The answer to this question is linked to a contradiction between theory and practice of governance. In theory, we are citizens and the governance system serves us. In practice, elites rule and we are subjected to their desires. How can this be? The solution is to define social issues as matters of policy instead of politics.

During the current era of reform, in viewing issues of diversity and education as matters of policy, our administrators and reformers tell at-risk youth and their parents what is good for them, and these youth and their parents are expected to acquiesce. To behave otherwise is a violation of the policy game rules.

On the other hand, if we were to look at contemporary issues of diversity and education as matters of "politics," then we would legitimate broad participation by directly affected at-risk groups. This, however, is what educational administrators have been taught to fear.

Matters having to do with educating at-risk students are legitimately defined as policy questions when we all know what needs to be done and the "experts" know the best way of getting it done. There is, however, no consensus about issues associated with diversity, and the traditional means of addressing these issues are ineffective. The perpetuation of culturally pluralistic policies under these circumstances only serves to maintain the illusion of consensus that does not exist and sustain belief in the effectiveness of methods that are counterproductive in educating at-risk youth.

To better understand the dynamics of a society and of the ways in which cultural politics contribute to those dynamics, we need to examine the "whole way of life" of the society. But studying the "whole way of life" of any society would seem to be a tall order (Bates, 1987). How might we approach such a task?

First, we need to expand the definition of culture. One of the useful ways of doing this is suggested by Bullivant (1989, p. 39), who defines culture as follows:

> The core of a social group's cultural program . . . knowledge and conceptions that are public, in the sense of being shared by most members of the social group.
>
> The knowledge and conceptions . . . embodied in the behaviors and artifacts of the social group's members . . . behaviors and artifacts are termed cultural forms.
>
> . . . the values a group subscribes to; these broadly control the group's preferences about how its cultural forms should be organized.
>
> knowledge, conceptions and values are transmitted among present members of the social group and those who are born into it through systems of communication, the most important of which are signs and symbols.

> ... [that which] has evolved historically as the social group has adapted to environments over time ... represent[s] how the social group has modified outdated adaptation strategies to suit its assessment of its present environmental conditions or has added to its own culture by borrowing from other groups and their cultures.
>
> ... the knowledge and conceptions that the group devises to anticipate and cope with its assessment of future problems.

A culture then is expressed through institutions, social relations, customs, material objects, and organizations. To this extent, culture is observable, and empirical descriptions can be provided of the ways in which the meanings, values, ideas, and beliefs of social groups are articulated through various cultural artifacts. These artifacts constitute the structures through which individuals learn a culture.

Learning can be thought of as the process by which the internal subjective experience and understanding of the individual are formed and shaped through interaction with the structures of the culture and the values, beliefs, mores, and meanings they anticipate. That is, becoming an individual entails the mastery of the blueprints of meaning contained in the social life and artifacts of a particular culture (Bullivant, 1989).

Becoming an individual, however, is not simply a passive process of soaking up the blueprints of meaning articulated through the social structures into which one is born. Culture is not something solely objective and external to the individuals who constitute a particular group. Culture is also carried, communicated, and shaped through individual attempts to understand, master, and participate in the life of a group. Learning a culture, or living a culture, is therefore not simply an inheritance of objects but a taking part in the processes of history (Giroux & Simon, 1984).

One of the most important circumstances invariably transmitted from the past is membership of particular social groups within the overall society. Most societies, and certainly all complex societies, contain within them a variety of social groups whose experiences of and relationships with the wider society are substantially distinct. Some of the most obvious differences are those based on class, ethnicity, gender, geography, race, and religion. As the experiences of members of these social groups differ, it is likely that their social consciousness will also differ; that is, that they will learn to understand and relate to members of their group, to members of other social groups, and to the society as a whole in particular ways.

It cannot therefore be assumed that all members and social groups within a society will share a "culture" equally. For instance, even where certain historical events have wide-reaching influence on all groups (such as the civil rights movement), the relationship of particular social groups to the event, their experience of it, and their understanding of its significance may well be different.

Consequently, the search for understanding of the "macro culture" of a particular community or school, the way of life shared to some degree by all members of that community or school, cannot succeed if it assumes a unitary pattern of beliefs, values, mores, understandings, relationships, institutions, and artifacts that are shared to some degree by all members of that community or school. This does not mean that particular cultures will not present themselves as the most comprehensive and therefore the most dominant culture within a community or school, one that embraces various micro cultures and provides the cultural underpinnings of the community or schools a whole. Dominant cultures make such claims continuously. Rather, a cultural politics perspective insists that the macro culture of a community cannot be understood unless the nature and organization of the relationships and struggles between dominant and subordinate cultures are taken into account. Indeed, it is the struggle between such cultures that constitutes some of the key dynamics of social and organizational change.

The outcome of such a perspective is that the search for the "way of life" of a specific community or school becomes the search for the various cultures within it and an examination of their relationships revealed through the struggles between them during concrete historical moments. It is this struggle between groups that constitutes the terrain of cultural politics, the object of which is the exercise of cultural dominance.

In the attempt to achieve and maintain a particular dominance pattern, the education system of any community is clearly crucial, because the socialization of the young into the existing sociocultural relationships within a community is essential to the reproduction of the privileged position of a dominant social group as well as the subordinate positions of less privileged social groups. By the same logic, the education system is also a crucial agency through which the existing sociocultural relationships can be contested and alternative sociocultural relationships at least partially achieved.

Schools can therefore be seen both as an ideological mechanism over which struggles for control will take place within the wider community and as sites within which struggles to maintain or challenge the existing structure of cultural dominance are likely to take place. This is clearly illustrated by the origins of mass education systems in the nineteenth century and the attempt to use such systems as mechanisms of moral and social control (Tyack & Hansot, 1982).

But, as a mechanism of ideological domination, schools have certain weaknesses. This is because, as we saw earlier, the learning of a culture is not simply determined by the presentation of that culture by history or by a dominant group in its own interests. Rather, the production and reproduction of a culture are crucially dependent on the interpretation of that culture by students within a context shaped through struggle between competing micro cultures. If the students' roots are in a different culture (e.g., female or Black, Spanish speaking or Muslim perhaps, instead of White, middle class, and Protestant), then their interpretations of the culture offered by the school may well be at variance with the controlling authority's intentions. If the looseness is too great, then students and parents may well lose faith in the school or even see it as an alienating experience. This clearly has been the response of at-risk students, many of whom have been of historically underserved sociocultural groups experiencing public education in the United States (Banks & Banks, 1989).

Educational Leadership and Cultural Politics

This kind of analysis, Bates (1984) notes, suggests that "successful" educational leadership can be defined in at least two ways. If the definition of culture adopted is derived from the notion of "high" culture, then leadership can be judged successful or not in terms of its ability to reproduce that culture among those who have inherited it and produce that culture among those who have not. Many traditional forms of educational leadership can be seen as elaborations of just such a rationale (Bates, 1984; Foster, 1984, 1986). This type of leadership has not been successful in schools with disproportionate numbers of at-risk students.

The second definition of successful educational leadership derives from the alternative "whole way of life" definition of culture, which takes account of the nature of cultural politics. It arises from an awareness that what people want from school is the manifestation of values that are central and meaningful in their lives. Therefore schools are cultural artifacts that people struggle to shape in their own image. For it is only when schools are in such form that people have faith in and can participate in them (Greenfield, 1973, p. 570). This leadership is more likely to be successful in schools serving at-risk students. Such a view of the purposes of schools implies that educational leadership can be judged as successful to the degree to which it assists in the articulation and development of the aspirations and blueprints of meaning that are the cultural heritage of a particular cultural group, thus helping members of the group to articulate and defend their interests in the wider social environment.

Schools differ significantly, Bates (1987) points out, in their furtherance or hindrance of various cultural aspirations and interests. The cultural politics perspective allows for an analysis of the different ways in which schools intervene in the cultural politics of society. For example, differences between dominant national interests and subordinate local interests are clearly shown in arguments over the conduct of schooling (Tyack & Hansot, 1982). In terms of promoting the existing dominance, the school is required to comply with the demands of the dominant culture (Callahan, 1962). In many at-risk schools, however, that culture may be distant from, unrelated to, or in disagreement with the local micro cultures of the school community.

Particular schools, Bates (1987) indicates, may be faced with conflicts resulting from being linked "vertically" to the requirements of the dominant macro culture and "horizontally" to the requirements of the local micro cultures. Where the local micro cultures are in agreement with the dominant macro culture, there is little discontinuity for pupils or teachers. Where the local micro cultures are distinct, things may be very different. In this situation, schools, especially where they are successful in inculcating the dominant macro culture in certain students, may serve to disconnect such students from their local micro cultures (Jackson & Marsden, 1966). On the other hand, among at-risk students, loyalty to their local micro cultures may be strong enough to disconnect these students from the dominant macro culture advanced by the school and provoke resistance and, inevitably, failure (Willis, 1977).

It is within a framework of the conflicts and struggles between sociocultural groups in a community, of their historical development, and of the structures of domination and subordination that exist between sociocultural groups that we can begin to understand the complex features of schools, the linkages that exist between various micro cultures in a community, and the limits and possibilities of cultural building in schools. The notion of corporate culture offered by advocates of the managerial tradition is a limited substitute for such understanding (Foster, 1986; Morgan, 1986). This may be particularly true of educational organizations.

It is evident that the cultural politics of an at-risk school are complex and the cultural artifacts brought to such a school by various sociocultural groups may result in serious conflicts over both ideology and technology. The negotiation of such conflicts can lead to a variety of accommodations, some of which are educational in their outcome, others of which give the illusion of being educational but are in fact little more than empty, if not misleading, rituals (Meyer & Rowan, 1977). The ritualistic forms of school organization often have paradoxical outcomes, pitting consensual against differentiating functions within the same structure, or bureaucratic against therapeutic forms of personal relations. The cultures of schools are both derivative of and contributors to stratification in terms of class, race, gender, religion, and age and other social factors that characterize the greater society. As a result, differing types of schools relate in differing ways to their clientele, and some schools articulate with the cultures and values of their clientele very successfully, contributing significantly to the production and reproduction of skills, attitudes, and relations in ways that confirm both school and class, gender, race, and other micro cultures. On the other hand, at-risk schools articulate with their communities in ways that fragment and disorient those communities, rejecting their skills, knowledge, values, aspirations, and interests and disconfirming the value of their activities. It is tempting to conclude that the former schools are well led and the latter poorly led. Such a conclusion depends very much upon the assumption that the purpose of schools is to articulate and confirm the cultures and aspirations of their communities.

There is, of course, support for such a position. For example, Greenfield (1973), as previously noted, argues that people expect schools to reflect central and meaningful values. Thus people struggle to shape schools in their own image. In such forms do people have faith in schools and can participate in them comfortably.

It is on the basis of such premises that the movement for community participation and governance grew and became enshrined in government policy. One of the major concerns voiced about such moves, however, is that participation of communities "politicizes" the work of the school, thus potentially interrupting its task of educating children in the skills required for employment and citizenship.

Thinking Differently About Leadership

There is little doubt that community participation in schooling can "politicize" the activities of schools in ways that are not conventional. The implicit argument that such politicization is an undesirable outcome of democratic participation, however, ignores the political settlement that has allowed schools to be structured in the ways they exist and to support the interests that they do. Schools are, in their very nature, political institutions, for they encourage and promote particular cultural views—views that are the outcome of political struggles between alternatives cultural perspectives. As Giroux (1985, p. 23) argues, "Schools are historical and structural embodiments of forms and culture that are ideological in the sense that they signify reality in ways that are often actively contested and experienced differently by various individuals and groups."

Therefore it is arguable that educational leadership is political in nature, enabling the articulation and, where possible, the resolution of conflicts contained within the cultural politics of the school. Tyack and Hansot (1982, p. 262) suggest that democracy and social justice need to be re-created in each generation and that the schools have a major role to play in such political action.

Recommendations for Preparing Educational Leaders of At-Risk Schools

Educational leadership, Foster (1986) suggests, is far from the "scientific," apolitical maxims of current administrative theory promoted by contemporary theorists, for it involves not just the formulation and implementation of reliable and neutral techniques of management but also the active adopting of political behavior involving analysis, judgment, and advocacy.

Analysis

To use the alternative approach of educational leadership, educational leaders must learn to analyze the culture of the school. What, an administrator might ask, is the nature of the school's culture? The analysis might well consist of the use of qualitative techniques such as those employed by Cusick (1983), Lincoln and Guba (1985), or Popkewitz, Tabachnik, and Wehlage (1982) and take into account the framework offered by Bernstein (1975) for distinguishing the effects of various ritual and ceremonial practices suggested by Meyer and Rowan (1977). For example, determining whether the culture of the school is technical, illusory, or constructive; whether its rituals are bureaucratic or therapeutic; and whether classroom relations are based upon principles of learning or solely on rituals of personal relations is important in arriving at an initial analysis. Within this analysis, the nature and effects of the organization and distribution of knowledge (Bates, 1980), evaluation systems (Bates, 1984), and pedagogy (Bernstein, 1975) are also important. The forms of relation through which students articulate with the existing culture of the school and the particular conflicts that result could then become the starting points for organizational change.

Accompanying the analysis of the culture within the school is an analysis of the communities from which the school draws its students. It is assumed that pupils carry with them into the culture of the school the micro cultures of their homes and community. These micro cultures are, as previously suggested, produced and reproduced continuously through the cultural politics of class, ethnicity, language, race, gender, and other cultural relations that occur in the greater society (Banks & Banks, 1989).

Such analysis is essential then both because it facilitates the development of curricular, pedagogical, and evaluative practices in the school that engage with the "whole way of life" of students but also because it has the potential for revealing to teachers, pupils, and parents alike the various ways in which power and culture relate and the ways in which schools are implicated in the production and reproduction of particular practices and relations.

Judgment

Following analysis of school and community cultures and their interaction within the cultural politics of the school, effective educational leadership depends very much upon judgment on particular courses of action. Educational leaders must be able to establish appropriate arenas that allow cultural politics to be articulated in ways that can imaginatively transform current practices. These arenas allow for the participation of representatives of various micro cultures that engage collaboratively (Gray, 1989) to arrive at and deliberate alternative courses of action. This does not, however, mean that school administrators, any more than teachers, students, or parents, are expected to withdraw from the process of decision making.

Administrative Advocacy

Informed advocacy, on the basis of cultural analyses, as suggested above, has an integral role to play in deriving and executing educational policy within the context of cultural politics. Administrative advocacy is inevitably saturated with values and ideology. The question then is this: What overriding values are to inform the work of the school? It is clear that, in any society that is democratic, principles of respect for individuals, social justice, and equity are fundamental. It follows then that an educational process for a democratic society is also based upon such principles.

If there is a fundamental connection between commitment to the individual, equity, and social justice, then effective educational leadership involves the continuous advocacy for and manifestation of such values in the cultural politics of schooling. The organization and culture of the at-risk school requires such ideals if at-risk schools are to be both effective and excellent.

Thus it would seem that, for at-risk schools to have more than a purely instrumental value, as reflected in the reform movement of the 1980s (Futrell, 1989), educational leaders must prepare to negotiate educational ideals through the processes of cultural politics. Such negotiation, as Dewey (1902) suggested, is in itself an educative process and one that is far removed from the manipulative imposition of a corporate culture (Deal & Kennedy, 1982).

In summary, it would seem that those involved in leading at-risk schools today and in the future must prepare to engage in cultural politics wherein educational and social ideals are involved as well as pragmatic decisions about the restructuring of those schools. Educational administrators must be prepared to decide, on the basis of a cultural analysis of their schools, whether the particular conjunction of cultural and political power in the organization of their school system serves the causes of democracy, social justice, and education less well than it does the maintenance of "at-riskness" on the basis of class, racial, or gender cultural relations that can be defended only on instrumental grounds that serve the interests of a dominant group. The challenge to administrators of at-risk schools will be to reorder their worlds so as to reassert the primacy of democratic principles in the cultural politics of schooling in the struggle toward providing equity and excellence in schooling of future generations of at-risk students.

References

Banks, J., & Banks, C. A. M. (1989). *Multicultural education: Issues and perspectives.* Boston: Allyn & Bacon.

Bates, R. J. (1980). Educational administration, the sociology of science and the management of knowledge. *Educational Administration Quarterly, 16*(2), 1-20.

Bates, R. J. (1984). Toward a critical practice of educational administration. In J. J. Sergiovanni & J. E. Corbally (Eds.), *Leadership and organizational culture: New perspectives on administrative theory and practice.* Urbana: University of Illinois Press.

Bates, R. J. (1987). Corporate culture, schooling and educational administration. *Educational Administration Quarterly, 23*(4), 79-115.

Bernstein, B. (1975). *Class, codes and control: Vol. 3. Towards a theory of educational transmissions.* London: Routledge & Kegan Paul.

Bullivant, B. M. (1989). Culture: The nature and meaning for educators. In J. A. Banks & C. A. M. Banks (Eds.), *Multicultural education: Issues and perspectives* (pp. 27-48). Boston: Allyn & Bacon.

Callahan, R. E. (1962). *Education and the cult of efficiency.* Chicago: University of Chicago Press.

Cusick, P. A. (1983). *The egalitarian ideal and the American high school: Studies of three schools.* London: Longman.

Deal, T., & Kennedy A. (1982). *Corporate cultures: The rites and rituals of corporate life.* Reading, MA: Addison-Wesley.

Dewey, J. (1902). *The educational situation.* Chicago: Chicago University Press.

Dychtwald, K., & Flower, J. (1989). *Age wave: The challenges and opportunities of an aging America.* Los Angeles: Jeremy P. Archer.

Dyer, W. G., Jr. (1982). *Culture in organizations: A case study.* Cambridge: MIT, Sloan School of Management.

Erickson, F. (1987, November). Conceptions of school culture: An overview. *Educational Administrative Quarterly, 23*(4), 11-24.

Foster, W. P. (1984). Toward a critical theory of educational administration. In T. J. Sergiovanni & J. E. Corbally (Eds.), *Leadership and organizational culture: New perspectives on administrative theory and practice.* Urbana: University of Illinois Press.

Foster, W. (1986). *Paradigms and promises: New approaches to educational administration.* Buffalo, NY: Prometheus.

Futrell, M. H. (1989). Mission not accomplished: Education reform in retrospect. *Phi Delta Kappan, 71*(1), 8-16.

Giroux, H. A. (1981). *Ideology, culture and the process of schooling.* Philadelphia: Temple University Press.

Giroux, H. (1985). Critical pedagogy, cultural politics and the discourse of experience. *Journal of Education, 167*(2), 22-41.

Giroux, H. A., & Simon, R. (1984). Curriculum study and cultural politics. *Journal of Education, 166*(3), 226-238.

Gollnick, D. M., & Chinn, P. (1986). *Multicultural education in a pluralistic society* (2nd ed.). Columbus, OH: Charles E. Merrill.

Goodlad, J. I. (1984). *A place called school.* New York: McGraw-Hill.

Gray, B. (1989). *Collaborating: Finding common ground for multiparty problems.* San Francisco: Jossey-Bass.

Greenfield, T. B. (1973). Organizations as social inventions: Rethinking assumptions about change. *Journal of Applied Behavioral Science, 9*(5), 551-574.

Griffiths, D. B. (1959). *Administrative theory.* New York: Appleton-Century-Crofts.

Hummel, R. P. (1982). *The bureaucratic experience* (2nd ed.). New York: St. Martin's.

Jackson, B., & Marsden, D. (1966). *Education and the working class.* Harmondsworth, United Kingdom: Penguin.

Kjolseth, R. (1983). The cultural politics of bilingualism. *Society, 20*(4), 40-48.

Lincoln, Y. S., & Guba, E. G. (1985). *Naturalistic inquiry.* Beverly Hills, CA: Sage.

McDermott, R., & Goldman, S. (1983). Teaching in a multicultural setting. In L. Van Der Berg, S. de Ryke, & L. Zuck (Eds.), *Multicultural education.* Dordrecht, the Netherlands: Faris.

Meyer, J., & Rowan, B. (1977). Institutionalized organizations: Formal structure as myth and ceremony. *American Journal of Sociology, 83*(2), 340-363.

Morgan, G. (1986). *Images of organization.* Beverly Hills, CA: Sage.

Plesser, D. R., Siegel, M. A., & Foster, C. D. (1987). *Immigration and illegal aliens.* Plano, TX: Information Aids, Inc.

Popkewitz, T. S., Tabachnik, B. R., & Wehlage, G. (1982). *The myth of educational reform: A study of school responses to a program of change.* Madison: University of Wisconsin Press.

Sergiovanni, T. J. (1984). Leadership and excellence in schooling. *Educational Leadership, 41*(5), 6-13.

Tyack, D., & Hansot, E. (1980). From social movement to professional management: An inquiry into the changing character of leadership in public education. *American Journal of Education, 88*(3), 291-319.

Tyack, D., & Hansot, E. (1982). *Managers of virtue: Public school leadership to America, 1820-1980.* New York: Basic Books.

Waller, W. (1967). *The sociology of teaching.* New York: John Wiley. (Original work published 1932)

Weber, M. (1947). *The theory of social and economic organization* (A. M. Henderson & T. Parsons, Ed. and Trans.). New York: Oxford University Press.

Weick, K. E. (1976). Educational organizations as loosely coupled system. *Administrative Science Quarterly, 21*(1), 1-19.

Willis, P. (1977). *Learning to labour.* London: Saxon House.

• 10 •

Multicultural Teacher Education: A Proposal for Change

MARILYNNE BOYLE-BAISE
CARL A. GRANT

We were asked to prepare a chapter on what was needed to train preservice teachers to work successfully with "at-risk" students. The label *at risk* concerned us so much that we also decided to investigate the use of the term and analyze its application. As we did so, we began to wonder *who* was really *at risk*. We used the term as a lens through which we examined students, teachers, and teacher educators.

During our examinations, we became further convinced that the current cohort of teachers and teacher educators are unprepared to work with diverse populations. In response to the conclusion we reached, we began to discuss changes that need to occur in teacher education programs. The following discussion chronicles our thoughts about multicultural teacher education.

The Mediocre Education Paradigm

Since the 1983 publication of *A Nation at Risk* (National Commission on Excellence in Education), the spotlight of publicity has shone—negatively for the most part—on education. In fact, our nation was considered to be at risk for accepting mediocrity in public schools (e.g., Education Commission of the States, 1983). "At risk" came to stand for a paradigm or set of explanations for and descriptions of mediocrity in schools. According to this paradigm, the decreasing test scores reflected mediocre standards: The schools needed to intensify kindergarten through grade-12 academic experiences, require demanding homework, improve and require science and math courses, and ensure English proficiency. The solution to mediocre education was "quality assurance" (Education Commission of the States, 1983) achieved by increased and intensified course work, homework, and standardized achievement testing across all levels. In general, to challenge mediocrity or stem failure, students were required to do more, test more, and try harder to get into college. For teachers, this meant teaching more of the same curriculum and instruction, or stressing the "basics."

Teachers were considered to be mediocre and in some cases not qualified to teach. The nation's "best and brightest" were not entering or remaining in a professional career that seemed to have no advancement beyond the classroom.

Teacher education programs were the object of severe criticism. In *A Nation At Risk* (National Commission on Excellence in Education, 1983), teachers in training were said to lack preparation in academic majors and to spend too much time in educational methods courses. In both *A Nation Prepared: Teachers for the 21st Century* (Carnegie Forum on Education and the Economy, 1986) and *Tomorrow's Teachers* (Holmes Group, 1986), it was posited that teacher training could not be completed within four years; a baccalaureate was required before pursuing professional graduate studies in education.

Implicit within *Tomorrow's Teachers* (Holmes Group, 1986) was the view that teacher educators were mediocre as well. The Holmes group proposed that teacher education should be more "intellectually solid." It was argued that education professors need to upgrade their course work.

We examined the paradigm of mediocrity to determine who was at risk. It was difficult to find indictments of students within the national reports cited above. Although test scores indicated students were "behind" those in other nations, students were not directly blamed for this failure. Hence "remediation" was not seen as necessary, rather school programs were criticized for offering and demanding too little of students.

During the 1960s and 1970s, however, students were blamed for school failure. *Compensatory language* (e.g., culturally deprived) commonly described poor students and students of color. While the term *at risk* was used originally to describe all students stunted by a mediocre system, that use has not held. Instead, it seems targeted at those students who continue to "fail" in schools.

Who are "those" children? According to Swadener (1991), the *at-risk* label is used to describe children who are poor and of color. She proposed that the label represents an updated version of the cultural deficit model of the 1960s—the 1990s equivalent of "culturally deprived."

Pallas, Natriello, and McDill (1989) supported Swadener. They list five indicators for the *educationally disadvantaged* label: "minority racial/ethnic group identity, living in a poverty household, living in a single-parent family, having a poorly educated mother, and having a non-English language background" (Pallas et al., 1989, p. 17).

Soto (1992, p. 7) pointed out that we "rarely read about fluent Spanish speakers; fluent Hmong speakers; fully proficient speakers; multilingual speakers." Instead, bilingual children are considered at risk because they are "limited English proficient." She argued that children continue to be viewed as "deficient language receptacles instead of enriched individuals" (p. 7).

We found that, in the education field (e.g., schools, journals), the term *at risk* usually referred to children considered to be educationally disadvantaged (even before they came to school). The term defined those who were second-language learners, poor, or racially "different" than the "norm." Differences were seen as a prelude to deficiencies. Countless times we heard statements about children similar to this: "Well, what can you expect from that kind of home."

It is certain that there is confusion and fluctuation in the use of the label *at risk*. At times, it is used to describe children who did not perform well in school; at other times, it refers to children who perform adequately in inadequate school programs. All children are said to need more of the "right stuff," but the right stuff is often defined as more rigorous versions of the same curriculum and instruction already in schools (e.g., Bennett, 1988; Bloom, 1987; Hirsch, 1987). Do schools need more rigorous application of questionable practices and policies?

The Multicultural Education Paradigm

Allow us to paint a different picture of the way things are and offer another paradigm. We will call this the "multicultural education point of view." Let us consider students who differ by group membership in terms of race/ ethnicity, gender, social class, and/or handicapping condition as merely different rather than deficient. From this perspective, *schools* are deficient to the extent programs and practices do not embrace and celebrate student diversity. Schools are at risk of depriving the very children they see as "deprived."

Multicultural education is not a new perspective. This point of view has been advanced by many educators for quite some time. Cardenas and Cardenas (cited in Swadener, 1991) argued that Anglo-American, middle-class students enjoyed a fair chance for success in schools because school policies, practices, and content were "compatible" with the language, culture, and social class experiences of this group. Many educators proposed incorporating these experiences within curriculum and instruction and integrating positive attention to racism, sexism, and classism within all aspects of the school day (e.g., Banks, 1987; Banks & Banks, 1989; Bennett, 1990; Grant, 1981; Grant & Sleeter, 1986; Sleeter & Grant, 1988; Tiedt & Tiedt, 1990). Research done in schools supported the multicultural education paradigm. There were also several reports and studies that linked student academic achievement to curriculum that was "compatible" with student interests, needs, and backgrounds. Merino, Politzer, and Ramirez (1979) found that bilingual teachers' proficiency in Spanish was positively related to bilingual students' achievement in both English and Spanish. Delpit (1988) reported success with "culturally compatible" teaching approaches for African American children. Freedman (1990) described the excitement and involvement of Lower East Side New York high school students as they learned to complete oral histories of their neighborhoods. Tailor and Dorsey-Gaines (1988) described the promotion of literacy even in the poorest homes, while schools undereducated the children in their study.

While educational reform is limited in terms of challenging inequality related to race, gender, social class, or handicapping conditions, we want to pose a series of questions about educating students from diverse backgrounds. What if . . . we relate student failure or mediocrity to lack of relevance in curriculum and variety in instruction? What if . . . we wonder about the effects of monocultural classrooms on multicultural students? What if . . . we define diverse students as at risk of invisibility and challenge the notion of "colorblind" or "sex blind" or "class blind" classrooms? What if . . . we question who is at fault here?

Within the report from the Holmes Group (1990), we found part of the answer to these questions. While the authors wrote about professional development schools, let us relate their comments to schools in general.

> A Professional Development School by itself cannot solve the problems arising from society, any more than any other public school can; neither can it evade them under the pretext that they are beyond its grasp. Although creating socially just learning communities in the long run will involve building a more equal and democratic society, school and university faculty can do a better job of disentangling social and class inequities from learning opportunities. (Holmes Group, 1990, p. 34)

Teachers, from this perspective, are considered "at risk" only to the extent they are unprepared to support student diversity. Many teachers we worked with defined providing equal opportunity as treating all students the same and giving all students equal access to the same material. Equal access, however, often is insufficient to achieve educational equity. For the latter, very different content and strategies may be needed to meet student needs and affirm student diversity. In addition, some teachers did not "see" group diversity; all students were individuals with individual differences. While noting differences is important, students are members of groups as well as individuals. Teachers deny students an important part of themselves when they gloss over group membership.

Teacher educators may be at risk as well as teachers. To what extent have professors been trained to provide an education that is multicultural? Soltis (1987, p. 1) wrote about teachers in a way that has relevance for this question: "The better a teacher is educated, the better an education that teacher potentially can provide." For our argument, this means that, the better educated professors are about multicultural education, the better they can teach education courses from a multicultural perspective. We are not the first to say this. In regard to professors, Conant (1963) argued that the quality of the professorship depended upon the extent to which professors were trained for what they were called upon to teach. For example, it was insufficient to assign an education professor to teach the history of education. Rather, the professor must understand both the disciplines of history and education. Similarly, professors must be well grounded in multicultural education and their special academic disciplines to teach subject matter from a multicultural perspective.

It is not surprising that Grant and Secada (1990) found little evidence of research on multicultural education within teacher education programs. These researchers reviewed 16 research studies completed between 1973 and 1988 that described course work related (in a broad sense) to multicultural education and investigated the impact upon preservice students. Most of these studies reported results related to course work lasting a semester or less. In general, the impact of multicultural training on education students was initially positive and increased awareness of group differences. Positive results, however, were lost or diminished over time. This resulted in little change in classroom teaching.

Researchers in quite a few of these studies urged teacher educators to realize that student teachers must receive continuous study in multicultural education to be able to affirm diversity in the classroom. They called upon professors to go beyond establishing a "comfort zone" about differences and to teach education students how to teach from a multicultural perspective.

The Perspectives of Teacher Educators

Teacher educators are not doing all they can to prepare preservice teachers to deal with diversity in the classroom. Why is this so? There are factors that Howey and Zimpher called "constraining," factors that may work against teaching about diversity. First, teacher education may not be enjoying the best of times. According to Schuster and Bowery (cited in Howey & Zimpher, 1990), the field has been fully staffed since the mid-1970s, few doors opened for new faculty, and thus a buyers' market prevailed. For those who got in the door, hiring and retention was based, increasingly, on research and publications. Dedication to these areas, along with a full teaching load, is a formidable task. Professors may see themselves as too extended to enter into curricular and/or programmatic change. Second, teacher educators were not a very diverse group: 90% of the faculty were Anglo-American, 5% were African American, 4% were Asian American; and 72% were male. A large proportion (44.7%) of the teacher education faculty were tenured and older (53 years of age; American Association of Colleges for Teacher Education [AACTE], 1987; Howey & Zimpher, 1990). These statistics suggest that most faculty were trained when monocultural and segregated schools were the norm. Unless these faculty received in-service training, they know little about multicultural education. Because no research and very few descriptive reports could be located on in-service programs for professors in regard to human diversity, this leads us to believe that the current core of teacher educators are asked to instruct students about multicultural education when they are not prepared to do so. In fact, given the demographics of teacher educators, the following questions are pertinent:

- To what extent will a largely white, male faculty deem it necessary and appropriate to teach about people different than themselves?
- To what extent will a heavily tenured faculty deem it necessary and appropriate to reconsider their teaching in regard to student diversity?
- To what extent is the faculty cognitively and attitudinally prepared to include information about diversity in their teaching?

Regardless of these constraining factors, universities and colleges are jumping on the "multicultural" bandwagon and pressing expectations for teacher educators to provide teacher training in multicultural education. As Schwebel (Howey & Zimpher, 1990, p. 352) explained, education faculty must choose between

> finding ways to make the schools work for larger proportions of children, or to follow a safer, more traditional academic path. If education faculty are to "make it" under the new priorities in the university, and if their research is to be useful to the schools, they must choose the riskier course.

Teacher educators share a quest for knowledge with the student teachers they teach; they are colleagues in an effort to gain multicultural competence. Therefore, as we talk of one group, we must simultaneously consider the other. In the next two sections, we suggest components that should be included in faculty in-service and preservice programs for multicultural education.

Multicultural Education for Teacher Education Professors

Professors are expected to engage in the formal and informal pursuit of knowledge on a continuing basis. Therefore they should be a group amenable to rethinking their instruction to prepare new teachers to work with diverse groups of students or to bring multiculturalism to monocultural schools. Professors need to talk to one another about their multicultural teaching.

Faculties need to work toward a goal of multicultural education as a group rather than as individual learners. As faculty wrestle with multicultural education together, they can react with the wisdom that comes from a collective and collegial effort. They can also create an integrated "across-the-curriculum" approach to multicultural education, and attention to diversity can become interwoven throughout the total program.

We would like to suggest a few approaches for helping professors learn about multicultural education. These approaches are based on our experiences with professors seeking multicultural information.

Almost forgotten in our age of computer searches are literary societies: meetings to discuss the significance of thought-provoking books. And yet, reading a new work opens eyes and minds in a time-honored way for professional literary buffs. Gomez (1991) wrote about promoting stimulating discussion and new revelations among teachers by organizing a course around several provocative questions and encouraging teachers to interact and react to these questions through readings. For example, Gomez (1991, p. 96) asked teachers: "What does it mean to be a literate person?" and "What curricula and what methods best serve diverse learners?" Readings included Rodriguez's *Hunger of Memory: An Autobiography, the Education of Richard Rodriguez* (1982), Rose's *Lives on the Boundary* (1989), and Tailor and Dorsey-Gaines's (1988) *Growing Up Literate: Learning from Inner-City Families*. Gomez (1991, p. 96) reported that, as a group, teachers "begin to view literacy and diversity as problematic, as historically and culturally defined, and as concepts which, transformed into school practices, have profound consequences for *who,* which learners, receive *what* instruction" (italics in original).

We propose that professors trained in multicultural education work with faculty members on an individual basis to analyze and suggest changes within course work that are explicit and relevant to the work of each professor. It is important that professors analyze the fundamental ways in which multicultural education affects their fields of study. They need to reexamine the basic questions asked, topics covered, research highlighted, authors emphasized, and assignments made in their courses. After professors have the opportunity to evaluate and modify their instructional curriculum, it would be worthwhile to share their modifications with colleagues. Professors need to let others know about their processes of learning and proposals for change. In this way, colleagues continue to work in their own way but toward the common goal of providing an education that is multicultural.

Also, professors need to communicate with colleagues at other institutions who they believe teach and research from a multicultural prospective. As the

Holmes Group (1990, p. 5) stated, "Much of what we would like to see is happening now: in the classrooms of isolated teachers, in schools inspired by principals who are lone entrepreneurs, in universities and colleges of education where a few maverick professors always turn up." Holmes's authors argued that it was time to challenge isolationism and "build communities of practice and inquiry that will endure over time" (p. 5). They call for publication of "stories" about "struggles and successes" in regard to "teaching and learning for everybody's children" (p. 43).

Faculty retreats for discussion of multicultural education are important. There needs to be a time for teaching faculty, administration, and support staff to come together to decide on multicultural education policies and practices. Resources, both human and financial, have to be discussed and allocation decisions made. Faculty groups should consider travel to urban centers to observe and consult with teachers, principals, and students. The possibility of working out exchange programs or field placements in cities is important.

The Perspectives of Teacher Education Students

One of the chapter authors works primarily with traditional university students, the "20-something" group (Gross & Scott, 1990). The other teaches in a nontraditional university setting where students may be "20-something" but that also includes a good number of those returning to school after raising families or working or receiving baccalaureate degrees in other fields—the "30-something and 40-something" group. Also, both authors have worked in an alternative certification program with a large population of students who had recently received their undergraduate degree from the nation's leading colleges and universities.

Our experiences were related to issues raised in a *Time* magazine (Gross & Scott, 1990) article and to comments by Bloom (1987) about his students. According to Gross and Scott (1990), the perspectives of the 20-something group did not coalesce around any central issues. In other words, there were no unifying themes or questions that bound the attention of this group. Rather, individuals tended to follow the beat of their own drummers.

Bloom (1987, p. 82) noted that students had "none of the longings, romantic, or otherwise, that used to make . . . society, in general, repugnant of the young." Bloom described students as "nice"; "students these days are pleasant, friendly, and if not great-souled, at least not particularly mean-spirited. Their primary preoccupation is themselves" (p. 83).

Gross and Scott (1990, p. 57) also portrayed students in this way: "They have few heros, no anthems, no style to call their own." These authors told us the 20-something group were the best educated group in U.S. history, yet they were not sure how to use their education. They did not want to join the rat race of Wall Street but did want to do good works—in small enough areas that they could see gains from goodness.

These propensities turned an increasing number of heads toward teaching. Enrollment in teacher education programs increased as more students claimed interest in public service careers. According to one *Time* respondent, "For our generation, teaching is the Peace Corps of the 1990's" (Gross & Scott, 1990, p. 57).

On the other hand, we noticed that passion for teaching as teaching did not generally abound among this group. Many were not sure why they chose teaching. Some were good students, and school seemed a comfortable place to which to return. Some were unsure about a career and teaching seemed an acceptable choice—at least for a while. Others chose the profession to "really help kids" or "give kids a better education than I got."

Even given a general attitude of goodwill toward students in an abstract sense, we experienced some difficulty moving this group toward appreciation of the diversity of human groups. After we introduced multicultural education, these prospective teachers responded in several ways.

The students of color often expressed anger about their past schooling and toward Anglo-American teachers for cultural omissions and benign neglect. They sought members of their own groups to champion their own heritage and issues. Others were alarmed by the separatist groups and sought a more integrationist posture. Still other students of color said little. This was true especially when there were few students of color in education classes.

The Anglo-American prospective teachers also varied in their responses to multicultural education. Some accepted it almost as a given and wanted to get on with teaching methods: "Well that's great but what do I do when children won't do what I say?" Others were stunned with a new awareness of human differences as they had had little experience with people different than themselves. This group spent most of their time expanding their awareness and dealing with themselves and were not ready to move toward education practices that affirmed diversity. This quote represents this view: "As a young child, in a small rural community, I didn't have any acquaintances with black people.... In high school again I was not acquainted with any other race.... But I am glad that this class is making me aware of the diversity that is in the world" (From a student paper, 1990). A few Anglo-American prospective teachers, especially White males, felt somewhat challenged by multicultural education and angered by the guilt that seemed placed at their feet for past wrongs to minority groups.

Bloom (1987) also talked of Anglo-American students when he said he found his students highly egalitarian; they believed all men and women were created equal and had equal rights. According to Bloom (1987, p. 89), students simply did not have prejudices against everyone; "everyone is an individual" and everyone is just a "person." Few felt oppressed; to them, doors were open for advancement for all.

Perhaps this helps explain the hurry of some 20-somethings to "get on with" the task of learning to teach. Why should they unpack cultural "baggage" when they felt they had none or deal with cultural legacies they deemed irrelevant? On the other hand, seeing everyone as "just a person" denied their group membership. For the Anglo-American students, the conviction that all individuals were equal lead them to perceive non-Whites in a colorblind manner.

Many students of color were experiencing their presence, in large numbers, at the university for the first time and tended to separate into their own groups. To some extent, they wanted others to recognize the value of their "differentness." These students were not looking for opportunities to integrate with those for whom equality seemed an easy matter.

Therefore, when both groups met in teacher education courses, they came with somewhat different agendas. Many people of color wanted to "help" the children of "their" group learn more about the history, language, and perspectives of their particular group. These prospective teachers wanted to succeed on their terms rather than according to the standards of the majority group. Even though they were novices within education, some of this group felt they had the "answers" to better schooling. The answers centered on promoting their particular group and left out "answers" for other groups of children.

Anglo-American students did not have the "answers," they had inclinations; they wanted to "be more creative than their teachers" and to "make school interesting." They tended to perceive educating children in terms of achievement of individual potential.

The 30-40 something group also were inclined toward public service—many wanted to "make a difference." Often, this group looked for success missed in other careers; they wanted to do more than just "put in hours," and teaching offered autonomy, good hours, good pay, and the opportunity for self-fulfillment through service. Many had children, enjoyed their company, and wanted to give each child chances for success.

All of our students in this group were Anglo-American women and men. Many students in this older group also had minimal educational or personal experience with people different than they are. Many attended segregated schools and colleges. This quote exemplifies these students: "I have been exposed to the concept of multicultural education in bits and pieces in other classes, but I never really considered it that pertinent to my situation. . . . I went to an all white grade school and high school. This is my first semester to ever be exposed to a black teacher" (From a student paper, 1990).

The 30-something/40-something group also thought of students' school success on individual terms. Many experienced sexism on the job, and this heightened their sensitivity to differences. They were receptive to discussions of multicultural education but did not necessarily transfer their experiences with sexism to racism. Our students told us they experienced sexism but did not investigate it, "It just happens, that's the way things are."

When we talked about social class, our students discussed what they could do in their families with limited incomes. But they did not think they experienced classism. They did not disdain poor people, yet they wanted, overwhelmingly, to teach in the suburbs. The suburbs were just closer to home or more convenient.

The responses were somewhat complex. There was sensitivity toward multicultural education but it only went so deep. It was still a concept pertinent to someone else's neighborhood. And yet this group wanted fervently to help *all* children prepare for and succeed in life. Also, this group advocated strongly treating *all* children equally in classrooms.

As we analyzed prospective teachers' responses about multicultural education, it seemed that most teachers, especially Anglo-American teachers-to-be, were comfortable with and prepared to advocate a human relations approach to differences—I'm OK, you're OK. This was a good first step toward affirming diversity, but so much of multicultural education was left untouched and, for us, unfinished. There are other, more dynamic aspects of providing an education that is multicultural; for example, teaching about the contributions and perspectives of other groups and challenging the institutions of racism, sexism, classism, and handicappism.

Five approaches to teaching multicultural education in relation to race, class, and gender were outlined by Grant and Sleeter (1986) and Sleeter and Grant (1988). These included human relations but also described single-group studies, multicultural education, and education that is multicultural and social reconstructionist. While we will not go into detail about each approach here, suffice it to say that each developed the study of diversity in much more depth than they did the promotion of positive human relations.

The question that needs to be raised is this: To what extent is attention to human relations adequate to the task of educating our nation's children? To answer this question, prospective teachers need to come to grips with their reasons for teaching. To "help kids" or to "give kids a better education than I got" are unclear reasons. While students' inclination toward public service and desire to make a difference should be applauded, more reflection needs to occur.

Prospective teachers need to ask themselves tough questions about the way they define what we call the moral mission of teaching. To what extent do their moral imperatives include an examination of their life histories and attitudes? To what extent do their moral imperatives include providing the best education for diverse students? To what extent is it necessary to provide equal access to educational opportunities? To what extent is equal access necessary and sufficient for achieving educational equity?

The moral mission of teaching needs to be considered within teacher education courses. Often, students' reasons for wanting to teach and definitions of teaching are assumed and left unquestioned. We challenge this position and urge teacher educators to help students define and decide upon which roads they will take toward good teaching. As they ponder the nature of good teaching, it is important they deal with the realities of student diversity in terms of group differences.

Multicultural Education for Teacher Education Students

Very important to the development of multicultural teacher education is the concept of "multicultural literacy." Hirsch (1987) and Bloom (1987) brought attention to the "lack of" cultural literacy among adults in the United States. Bloom argued for a return to the study of "great books." Hirsch (1988) held that Americans (U.S. assumed) needed a shared background of literate knowledge to communicate with one another. Hirsch, Kett, and Trefil (1988) compiled a list of 5,000 names, quotes, events, and concepts Americans "needed to know."

The problem with these works was that the concept of culture was not seen as problematic. "Whose" culture was considered "traditional" was unquestionably weighted toward White males. Also, most of our cultural heritage was considered to be determined years ago.

The editors of the *Graywolf Annual Five* (Simonson & Walker, 1988, p. xi) took issue with the Hirsch/Bloom worldview:

> Most Americans are now aware of the contributions of repressed cultures, more alert to how history has been rewritten and molded to the vision of the majority population, and accustomed to the notion that culture, like language, changes, and that we ought to be sensitive to those changes. Though Hirsch is right, as far as he goes, ... he doesn't go far or deep enough. We need to know much more.

Multicultural literacy describes our diverse cultural heritage in terms of languages, traditions, and contributions of Anglo-Americans, people of color, and men and women representing various social classes. Multicultural literacy defines the "literatures, histories, mythologies and politics" (Simonson & Walker, 1988, p. xii) of these groups as valuable and fundamental aspects of our literary traditions. To perceive cultural literary as multicultural literacy is to appreciate and acknowledge cultural diversity.

For educators, acknowledgment of cultural diversity includes positive attitudes and actions toward all students, some or many of whom may differ from the teachers themselves. In classrooms in the United States, where desegregation and mainstreaming are norms, this means positive responses to students who differ by race/ethnicity, language, gender, social class, and handicapping conditions. Literacy, from a multicultural perspective, is a foundation for positive intergroup communication, respect, and inclusion. Multicultural literacy is what U.S. teachers "need to know."

To become "multiculturally literate" is to be educated about human diversity in the fullest sense. This means that recognition and appreciation of human differences permeates all that we teach and learn. As we teach history, we include multiple perspectives and Western and non-Western traditions. As we teach science, we help students to learn that science is all around them, that they can do science and think like a scientist without being in a laboratory or having a microscope or test tubes. We explain to them that they can be scientists and that men and women representing diverse groups have contributed to scientific knowledge. As we teach English, we explain how language and the people who speak the language have been enriched by the diversity of tongues that are includes when we say, "We the people . . ."

For teacher education, the promotion of multicultural literacy is based upon shared programmatic values and common goals in regard to diversity, course work from a multicultural perspective, and field experiences in diverse settings. Let us describe what we mean more fully. While some teacher educators may work alone to integrate multicultural education into their courses, that effort is insufficient to promote multicultural literacy. At best, we know that individual efforts may heighten awareness and acceptance of diversity for a short time. To develop and maintain the multicultural point of view, this perspective, including information about race, class, gender, and disability, must be infused in an ongoing way throughout the teacher program. This includes foundations and educational psychology courses, curriculum and instruction courses, and field experiences.

Multicultural literacy is built upon an attitudinal foundation of awareness, acceptance, and affirmation of differences. Many teacher education students have had minimal experiences with diverse groups. They have not had much opportunity to confront and grapple with their knowledge, feelings, and attitudes about people different than themselves. The following quote exemplifies responses from students in our education courses:

> When I was in third grade, our school was all Anglo-Saxon. There were no Latinos, no Asians, and no African-Americans. Everyone knew who the few really poor kids were. We were all treated pretty much the same. There was a high reading group, middle reading group and a slow reading group. The smart kids got to go to an enhancement group once a week. There was very little in the way of special education. Once, my girlfriends and I got in trouble for playing football. That was a boys' sport. None of my friends ever moved away. In fact, very few kids in our school moved. Most of us had stable, loving, secure homes. (From a student paper, 1990)

Students of color may have had minimal contact with people different than themselves as well and/or look upon others with disdain. This comment from one of our African American students illustrates this point:

> The student composition of the schools I have attended was primarily segregated. My student body was 99% African-American with about .5% Hispanic and White-American students. After carefully answering the questions . . . [in an autobiographical questionnaire] and hearing the answers of my classmates, it made me aware of the difference in the education I received as opposed to . . . my classmates. This helps me to understand why more minorities should be encouraged to enter the profession of education. (From a student paper, 1990)

As we prepare prospective teachers to work with diverse student populations, let us not assume that they come ready to deal with diversity. We have found that we have to spend considerable time helping students critically examine their knowledge, beliefs, and attitudes toward people who differ from them. This help requires patience, knowledge, and sensitivity on the part of the instructor. Also, this help requires the ability to get students to feel at ease as well as the ability to make the classroom a psychologically safe environment when issues and events become tense. We have also found that we must spend time helping students to understand the concept of institutional oppression in terms of racism, classism, sexism, and handicappism.

In addition, let us not assume that prospective teachers of color are prepared to deal with the diversity of other groups. Also, it is problematic to assume that people of color automatically know how to teach minority students. While students of color usually understand the denigration of their own group, they may not transfer this awareness to other groups. Additionally, because individuals differ within a group, assumptions cannot be made regarding the comprehensiveness of understanding. For example, an African American person who has grown up in a middle-class environment may not completely understand the life ways of an African American who has grown up in poverty. All prospective teachers need to know what they do *not* know. In this way, they prepare to learn about diversity from a point of view larger than their own.

We propose that these preliminary attitudinal investigations could be accomplished better in a multidisciplinary course perhaps taught by faculty with expertise in psychology, sociology, and multicultural education. This course should focus on exploring the attitudes and behavior prospective teachers bring with them to the university. It would be important to offer such a course early or even prior to the teacher education sequence of courses as the awareness gain here would help ease pressure in subsequent courses to discuss *why* we teach about multicultural education. This would allow professors to focus on *what* teachers can do to provide multicultural education.

Another important dimension of multicultural literacy is bilingualism. "Spanish is the second most widely spoken language in the United States, with estimates of up to 11 million speakers and still growing" (Tiedt & Tiedt, 1990, p. 146). It is commonplace in some areas for students to speak English as a second language. Yet, currently, educators see this as a deficiency and emphasize training in English and deemphasize second-language maintenance. Why is this so? Certainly students need to know the primary language of our country, but, if teachers could communicate in the students' language, perhaps students would be able to maintain their native language as well. As it is, we promote foreign language acquisition while, at the same time, deny second-language speakers opportunities to sustain and build bilingualism. We propose that the promotion of language diversity take place within liberal arts courses.

Multicultural literacy includes knowledge about different cultural groups. We propose that subject matter in general education courses and teacher education courses include multiple perspectives. What is the "true" story? Truth is different to different groups and history is an interpretation of the truth. But, unless prospective teachers have the opportunity to study several definitions of truth or several versions of the story, they will not be prepared to critically examine new information and events.

As we approach the teaching of methods for various subjects, we need to consider the student diversity that makes up multicultural classrooms. In what ways can teachers affirm student differences in terms of race, ethnicity, gender, social class, or handicapping conditions? Teachers affirm diversity through including information about various groups in curriculum and varying the processes of instruction. Methods for realizing the affirmation of diversity can be taught systematically. We propose that professors examine methods for teaching and learning to determine ways to integrate attention to diversity within teaching strategies and management techniques. For example, room environments should reflect diversity in displays, pictures, and posters. The social organization of the class should support mixed seating and grouping arrangements. Also, the instructional organization of the class should include a variety of approaches (e.g., large group recitation, panels, peer tutoring, cooperative learning) that suit different students and groups of students.

Subject matter areas such as the teaching of language arts methods should include the concept of diversity within the content of language arts. For example, a study of children's literature should include multicultural selections. Also, attention to diversity should be integrated into processes for teaching language arts. For example, methods to teach English as a second language should be included.

Clinical or field experiences are vital to teacher training programs. Field experiences should be organized around the goal of placing students in school settings with diverse populations. While it may difficult to find enough placements for students for *all* clinical experiences, *some* experience in a diverse setting should be required. Also, the cooperating teachers should be individuals who encourage multicultural teaching.

Summary and Conclusion

We argued that we are at risk of denigrating diversity at the very time differences are defining our nation's classrooms. We proposed that students should be "at promise" of success and can be to the extent we are willing to take a hard look at ourselves and make changes necessary to celebrate human differences. This means educating teacher education professors to lead change; we cannot assume professors understand multicultural education. Also, this means revamping teacher education programs to train teachers from a multicultural perspective within university and field experiences. And, in the broadest sense, the promotion and support of multicultural education should extend to the entire baccalaureate program. This calls for a dramatic change in the way educators perceive teacher education. Once educators embrace the concept of multicultural education, however, possibilities to define it within a specialty seem unlimited. This is possible; teacher educators can make it probable by taking steps in their own way to prepare teachers to celebrate human diversity.

References

American Association of Colleges for Teacher Education (AACTE). (1987). *Teaching teachers: Facts and figures*. Washington, DC: Author.

Banks, J. A. (1987). *Teaching strategies for ethnic studies* (4th ed.). Boston: Allyn & Bacon.

Banks, J. A., & Banks, C. M. (1989). *Multicultural education: Issues and perspectives*. Boston: Allyn & Bacon.

Bennett, C. I. (1990). *Comprehensive multicultural education: Theory and practice*. Boston: Allyn & Bacon.

Bennett, W. J. (1988). *Our children and our country: Improving America's schools and affirming the common culture*. New York: Simon & Schuster.

Bloom, A. (1987). *The closing of the American mind*. New York: Simon & Schuster.

Carnegie Forum on Education and the Economy. (1986). *A nation prepared: Teachers for the 21st century* (Report of the Task Force on Teaching as a Profession). New York: Author.

Conant, J. (1963). *The education of American teachers*. New York: McGraw-Hill.

Delpit, L. D. (1988). The silenced dialogue: Power and pedagogy in educating other people's children. *Harvard Educational Review, 58*(3), 280-298.

Education Commission of the States, Task Force on Education for Economic Growth. (1983). *Action for excellence: Comprehensive plan to improve our nation's schools*. Denver, CO: Author.

Freedman, S. G. (1990). *Small victories: The real world of a teacher, her students and their high school*. New York: Harper & Row.

Gomez, M. L. (1991). Teaching a language of opportunity in a language arts methods course: Teaching for David, Albert and Darlene. In B. R. Tabachnick & K. M. Zeichner (Eds.), *Issues and practices in inquiry-oriented education*. London: Falmer.

Good, T. L., & Brophy, J. E. (1987). *Looking in classrooms*. New York: Harper & Row.

Grant, C. A. (1981). Education that is multicultural and teacher preparation: An examination from the perspective of preservice students. *Journal of Educational Research, 75*(2), 95-99.

Grant, C. A., & Secada, W. G. (1990). Preparing teachers for diversity. In W. R. Houston (Ed.), *Handbook of research on teacher education* (pp. 403-421). New York: Macmillan.

Grant, C. A., & Sleeter, C. E. (1985). The literature on multicultural education: Review and analysis. *Educational Review, 37*(2), 97-118.

Grant, C. A., & Sleeter, C. (1986). Race, class and gender effects in education: An argument for integrative analysis. *Review of Educational Research, 56*, 195-211.

Gross, D. M., & Scott, S. (1990, July). Proceeding with caution. *Time*, pp. 57-62.

Hirsch, E. D. (1987). *Cultural literacy: What every American needs to know*. Boston: Houghton Mifflin.

Hirsch, E. D., Kett, J. F., & Trefil, J. (1988). *The dictionary of cultural literacy*. Boston: Houghton Mifflin.

The Holmes Group, Inc. (1986). *Tomorrow's teachers*. East Lansing, MI: Author.

The Holmes Group, Inc. (1990). *Tomorrow's schools: Principles for the design of professional development schools*. East Lansing, MI: Author.

Howey, K. R., & Zimpher, N. L. (1990). Professors and deans of education. In W. R. Houston (Ed.), *Handbook of research on teacher education* (pp. 349-372). New York: Macmillan.

Merino, B. J., Politzer, R., & Ramirez, A. (1979). The relationship of teachers' Spanish proficiency to pupils' achievement. *National Association of Bilingual Education Journal,* 3(2), 21-37.

National Commission on Excellence in Education. (1983). *A nation at risk: The imperative for educational reform.* Washington, DC: Author.

Pallas, A., Natriello, G., & McDill, E. (1989). The changing nature of the disadvantaged population: Current dimensions and future trends. *Educational Researcher,* 18(5), 16-22.

Rodriguez, R. (1982). *Hunger of memory: An autobiography, the education of Richard Rodriguez.* Toronto, Canada: Bantam.

Rose, M. (1989). *Lives on the boundary.* New York: Penguin.

Sikula, J. (1990). National commission reports of the 1980's. In W. R. Houston (Ed.), *Handbook of research on teacher education* (pp. 72-82). New York: Macmillan.

Simonson, R., & Walker, S. (1988). *The Graywolf Annual five: Multicultural literacy.* Saint Paul, MN: Graywolf.

Sleeter, C., & Grant, C. A. (1988). *Making choices: Five approaches to race, class, and gender.* Columbus, OH: Charles E. Merrill.

Soltis, J. F. (1987). *Reforming teacher education: The impact of the Holmes Group Report.* New York: Teachers College Press.

Soto, L. D. (1992). Success stories. In C. A. Grant (Ed.), *Research and multicultural education: From the margin to the mainstream.* London: Falmer.

Swadener, E. B. (1991). Children and families "at risk": Etiology, critique, and alternative paradigms. *Educational Foundations,* 4, 17-39.

Tailor, D., & Dorsey-Gaines, C. (1988). *Growing up literate: Learning from inner-city families.* Portsmouth, NH: Heinemann Educational.

Tiedt, P. L., & Tiedt, I. M. (1990). *Multicultural teaching: A handbook of activities, information, and resources* (3rd ed.). Boston: Allyn & Bacon.

PART IV

Effective Programs for Students in At-Risk School Environments

HERSHOLT C. WAXMAN, EDITOR

In recent years, there have been a large number of school-based programs that have been developed and implemented specifically for students in at-risk school environments. Some of these programs are research based (i.e., designed, modified, and implemented based on research findings), while others are based on theoretical/conceptual models that are implemented and sometimes evaluated afterward. Furthermore, some compensatory and remedial programs could be classified as "funding programs" because they specify *which* students are to be served rather than *how* students are to be served.

A growing number of educators have become disillusioned and concerned with some of these theoretical/conceptual and funding programs because the evaluative evidence about their effectiveness is mixed at best (Anderson & Pellicer, 1990; Slavin & Madden, 1989). For example, a summary of the evaluations conducted on one of the most widely used applications of computer technology, IBM's "Writing to Read" program, has found no consistent achievement results (Slavin, 1991). Although it could be argued that these findings show that this program is not detrimental for students, one also needs to consider that this program is quite costly to implement and is being used instead of other programs that have been empirically found to improve students' achievement. We need to be especially cautious of programs that are being widely publicized and disseminated yet have questionable empirical results on their effectiveness.

In Part IV, successful instructional and school-based programs that have been specifically developed for students in at-risk school environments are discussed. The programs and school-based approaches addressed in this part are representative of some of the widely implemented models. Although there are a number of other programs like "Success for All" (Slavin, Madden, Karweit, Livermon, & Dolan, 1990) and James Comer's "Child-Parent Center Model" (Comer, 1987) that have been found to be successful in improving the education of students at risk, these programs have not been as widely implemented as other programs. Consequently, the chapters included in this part represent some of the more widely publicized and/or implemented programs that are currently designed for students in at-risk school environments.

Successful Compensatory Education Programs

In their chapter, Sam Stringfield and Nancy Yoder provide a brief history of Title I/Chapter 1 research and then describe the results of two specific studies that examined programs that were successful in providing effective services to students in disadvantaged populations. They begin by explaining why research on the effectiveness of compensatory education has lagged behind teacher and school effectiveness research. They describe the complexity of measuring Chapter 1 effects because of the difficulty of conducting randomized experiments and due to the fact that Chapter 1 effects are neither nested within nor crossed with school effects and related to teacher, school, and other program effects.

Stringfield and Yoder continue to describe the research on Title I/Chapter 1 as having gone through three generations. The first generation of research was conducted by researchers who typically evaluated programs and generally found no cohesive conclusions. The second generation of research included large-scale studies like the Sustaining Effects Study, which found that low-achieving students did not seem to benefit from Title I programs. The third generation of research consisted of smaller studies and applied reviews of research from areas related to Chapter 1. This generation of research found that (a) continuous-progress programs, (b) cooperative learning, (c) preventive and remedial tutoring programs, and (d) some types of intensive, integrated computer-assisted instruction programs achieved greater than average gains for students from disadvantaged populations.

In the next part of their chapter, the authors described two studies in which they were (a) determining which Chapter 1 programs were succeeding and then (b) describing how these programs provided exemplary services to students from highly disadvantaged populations. They uncovered nine organizational/leadership themes that were common among the exemplary programs: (a) a primary goal that *every* student could learn; (b) instructional leaders; (c) highly qualified, experienced teachers; (d) an emphasis on staff development; (e) teachers held accountable for students' learning; (f) mandated coordination between Chapter 1 and classroom teachers; (g) a monitored program for success; (h) discontinuance of methods, materials, and staff that were not effective; and (i) parents involved in the students' learning processes. They also uncovered six instructional/classroom practices that were common among the exemplary programs: (a) instruction was geared to improving academic skills of individual students; (b) diagnosis, prescription planning, instruction, and evaluation were integrated; (c) lessons were structured to provide success *and* challenge; (d) there was frequent use of praise and rewards; (e) there was frequent coordination between Chapter 1 instructors and classroom teachers; and (f) many nationally recognized approaches to instruction were used.

In the next part of the chapter, the authors develop a complex model of Chapter 1 effects that specifies that the four direct influences of (a) parents, (b) regular classroom time, (c) additional special programs, and (d) Chapter 1 instruction significantly affect students' outcomes. The model also includes the six indirect effects of the (a) school, (b) community, (c) district, (d) compensatory education programs, (e) federal laws and regulations, and (f) state laws and regulations. Finally, the authors describe a research agenda for Chapter 1 that includes (a) more descriptive studies, (b) large-scale correlational studies, (c) well-controlled change studies, and (d) the testing and development of more complex models.

Effective Reading Programs for Students at Risk

In her chapter, Yolanda N. Padron begins by describing how schools have been successful in improving students' basic skills achievement but have not been successful in fostering students' higher-level thinking skills. She then summarizes the recent findings from cognitive strategy research and explains how reading comprehension may be enhanced through the explicit instruction of cognitive reading strategies.

The next sections of the chapter describe the applicability of three instructional approaches that are aimed at improving at-risk students' reading comprehension: (a) reciprocal teaching, (b) Reading Recovery, and (c) the Kamehameha Early Education Program (KEEP).

Reciprocal teaching is a cognitive strategy training approach that takes place in a cooperative instructional environment. Students received instruction in four specific comprehension-monitoring strategies: (a) summarizing, (b) self-questioning, (c) clarifying, and (d) predicting. The teacher begins by modeling the strategies for students, but gradually the students take on the role of the teacher.

Reading Recovery is an early intervention program designed to help students who are in the lowest 20% in reading. Teachers in this program provide supplemental one-on-one tutoring with individual students for 30 minutes each day. The goals of the program are to teach students to (a) understand the reading process, (b) learn letter-sound relationships, and (c) gain fluency.

The Kamehameha Early Education Program (KEEP) is a language arts program that has incorporated the native cultural patterns of Hawaiian children into the instruction. Patterns of culture pertaining to social organization, sociolinguistic patterns, cognitive patterns, and motivation have all been taken into account in the program. Lessons in this program are about 25 minutes long and are conducted in groups of five. Students (a) discuss what they know about a topic before they read it, (b) silently read the text to answer questions, and (c) discuss the text integrating their prior experience into the discussion.

In the next section of the chapter, the needs of culturally and linguistically different students are addressed. In particular, the important role of prior knowledge is discussed. Culturally different students, for example, may need more help and guided instruction because they may not have the prerequisite knowledge needed to understand a particular topic being discussed.

In the next section, the issue of teacher training is discussed. The three approaches discussed in this chapter are all very demanding from the point of view of the teacher. Staff development is crucial to the implementation of these programs because teachers' attitudes and beliefs as well as practices have to be changed.

In the last section of the chapter, some similarities and differences among the three programs are discussed. Implications for future research are also addressed.

School-Within-a-School Approach

In his chapter, Daniel U. Levine describes the school-within-a-school (SWAS) unit as an alternative approach for making education more meaningful for at-risk students. He reports on several sites across the country where SWAS approaches have been successfully implemented and then provides a detailed description of the ninth-grade SWAS program in the Kansas City, Missouri, School District.

The Kansas City SWAS program was established to help ninth-grade students improve their reading comprehension and motivate and prepare them to succeed in academic courses. Students are placed in the SWAS based on grades, teacher and counselor judgment, attendance, and reading comprehension scores. Teachers are appointed to SWAS based on their willingness and capacity to work with at-risk students.

The major program characteristics are (a) teachers having common planning periods to coordinate instruction; (b) teacher teams agreeing on the selection and use of texts, grading, and communication with parents; (c) motivating learning experiences for students including academic competition between teams and schools; and (d) intensive staff development. One of the central components in the SWAS approach is to coordinate curriculum and instruction across subject areas. This "Linking Learning" component facilitates coordination among teachers and helps students acquire the appropriate "schema for thinking and comprehending."

In the next section of the chapter, Levine carefully describes the Degrees of Reading Power (DRP) approach, which has been a basic focus for instruction and continuing staff development in SWAS since 1984-1985. The DRP three-step approach consists of (a) administering the test to measure students' ability, (b) analyzing the readability of instructional materials and selecting materials that match students' current comprehension levels, and (c) providing instructional materials to help teachers use instructional strategies for improving students' comprehension.

In the next section, Levine describes some of the problems and deficiencies in implementing the SWAS program. In particular, he summarizes some of the results from formal evaluations of the project, which found that the following considerations reduced the effectiveness of the program: (a) there was inadequate staff development, (b) the district coordinator could only provide assistance when invited, (c) direct coordination and assistance from the superintendent's office were unavailable, (d) teachers were not provided with systematic instructional feedback, (e) there was insufficient time for teachers to acquire appropriate skills, (f) insufficient attention was given to teachers and student schedules, (g) administrators failed to adjust program delivery, and (h) too little technical assistance was provided.

In the last section of the chapter, Levine summarizes the district evaluation reports of the SWAS program and describes some of his research on the program. Overall, there have been impressive gains in student performance for well-functioning units. For the most part, teachers also indicated that they often used the 13 comprehension-improvement strategies emphasized in staff development.

Accelerated School Approach

In their chapter, Jane McCarthy and Henry M. Levin vividly describe an example of what an accelerated school would look like. They describe how one elementary school in Houston, Texas, successfully implemented the Accelerated School approach and then discuss the success of some other schools across the country.

In the next sections of the chapter, the authors describe what accelerated schools are and the three basic schoolwide principles that guide this approach: (a) unit of purpose, (b) building on strengths, and (c) school-site empowerment with responsibility. They further explain how everyone is involved in the program and how every aspect of the school is affected by this approach. Collaborative inquiry is the process for implementation to which all participants adhere.

The next section describes the curriculum, instruction, and organization of the Accelerated School approach. The curriculum builds on students' strengths and is designed to enable students to think and act at high levels of complexity. It places heavy emphasis on manipulatives, student research, and school-based instructional materials. An important aspect of the curriculum is that each accelerated school develops its *own* curriculum according to its own personal visions. Instruction in accelerated school focuses on active instruction and problem solving. A variety of instructional activities are used in the classroom and the teacher's role becomes one of arranging learning environments, selecting materials, and providing activities that allow students to use several modalities. The organization of the accelerated school allows for teachers, administrators, parents, students, and the community to collaboratively determine the activities in which the school partakes.

The authors maintain that there must be an integrated approach to change that affects the curriculum, instruction, and organization of the school simultaneously. They argue that the lack of additional funding does not impede the change process, and schools can reallocate existing resources to implement the program. Finally, they estimate that the process of transforming a school into an accelerated school will take about six years, but they feel that this program holds promise for lasting and meaningful educational reform.

Summary

The main purpose of Part IV of this book is to provide some potential solutions to the educational problems of students in at-risk learning environments by looking at effective instructional programs and school-based programs that have worked in other settings. Several key elements or components that have been successful in many different settings are discussed here, but it should be clear that these are only meant as suggestions, not simple recipes for improving schools. No program, even though it may be ideally or perfectly implemented, will prove a panacea for all the educational problems of students in at-risk school environments (Boyd, 1991). For the most part, each school must concern itself with the resolution of its own specific problems (Schubert, 1980). In that sense, every situation or problem should be considered unique, and educators should search on their own for the knowledge that is most valuable for them to improve educational practice (Schubert, 1980). Furthermore, we also need to address the critical out-of-school factors that affect the outcomes of schooling. If we only focus on school factors and ignore the importance of family and community influences on the education of students, we will clearly fail in our endeavors.

References

Anderson, L. W., & Pellicer, L. O. (1990). Syntheses of research on compensatory and remedial education. *Educational Leadership, 48*(1), 10-16.

Boyd, W. L. (1991). What makes ghetto schools succeed or fail? *Teachers College Record, 92,* 331-362.

Comer, J. P. (1987). New Haven's school community connection. *Educational Leadership, 44*(6), 13-16.

Schubert, W. H. (1980). Recalibrating educational research: Toward a focus on practice. *Educational Researcher, 9*(1), 17-24.

Slavin, R. E. (1991). Reading effects of IBM's "Writing to Read" program: A review of evaluations. *Educational Evaluation and Policy Analysis, 13,* 1-11.

Slavin, R. E., & Madden, N. A. (1989). What works for students at risk: A research synthesis. *Educational Leadership, 46*(5), 4-13.

Slavin, R. E., Madden, N. A., Karweit, N. L., Livermon, B. J., & Dolan, L. (1990). Success for all: First-year outcomes of a comprehensive plan for reforming urban education. *American Educational Research Journal, 27,* 255-278.

• 11 •

Toward a Model of Elementary Grades Chapter 1 Effectiveness

SAM STRINGFIELD
NANCY YODER

Far and away the largest federal investment in improving the education of at-risk students is Chapter 1. Begun in 1965 as the first bill of President Johnson's "War on Poverty," Title I (Chapter 1 since 1981) has provided more than $80 billion in funding for compensatory education services to America's at-risk children. For the 1991-1992 school year, Chapter 1 services will be supported by $6.1 billion in federal money. More than two thirds of these funds will be spent providing services to students from prekindergarten through grade 6.

Since its inception, the goal of Title I/Chapter 1 of the Elementary and Secondary Education Act (ESEA) has been to "break the cycle of poverty" by enhancing the educational opportunities provided to low-achieving children in schools serving disadvantaged communities. ESEA's authors believed that local educators were more likely to know what was best for their children than was the federal government, so Title I and Chapter 1 have always been funding programs. The programs have never prescribed particular instructional interventions. Due in part to restrictive interpretations of federal regulations, however, most funds have been used to provide diagnostic/prescriptive services to low-achieving students pulled out of their regular classes or to provide instructional aides within classrooms to help identified children (Birman et al., 1987).

This chapter provides a brief history of Title I/Chapter 1 research. We then describe two Chapter 1 Technical Assistance Center (TAC) Technical

Investigations (TIs) of programs that appeared to be providing effective services to highly disadvantaged student populations. Using the TIs as a base, we present a model of Chapter 1 effects. The chapter closes with a Chapter 1 research agenda.

To study Chapter 1 is to study paradox. From its inception, it has been the source of great optimism and equal pessimism. After 25 years of analyses, evaluators have declared it to be "a program that works" (Birman et al., 1987), a program that has produced modest gains (Slavin, 1987), and a waste of taxpayers' money. Chapter 1 is simultaneously among the most and least studied social programs in history. It has been extensively evaluated in the sense that, from the inception of Title I, local programs have been required by law to conduct evaluations of their services. Yet, for a program of such size and duration, very few systematic studies of Title I/Chapter 1 effectiveness have been conducted.

The development of effectiveness research has proceeded along a slow but understandable path. Compensatory education effectiveness research has lagged behind teacher and school effectiveness research. Although frustrating, the reasons for this lag time in developing a Chapter 1 effectiveness research base are not surprising. Regular classroom teachers have the greatest amount of daily and yearly contact with students; measurement of their impacts can be based on observations of students and teachers in classrooms during a one-year period. This is an expensive but manageable process, and one that has made considerable progress during the last 30 years (Brophy & Good, 1986; Rosenshine & Furst, 1973). Research on school effects is inherently more complex. Students learn reading and math in classrooms, not at the knee of a principal. Accurate measurement of a single unit of interest (e.g., the processes that contribute to the effects of one school) are inherently complex and expensive. Gathering a process-outcome data base on even a moderate number of schools is necessarily a large-scale, multiyear undertaking. Relative to teacher effects, progress in the school effects area has been slower (Purkey & Smith, 1983; Stringfield & Teddlie, 1991).

Measuring Chapter 1 effects is more complex yet. Some programs are uniform across districts (e.g., "pullout" computer-assisted instruction or aide-based, in-class assistance). Others vary from school to school within a district. Most students who receive Chapter 1 services do so for only 15-40 minutes per day (Rowan, Guthrie, Lee, & Guthrie, 1986) and participate in regular classroom instruction during the remaining five-plus hours of their school days. Whatever the effects of Chapter 1, they necessarily are crossed with regular classroom teacher effects. Depending on the question being asked and the specific district under study, Chapter 1 effects are either nested within or crossed with school effects. In those schools and districts in which teachers and principals coordinate programs closely, Chapter 1 effects can be expected to be multicollinear with teacher, school, and other special program effects. Moreover, it would be extremely difficult to perform a truly randomized experiment on Chapter 1 effectiveness. Federal law and regulations require nearly uniform service delivery within a district. Even the most optimistic observers could hardly be surprised that the field of Chapter 1 effectiveness research is evolving slowly.

The research that has been conducted may be thought of as having occurred in three generations. McLaughlin (1975) found that the first 10 years of Title I research was conducted by researchers attempting to evaluate programs with diverse components who encountered problems in obtaining local cooperation. It is not surprising that McLaughlin concluded that those early efforts had achieved no cohesive conclusions.

A second generation of Title I studies included the Sustaining Effects Study (SES; Carter, 1984), reanalyses of the SES data (e.g., Frontera, 1986), a moderate-scale attempt at independent replication of SES (Gabriel et al., 1985), and a U.S. Department of Education analysis of local, state, and national program data (Anderson & Stonehill, 1986). Based almost entirely on analyses of achievement test data and questionnaire-based, distal measures of programs, these second-generation studies produced five tentative conclusions:

1. The average Title I program appeared to have modest, positive effects on the achievement of disadvantaged students.
2. Achievement gains made by Title I students appeared to be greater in earlier grades.
3. Achievement gains were not consistently associated either with federal dollars spent or with the application of any one educational approach.
4. Students who exited Title I continued to perform at their enhanced levels and did not seem to revert to lower achievement levels during the first year after compensatory education services had been discontinued. But gains were generally not sustained over a period of more than two years following program participation.
5. Title I programs appeared to be most effective for students who were only moderately disadvantaged, but Title I did not appear to substantially improve the relative achievement of the most educationally disadvantaged part of the

school population. As Carter (1984, pp. 11-12) stated: "Low-achieving students did not seem to benefit from the Title I program, and we believe that a new program with more intensive and innovative techniques of instruction should be devised for these students."

The compensatory education research of the 1970s and early 1980s was not able to provide clear guidance for compensatory education programs. That situation was not aided by the fact that 1980s did not witness a single, integrated, large-scale process-outcome study of the effects of Chapter 1. Rather, the past decade produced a third generation comprising smaller studies and applied reviews of research from areas related to Chapter 1. Beyond the 1970s findings, Chapter 1 research and literature reviews of the last 10 years have tended to justify six additional conclusions:

6. The setting in which Chapter 1 services are delivered (in class versus pullout) is not as important as the quality of services provided in either setting.
7. Research on instructor type (such as types of specialists or instructional aides) is equally inconclusive.
8. Research relating teaching behaviors to disadvantaged students' achievement gains found several stable predictors of gains: high content coverage, maximum time allocated to instruction, high engaged time, consistent student success, active teaching, teachers structuring information, and frequent questioning with relatively high correct response rates (Brophy, 1986).
9. A carefully conducted study of Chapter 1 instructional effectiveness indicates that Chapter 1 teachers obtain greater achievement gains when they provide considerable challenge to their students, praise perhaps 10%-15% of students' correct responses, and provide fast feedback for incorrect student responses (Crawford, 1989). Whereas previous teacher effectiveness studies had found negative correlations between achievement gain and teachers' working one-to-one with students, Crawford found that, in the often quite small Chapter 1 groups, one-to-one instruction was positively correlated with achievement gain.
10. Allington and Johnston (1986) concluded that improved coordination was one key to improved compensatory education.
11. In an extensive search for programs that achieve greater than average effects on disadvantaged students' progress, Slavin (1987) identified four broad types of most promising programs. These were continuous-progress programs (e.g., DISTAR, U-SAIL), cooperative learning, preventative and remedial tutoring programs, and some types of intensive, integrated computer-assisted instruction programs.

These third-generation studies offer more grounds for optimism regarding a meaningful Chapter 1 effectiveness literature. None of them, however, directly addressed the most troubling of the second-generation research conclusions: that Title I did not help the students most in need. Our experience as Chapter 1 Technical Assistance Center (TAC) service providers ran counter to that darkest of the second-generation conclusions. We had worked with many local Chapter 1 programs that appeared to be having considerable success educating highly disadvantaged student populations. The more programs we worked with, the greater was our sense that those programs contained common characteristics not adequately tapped by previous research.

To test the hypotheses (a) that such programs existed and (b) that they shared many characteristics, staff from four regional TACs conducted two TAC Technical Investigations (Hepler et al., 1987; Stringfield, Yoder, & Quilling, 1989). The initial goal of the first Technical Investigation (TI) was simply to find programs that were succeeding. We were not searching for evidence in support of a particular model or group of nationally recognized programs. Rather, we were looking for success and were willing to allow common features of success to emerge over time. We were seeking a more overarching model. In the second TI, we were seeking rich, qualitative descriptions of a few programs clearly providing exemplary services to extremely disadvantaged children.

Method

Two studies were conducted by staff of the regional TACs. The first involved the identification of 20 local Chapter 1 programs that were obtaining unusually large achievement test score gains from highly disadvantaged student populations. All 20 projects met five criteria. First, the projects served high-need students. The definition of "high need" included two components: high concentrations of students receiving free or reduced-price lunch and student populations that had historically low entry-level skills. Second, the projects were selected from programs across the nation in urban, suburban, and rural areas. Third, the projects had multiple sets of data to document their effectiveness for at least two consecutive years. The projects had received formal federal or state recognition as exemplary programs or had been invited by their state departments of education to seek such recognition. Fifth, regardless of their total range of service, the projects included services in grades 3 to 6.

The sampling process resulted in the selection of 14 districtwide programs (with average district mean pretest performance ranging from the 4th to the

24th percentile) and six single or multischool projects operating within larger district programs. The later six were selected as providing exemplary services to high-need students within somewhat more affluent, larger districts. The programs sampled were from districts ranging in student body size from 265 to more than 90,000. Five of the programs were located in the northeast United States, five in the Southeast, five in the Midwest, and the remaining five in the western United States. Student body racial/ethnic composition ranged from as high as 97% Black to 83% Native American, 50% Hispanic, and, at one site, 98% Caucasian. Free lunch counts ranged upward to 98%.

Each site was visited for a minimum of two days. Site team members were asked to obtain information regarding the community, district, and other contextual variables and to spend at least half of their time visiting classrooms. They were instructed to look for evidence of each of the "13 characteristics of effective compensatory education programs" (Griswold, Cotton, & Hansen, 1986) and were instructed to try to look for additional components that contributed to the programs' successes.

The follow-up study (Stringfield et al., 1989) involved extended second visits to three programs that served more than 75% free lunch populations, provided services to elementary school students, had several years' data indicating achievement gains considerably above the national average, had conducted studies indicating that gains were maintained over at least two years, and had received the U.S. Secretary of Education's National Compensatory Education Recognition award. In the second TI, detailed interviews were conducted with teachers, principals, and Chapter 1 coordinators. Chapter 1 and regular classrooms were observed, and Chapter 1 students were shadowed for whole days in an effort to understand the connections between Chapter 1 and students' larger academic lives.

Results

Achievement Results

As Table 11.1 indicates, the 20 projects serving high-need children were obtaining student achievement gains that were consistently above the national average for Chapter 1 programs. In the cases of the six projects serving schools with 50% or higher free lunch counts, those gains averaged more

Table 11.1 Mean NCE Gains for High-Need Exemplary Projects, Highest-Need Exemplary Projects, and the National Average

Type of Project	Fall to Spring Testing		Annual Testing	
	Mean NCE Gain	Gain as a Percentage of National X̄ Gain[*]	Mean NCE Gain	Gain as a Percentage of National X̄ Gain
Six-project highest-need sample	11.20	164	7.66	250
High-need study, total sample	9.94	145	7.33	239
National average	6.83	—	3.07	—

NOTE: Unweighted national average for grades 4-6 derived from Carpenter and Hopper (1985).
[*](Sample gain/national mean gain) × 100.

than double the national average. In terms of conventional measures of Chapter 1 achievement gain (e.g., normal curve equivalent gains across school years), the programs serving high proportions of at-risk students were unusually effective.

Process Results

Cross-case study analyses of the 20 programs and the more in-depth analyses from three sites indicated considerable commonality in processes among the programs providing exemplary services to highly disadvantaged populations. These themes were grouped at two levels: organizational/leadership and classroom/instructional practices.

Organizational/leadership level. Nine themes ran across the organizational/leadership level. First, the leaders' primary goal was that *each* student would learn. Two of the clearest messages sent to teachers from these programs were that all children can learn and that all children can learn more than they have learned in the past. The objectives for the program followed from this goal and were often communicated in writing to the teachers at the beginning of every school year. Handbooks were often developed that included a clear statement of this goal, and resources were provided to aid the teachers in accomplishing this goal.

Second, the Chapter 1 directors were unusually well grounded in effective instructional techniques. They functioned as *instructional leaders*. They kept in touch with current trends in curriculum and instruction and were skilled at sifting promising innovations from simple, although glittering, fads. The leaders were involved in ongoing efforts to find and experiment with new, potentially useful organizational and instructional options.

Third, the directors employed highly qualified, experienced teachers. They "kept an eye out" within their districts for excellent teachers and then recruited those natural instructional leaders to Chapter 1 programs. They gave their teachers support and encouragement for providing quality instruction.

Fourth, the leaders took staff development very seriously. Individual teacher needs were assessed, and effective training strategies were used. Both formal and informal staff support systems were set up. There were unusually large numbers of regularly scheduled training sessions and faculty meetings in these Chapter 1 programs. Time was set aside for teachers to plan together. It is not surprising that the teachers came to believe in their programs.

Fifth, the leaders held teachers accountable for students' learning, requiring that time be used for instruction.

Sixth, regular, often formalized coordination between the Chapter 1 and regular classroom teachers was mandated. An emphasis was placed on sharing among teachers. The education of disadvantaged students was seen as a schoolwide responsibility—not solely a Chapter 1 responsibility.

Seventh, the leaders constantly monitored the program for success, with emphasis placed on instruction. Monitoring was conducted through classroom visits and close examination of student progress data. The programs were adjusted as a result of the monitoring. Once successful practices were in place, they were maintained and formalized.

Eighth, the leadership discontinued those methods, materials, and staff that were not effectively meeting the needs of the students. If honest attempts to improve nonproductive curricula or instruction failed, the programs were replaced with more promising options. Staff who were not willing to put forward the efforts required to help highly disadvantaged students progress received both one-to-one counseling with the principal or Chapter 1 director and targeted staff development opportunities. Almost every leader described circumstances in which they had counseled one or more teachers out of Chapter 1. This was invariably viewed as a last resort. It indicated not only that there were minimum standards for *all students* but there were also professional standards for *all staff.*

Finally, the leadership encouraged the intelligent involvement of parents in students' learning processes. School- or districtwide Chapter 1 newsletters were often sent home. It was not uncommon to find a programwide effort to "catch a child doing something good" and send a note home to the parents describing the child's success. Parents were often sent detailed explanations of why their child was in Chapter 1 and how they, as parents, could be partners in their child's educational growth.

Instructional/classroom practices. The nine leadership orientations and actions were accompanied by six instructional/classroom practices. First, instruction was clearly dedicated to improving the academic skills of individual students. An organizational goal of "all children learning" becomes a mere truism if not coupled with support for instructional thoroughness. Repeatedly, observation notes from the 20 programs indicated that leaders challenged teachers to be sensitive to individual students' strengths and weaknesses. The observers noted that teachers were provided with the wherewithal to assist students and that the teachers often made remarkable efforts on the students' behalf. When a student did not learn through one approach, a variety of resources were brought to bear in efforts to find workable alternatives.

Second, diagnosis, prescription planning, delivery of instruction, and evaluation of student progress were integrated into continuous, interlocking processes. This was not a finding that favored a specific type of program. Rather, TAC researchers found specific *processes* across the 20 sites: Student progress was closely and regularly monitored. For example, every new student at one school passed through a five-step process before receiving even tentative placement within the school. Each student received an initial assessment in reading, language arts, and mathematics. Assessment results were evaluated by program management staff, and a conference was held between the program manager and parents. The regular classroom teacher observed the new student in a variety of situations, and teamwide comparisons were made between previous school records and current assessments and observations. The sum of the above processes led to a "final" placement of the student in a class. If later data indicated that the placement was not as desirable as had been hoped, the process was repeated.

Third, lessons were structured to provide both success and challenge.

Fourth, there was frequent use of praise and rewards associated with the accomplishment of instructional objectives. Awards ranged from stickers to extended field trips to simple acknowledgment of jobs well done.

Fifth, there was frequent and intensive coordination between the Chapter 1 instructors and the regular classroom teachers. Just as there were many levels of program coordination in the various contexts, Chapter 1 and regular classroom teachers found a multitude of methods for communicating about the needs and services provided to individual students.

Finally, many of the Chapter 1 classrooms used nationally recognized approaches to instruction. "Assertive discipline," "TESA: Teacher Expectations and Student Achievement," "Writing to Read," and other nationally recognized programs were regularly noted as components of the exemplary projects. In none of the 20 high-gain cases was a local Chapter 1 program exclusively identified with one national program. Rather, the local schools seemed to view national programs as individual vegetables on a salad bar of alternatives. National programs were used when and where they were judged to be locally appropriate, but the local program reserved the option to choose which nationally recognized "program" to plug into each situation.

In summary, the two technical investigations were successful in identifying local programs that were consistently obtaining much higher than average achievement gains from highly disadvantaged students. Those local programs had several common characteristics at both the organizational/leadership and the classroom/instruction levels.

The Evolution of a Model of Chapter 1 Effects

Based on our experiences in the Technical Investigations and the previously noted literature reviews, we have developed a more complex model of Chapter 1 effects. We believe that a useful point of departure is with the model assumed by the Title I/Chapter 1 Evaluation and Reporting System (TIERS Model A). For 25 years, researchers have attempted to ascertain simple program effects on students through this model. The implicit TIERS model assumes that Chapter 1 programs have a direct effect upon student

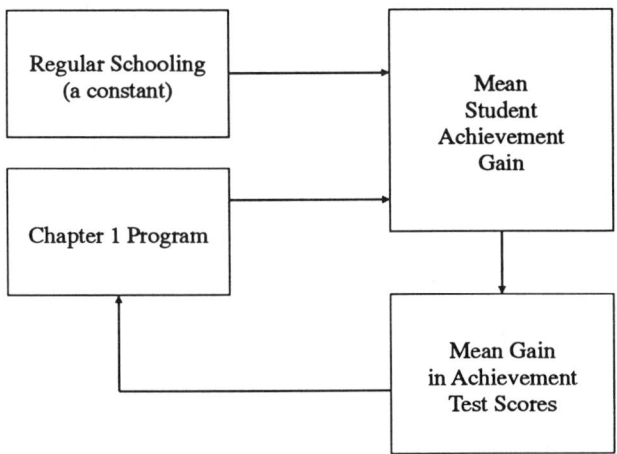

Figure 11.1. The Implicit Model of Group Growth in TIERS

outcomes, with all other factors neatly canceling each other's effects (see Figure 11.1). Using a model that is not notably more complex, it is hardly surprising that second-generation studies found little evidence of Title I program effects. Pupils do not attend Chapter 1 programs in a vacuum; nor are all other events equal in the lives of various children. Typical Chapter 1 students spend only 25-40 minutes of each six-hour school day in compensatory education programs. They spend the remainder of their school days in more or less effective classes, in more or less effective schools. The students' parents differ substantially in their support for their children's educations, and none of this is reflected in Figure 11.1.

Attempting to understand the effects of Chapter 1 programs requires a more complex model. In Figure 11.2, the academic gains of students participating in local Chapter 1 programs are seen as being directly influenced by at least four factors: parents, regular classroom teachers and curricula, Chapter 1 curricula and instruction, and other school programs.

Each of those four direct influences on student learning is supported (or hindered) by several other forces. Among those supporting institutions and groups are the federal and state laws and regulations, the local community, the school district administration, the school, and the local compensatory education program.

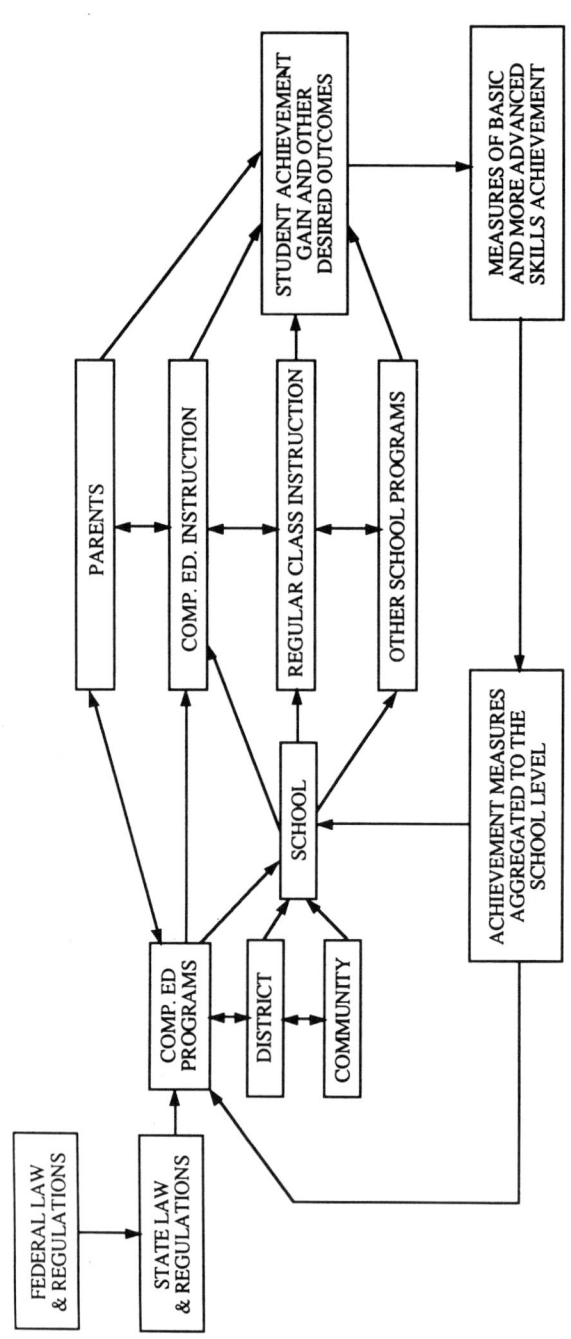

Figure 11.2. A More Realistic Compensatory Education Program Effects Model

Direct Influences on Chapter 1 Students' Achievement and Other Desired Outcomes

In the programs visited, Chapter 1 teachers and administrators tended to assume that there were four groups of people capable of having direct influences on students' achievement, attendance, academic self-concept, and other desired outcomes. The first of those was *parents*. Children spend 18 hours of every school day and 48 hours every weekend away from school. In the case of elementary students, parents are the people most directly able to influence children's use of those hours. There is a rapidly evolving literature on parent involvement (e.g., D'Angelo & Adler, 1990; Epstein, 1990) that is consistent with the observations of the case study researchers. TAC staff visited schools that had found a multitude of methods for keeping parents informed and involved in their children's educations. Mailings, signed homework, teacher-parent meetings, calls home, and home visits—each district attended to parent involvement.

The second direct influence on students' learning is *regular classroom* time. Chapter 1 children spend over five hours per day under the instructional supervision of regular classroom teachers. An important measure of children's academic success is success in the regular classroom. There is a substantial literature on effective classroom practices for working with disadvantaged children. This research does not directly address one of the important problems faced by many regular classroom teachers, however, which is how to find sufficient materials that are at the appropriate difficulty levels for Chapter 1 students while continuing to move the average- to above-average-achieving students forward. At most of the exemplary sites visited, Chapter 1 personnel actively assisted regular classroom teachers in attending to the daily academic needs of children who were in danger of falling behind academically.

Chapter 1 students often qualify for additional special programs. Bilingual, migrant, special education, and a variety of other categorical programs often overlap in the services they provide to students. These have the potential to become a bewildering and dysfunctional maze for elementary school children. In the sites visited by TI staff, time was found to coordinate the instructional efforts of these programs as they related to Chapter 1 children.

Fourth, Chapter 1 instruction itself has the potential to have positive effects on students' achievement and attitude gains. The instructors that the researchers observed and interviewed tended to be dedicated, well informed, and multiskilled. Chapter 1 time was intense work time for their students. In general, Chapter 1 teachers at the exemplary sites provided materials at the appropriate difficulty levels for individual students, used multiple methods of presentation of material, and provided many types of student rewards. As a result, the students almost invariably reported enjoying it. Several of the exemplary programs faced the "problem" that high-achieving children wanted to receive compensatory education services.

Supporting Influences on Chapter 1 Students' Achievement and Other Desired Outcomes

Investigators visited almost no sites at which regular teachers, parents, Chapter 1 programs, and "other" programs all appeared to be working well in isolation. Rather, a variety of forces were actively guiding and coordinating services to children.

The most distant but not least important of those supporting roles is played by the federal government. Congress passes laws that both enable and constrain the delivery of Chapter 1 services. The U.S. Department of Education creates regulations and "nonregulatory guidance" designed to further restrict uses (and abuses) of federal funds. The congressionally mandated increases in school-level Chapter 1 accountability for student achievement gain is an example of the occasionally considerable federal role in local Chapter 1 processes.

An example of the power of shifts at the federal level to affect local service delivery was provided in the 1988 Hawkins-Stafford amendments to the Chapter 1 legislation. Among other changes, the new law called for school-level analysis of student achievement gains. If a school's Chapter 1 students do not show pre- to post-treatment gains, that fact now must be reported to the local school board and the school is required to enter into a period of "Chapter 1 program improvement." Some principals appear to infer from that designation that they are operating "ineffective" schools. As a result, many principals are attending to their Chapter 1 services and test scores much more closely than in the past.

The actual funneling of Chapter 1 funds and responsibility for guidance and oversight of local programs is the responsibility of state departments of education. Most state directors of Chapter 1 actively exercise the discretion allowed them. In some states, Chapter 1 teachers told site visitors that the law forces them to focus on basic skills. In other states, teachers seemed to believe that the same federal law required them to focus on higher-order skills. As TAC service providers, we were often aware that these local understandings were derived from state-level meetings in which various aspects of federal mandates were emphasized and others glossed over.

Community conditions often set parameters within which Chapter 1 programs operate. In middle-class districts, Chapter 1 is often a very small part of the overall program. In highly disadvantaged communities, Chapter 1 can represent 10%-25% of the total district budget. In some districts, compensatory education has rarely been discussed and project directors are free to design services as they see fit. In others, community action groups form around decisions to add or subtract schools from those receiving services, or unions and parents' groups become involved in decisions to move to more teacher- (or aide- or computer-) based programs.

District-level personnel are often acutely aware of community concerns and attempt to address them. Similarly, many superintendents and curriculum coordinators seek to create districtwide curricular foci. These may or may not include components that are well matched to the federal goals for Chapter 1.

Both within the TI sites and in our broader experiences with compensatory education programs, typical local Chapter 1 programs were allowed considerable freedom to create administrative and instructional systems. There are many technical aspects unique to the administration of Chapter 1, and many ways to obtain an unwanted audit exception. Superintendents and curriculum coordinators are often eager to give Chapter 1 directors considerable autonomy in exchange for bureaucratic relief from responsibility. This freedom can be used in a variety of ways. In some of the exemplary sites, district Chapter 1 personnel mandated a particular set of options to all qualifying schools. In others, the freedom and responsibility were passed on to each individual school, and schools responded with a colorful mosaic of programs.

Typically, the options for prescribing or offering Chapter 1-funded staff development were retained at the district level. Several of the exemplary programs mandated districtwide training of Chapter 1 personnel in a variety of specific programs (e.g., Mastery Learning, TESA, cooperative learning, use of microcomputers in instruction). In some districts, Chapter 1 hiring and teacher evaluation responsibilities were held at the district level. In others, those options were controlled at the school. In all of the exemplary programs, there was informal give-and-take between schools and district Chapter 1 personnel.

In almost all of the TI sites, schools were the final arbitrators of all student services offered. Schools have the potential to provide the most unifying source of support for high-quality instruction. Although the TIs were not studies of school effects, the majority of observers reported the impression that they were visiting very good schools. In at least one case during the second TI, however, there was clear evidence that the school within which exemplary Chapter 1 services were being offered was anything but exemplary. Even in that extreme case, there was evidence of solid communication between the district-level Chapter 1 program, the principal, and the Chapter 1 staff.

The preceding paragraphs have examined the "boxes" in Figure 11.2. The TI observers repeatedly noted the importance of the connections among the boxes. It was clear to the observers that at some sites many of the isolated components were not extraordinary. The school districts visited were not always noteworthy. The communities and schools often seemed typical of those with large concentrations of disadvantaged students. The observed quality of regular instruction varied greatly and, even in these exemplary programs, the quality of Chapter 1 instruction was occasionally uneven. What was universal was a deliberately developed and maintained set of connections. Leadership; shared, systematic evaluation procedures; staff development; and an awareness that no mandated program can, in isolation, solve the problems of disadvantaged students all seemed to auger for information flow—for coordination among the involved components.

The presence of highly charged connections among components of programs achieving exemplary results while working with extremely disadvantaged populations points back to the critical role of leadership. Each of the exemplary programs had strong, stable, instructionally focused leadership. Virtually all the Chapter 1 directors held high levels of what Greenfield (1987) described as "moral imagination and interpersonal competence." They worked at maintaining productive relationships with parents, their superintendents, and their schools' principals and teachers. Though each completed their bureaucratic tasks effectively, each provided guidance and hands-on communication and allowed freedom to dream and experiment. The directors of the exemplary programs had carefully nurtured, positive relationships with their state's education department colleagues. Maximizing the active coordination among the four groups in direct contact with children was one of the critical roles of program leadership.

A Research Agenda for Chapter 1

The Chapter 1 budget for the 1991-1992 school year is just over $6.1 billion. That budget is scheduled to rise in the years to come. This is a very large investment in compensatory education services for at-risk students. Slavin (1987) has called for the federal government to invest "a penny on the dollar" for research on the effectiveness of compensatory education programs. In industry or the military, a 1% investment in research and development would be viewed as disastrously low. Yet, for research on Chapter 1 to reach that level would require an increase of several magnitudes over current investments.

It is possible that one of the reasons for remarkably small federal investment in compensatory education research has been the lack of an active research agenda. To that end, we propose the following agenda for research on Chapter 1. Four types of work are needed within this field.

(1) More descriptive studies. The department of education has recently funded several descriptive studies of exemplary programs (Plisko & Scott, 1991). Many more are needed. There are large numbers of innovations currently evolving in Chapter 1. In the Netherlands, the national government funds a thorough, independent evaluation of an innovation before supporting replications. Such sensible analyses are needed in the United States.

Federal law requires that schools found not to be producing gains on the TIERS evaluation system undergo "program improvement." Given that research on the effects of schools indicates that the road to ineffectiveness is not simply the mirror image of school effectiveness (Stringfield & Teddlie, 1988), it would appear to be in the best interest of the Chapter 1 program to obtain a better understanding of ineffective programs. How have they come into being, how are they sustained, and how can they be improved? Detailed descriptive studies of both innovations and problem schools are needed.

(2) Large-scale correlational studies. The Department of Education is currently planning the first large-scale, questionnaire and test-based, longitudinal study of the Title I/Chapter 1 program in 15 years. It will be a welcome addition to the research base. It is worth noting, however, that, to reach consensus, the field of teacher effectiveness required a half dozen such studies. Chapter 1 deserves similar efforts.

(3) Well-controlled change studies. Once correlational analyses and descriptive studies of promising and problematic programs have been completed, the Department of Education should fund a series of independently conducted, well-controlled change studies. Chapter 1 students deserve more than an eternally swinging pendulum of fads. Controlled experiments are extremely valuable and far too rare in education. Madden, Slavin, Karweit, Dolan, and Wasik (1991) offer a clear and unusual example of the potential benefits of such programmatic research.

(4) Work toward the evolution of a more realistic, probably more complex model. In this chapter, we have proposed a model of Chapter 1 effects that is considerably more complex, and we believe more accurate, than TIERS. Beyond our own research, it is untested. Advances in the field of Chapter 1 effectiveness will come through the development and testing of a variety of effectiveness models. That research, in turn, could be used to improve practice.

The recent congressional reauthorization of Chapter 1 requires poorly performing programs and schools to make concerted efforts to become more effective. Rationally, such a requirement would be linked to a strong Chapter 1 research base. After nearly $100 billion have been spent on Title I/Chapter 1 programs, the federal government has funded only a handful of reasonably sophisticated studies of Chapter 1 effectiveness. Over the last 25 years, teacher and school effectiveness studies have demonstrated that such research can yield practical results. Research on Chapter 1 is beginning to hold similar promise. The time for funding and learning from sophisticated, large-scale studies of compensatory education effectiveness is at hand.

References

Allington, R., & Johnston, P. (1986). The coordination among regular classroom reading programs and targeted support programs. In B. Williams, P. Richmond, & B. Mason (Eds.), *Designs for compensatory education: Conference proceedings and papers.* Washington, DC: Research and Evaluation Associates.

Anderson, J., & Stonehill, R. (1986, August). *Twenty years of federal compensatory education: What do we know about the program?* Washington, DC: U.S. Department of Education.

Birman, B., Orland, M., Jung, R., Anson, R., Garcia, G., Moore, M., Funkhouser, J., Morrison, D., Turnbull, B., & Reisner, E. (1987). *The current operation of the Chapter 1 program.* Washington, DC: U.S. Department of Education, Office of Educational Research and Improvement.

Brophy, J. (1986). *Research linking teacher behavior to student achievement: Potential implications for Chapter 1 students.* East Lansing: Michigan State University, Institute for Research on Teaching.

Brophy, J., & Good, T. (1986). Teacher behavior and student achievement. In M. Wittrock, *Handbook of research on teaching* (3rd ed.). New York: Macmillan.

Carpenter, M., & Hopper, P. (1985, September). *Synthesis of state Chapter 1 data: Summary report.* Indianapolis: Advanced Technology.

Carter, L. (1984). The sustaining effects study of compensatory and elementary education. *Educational Researcher, 13*(7), 4-13.

Crawford, J. (1989). Instructional activities related to achievement gains in Chapter 1 classes. In R. E. Slavin, N. L. Karweit, & N. A. Madden (Eds.), *Effective programs for students at risk.* Boston: Allyn & Bacon.

D'Angelo, D., & Adler, R. (1990). Chapter 1: A catalyst for improving parent involvement. *Phi Delta Kappan, 72*(5), 350-354.

Epstein, J. (1990). Paths to partnership: What we can learn from federal, state, district, and school initiatives. *Phi Delta Kappan, 72*(5), 344-349.

Frontera, L. (1986). *Compensatory education and achievement growth in elementary school: Title I of the Elementary and Secondary Act of 1985.* Unpublished doctoral dissertation, University of Delaware.

Gabriel, R., Anderson, B., Benson, R., Hill, J., Pfannensteil, J., & Stonehill, R. (1985). *The sustained achievement of Chapter 1 students.* Washington, DC: U.S. Department of Education.

Griswold, P., Cotton, K., & Hansen, J. (1986). *Effective compensatory education sourcebook.* Washington, DC: Government Printing Office.

Greenfield, W. (Ed.). (1987). *Instructional leadership.* Newton, MA: Allyn & Bacon.

Hepler, N., Stringfield, S., Seltzer, D., Fortna, R., Stonehill, R., Yoder, N., & English, J. (1987). *Effective compensatory education programs for extremely disadvantaged students.* Portland, OR: Northwest Regional Educational Laboratory.

Madden, N., Slavin, R., Karweit, N., Dolan, L., & Wasik, B. (1991). Success for all. *Phi Delta Kappan, 72*(8), 593-599.

McLaughlin, M. (1975). *Evaluation and reform: The Elementary and Secondary Education Act of 1965, Title I.* Cambridge, MA: Ballinger.

Plisko, V., & Scott, E. (1991). Planned evaluations of Chapter 1. *Phi Delta Kappan, 72*(8), 590-592.

Purkey, S., & Smith, M. (1983). Effective schools: A review. *Elementary School Journal, 83,* 427-452.

Rosenshine, B., & Furst, N. (1973). The use of direct observation to study teaching. In R. Travers (Ed.), *Second handbook of research on teaching.* Chicago: Rand McNally.

Rowan, B., Guthrie, L., Lee, G., & Guthrie, G. (1986). *The design and implementation of Chapter 1 instructional services: A study of 24 schools.* San Francisco: Far West Laboratory.

Slavin, R. (1987). Making Chapter 1 make a difference. *Phi Delta Kappan, 69*(2), 110-119.

Stringfield, S., & Teddlie, C. (1988). A time to summarize: Six years and three phases of the Louisiana School Effectiveness Study. *Educational Leadership, 46*(2), 43-49.

Stringfield, S., & Teddlie, C. (1991). Observers as predictors of schools' multi-year outlier status. *Elementary School Journal, 91*(4), 357-376.

Stringfield, S., Yoder, N., & Quilling, M. (1989, March). *Effective compensatory education programs for extremely disadvantaged students.* Paper presented at the American Educational Research Association, San Francisco.

• 12 •

Instructional Programs That Improve the Reading Comprehension of Students at Risk

YOLANDA N. PADRON

In an effort to improve the education of students who are at risk of dropping out of school, there has been an emphasis on the development of basic skills. Schools, for the most part, have been successful in improving students' basic skills achievement. For example, schools have done a fairly good job of teaching children how to decode text and comprehend simple text (Applebee, Langer, & Mullis, 1988). Nonetheless, there is growing evidence to suggest that the focus on basic skills has prevented or limited students' learning other cognitive skills such as higher-level thinking skills (Knapp & Shields, 1990; Waxman, Padron, & Knight, in press). In reading, for example, results from the National Assessment of Educational Progress, *Who Reads Best*, indicated that, after reading a page-long passage, 81% of third graders, 54% of seventh graders, and 36% of eleventh graders were not able to state what the author was intending to say (Applebee et al., 1988). Overall, these results indicated that students were not doing well on higher-level thinking skills (Applebee et al., 1988).

A possible explanation for differences in the academic achievement between high- and low-achieving students may be that lower-achieving students are often denied the opportunity to learn higher-level thinking skills (Coley & Hoffman, 1990; Farr, 1986; Foster, 1989; Moll, 1986; Padron & Knight, 1990; Stein, Leinhardt, & Bickell, 1989). The lack of exposure to higher-level thinking skills may be due to the assumption that students must demonstrate the ability to learn the basic or lower levels of knowledge before they can be taught higher-level skills (Foster, 1989; Stein et al., 1989). In the case of limited-English-proficient students, higher-level skills are generally not taught until the student has mastered English fully because it is believed that students are not able to comprehend until they can speak the language well (Garcia & Pearson, 1991).

Cognitive Reading Strategy Instruction for At-Risk Students

Recent findings from cognitive strategy research have important implications for the instruction of students who are at risk of academic failure. These studies have examined the processes used to evaluate understanding while reading text and to correct perceived difficulties or comprehension monitoring (Collins & Smith, 1982; Mier, 1984). This research, for example, has found that good readers actively construct meaning and monitor their own comprehension by questioning, reviewing, revising, and rereading (Baker & Brown, 1984). Furthermore, there is evidence that indicates that knowledge about the cognitive strategies used during reading helps students acquire a better understanding of the reading process (Saracho, 1983). A cognitive strategy is "a goal-directed sequence of mental operations" (Gagne, 1985, p. 140). When considered in relation to reading, the goal of the mental operations becomes the comprehension of text, and reading is viewed as a problem-solving process in which the reader applies strategies in relating the author's meaning to prior knowledge (Olshavsky, 1976-1977). The teaching of comprehension-fostering skills suggests that reading comprehension may be enhanced through explicit instruction in strategies (Forrest-Pressley & Gillies, 1983; Palincsar & Brown, 1984, 1985; Palincsar & Klenk, 1991) by providing students with better awareness and self-control of the reading task (Paris, Wixson, & Palincsar, 1986).

The above research suggests that, for at-risk students, comprehension instruction needs to be based on constructivist principles (Flood & Lapp, 1990). That is, instructional approaches need to be based on the assumption that students must be actively involved in creating meaning out of the information presented. This approach builds on the reader's experiences, knowledge, and values in constructing meaning while reading text (Flood & Lapp, 1990). The instructional approaches described are based on constructivist principles.

Viable instructional programs can be developed to assure that all students learn. There is ample research evidence that indicates that reading comprehension instruction programs have been effective for many at-risk students (Flood & Lapp, 1990). Nonetheless, effective instruction for culturally diverse, at-risk students may need to match those students' cultural patterns. According to Tharp (1987, 1989), improvements in basic skills acquisition, social skills, and problem-solving abilities take place when the students' cultural patterns are matched with instruction. Because individuals from different cultural groups perceive experiences differently, students' cultures may affect their preferred modes of learning (Escobedo & Huggans, 1983).

The purpose of this chapter is to discuss the applicability of instructional approaches aimed at improving at-risk students' reading comprehension. Only a few instructional approaches have been selected to provide an overview of effective instructional programs that can enhance the reading comprehension of culturally and linguistic different students who are at risk of dropping out of school. The approaches discussed are (a) reciprocal teaching, (b) Reading Recovery, and (c) the Kamehameha Early Education Program (KEEP).

Reciprocal Teaching

One of the most frequently cited approaches to cognitive strategy training is reciprocal teaching. This procedure takes place in a cooperative instructional environment where the teacher and students engage in a dialogue. The students are instructed in four specific comprehension-monitoring strategies: (a) summarizing, (b) self-questioning, (c) clarifying, and (d) predicting. The teacher begins by modeling the strategies for the students. Gradually, the students take the role of the teacher while the teacher takes on a supporting role.

The reciprocal teaching procedure provides an important component that can promote the improvement of reading comprehension of students at risk. Either the text may be read by the students or the teacher may read the text aloud to students. This technique can be very useful when teaching students who are poor readers or are learning English as a second language (Padron, 1991). Having the teacher read the text provides the students with the opportunity to learn the four comprehension strategies presented in reciprocal teaching without having to wait until they learn to decode.

Studies using reciprocal teaching have found that strategies can successfully be taught to low-achieving students and that, once these are learned, use of these strategies increases reading achievement (Lysynchuk, Pressley, & Vye, 1990; Padron, 1989; Palincsar & Brown, 1984, 1985; Palincsar & Klenk, in press).

Reading Recovery

Reading Recovery is a short-term early intervention program developed by the New Zealand psychologist Marie Clay. It is designed to assist students before problems develop. Students who participate in the program are in the lowest 20% in reading. In Reading Recovery, teachers are trained in techniques to help students develop effective strategies that good readers use (Lyons, 1989; Pinnell, 1990). The teacher works one-on-one with the student for 30 minutes each day. This supplemental instruction is in addition to the student's regular classroom reading instruction (Pinnell, 1990). In this approach, students engage in reading and writing with the support of the teacher. Skills are learned in an integrated manner.

Reading Recovery lessons consist of (a) rereading books introduced in previous lessons, (b) reading a new book at the student's appropriate level, (c) composing and writing a brief story, and (d) word study and analysis (Anderson & Armbruster, 1990; Pinnell, 1990). The goals of the program are to teach students to understand the reading process, learn letter-sound relationships, and gain fluency through reading and writing of progressively more difficult text (Cohen, McDonnell, & Osburn, 1989).

A key to the program is the teacher. The teachers in this program receive a full year's training (Pinnell, 1990). These teachers are selected from among experienced elementary school teachers. The teachers are trained to become sensitive observers of children's reading and writing and to develop facility in making moment-to-moment diagnoses on which to base instructional decisions.

Data from research studies indicate not only that students in the program catch up with their classmates but that the effects persist for at least two to three years (Lyons, 1989; Pinnell, 1990; Slavin & Madden, 1989). In addition, research has found that students who participate in Reading Recovery programs are more likely to attribute their success in various school tasks to their own ability and hard work than students who do not participate in the program. Students who have participated in Reading Recovery programs also expressed greater feelings of competence to carry out various reading and writing tasks in the classroom than do other at-risk students (Cohen et al., 1989).

Kamehameha Early Education Program (KEEP)

The Kamehameha Early Education Program (KEEP) has developed a language arts programs where native cultural patterns of Hawaiian children have been incorporated into the instruction. Lessons are 20 to 25 minutes long for groups of five students that are at about the same instructional level. The program focuses on (a) students' discussion of what they know about a topic before they read about it, (b) silently reading the text to answer questions, and (c) discussion to integrate students' prior experience with the text read (Au, 1981).

In this program, elements of culture pertaining to social organization, sociolinguistic patterns, cognitive patterns, and motivation have been incorporated in the instruction. For example, more informal patterns of group interaction have been adopted in the classroom setting because these patterns are more compatible with Hawaiian storytelling traditions. Traditional classroom turn-taking practices are relaxed during reading lessons to allow students to interrupt when they want to contribute to the discussion (Charbonneau & John-Steiner, 1988).

More than a decade of extensive field testing has shown that the emphasis on comprehension and teacher mediation factors within a context of culturally compatible systems of social interaction enhances literacy acquisition for students participating in KEEP (Au & Mason, 1981; Tharp, 1987, 1989; Tharp & Gallimore, 1988). Students participating in the program have exhibited improvements in basic skills acquisition, social skills, and problem-solving abilities when the native culture patterns are matched with instruction (Tharp, 1987, 1989). Not only is student achievement higher, but there is also increased satisfaction with school for students participating in the program. In addition, risk taking by students increases, because the teachers create a classroom climate where there is not a fear of being punished for having an incorrect response (Au & Kawakami, 1986).

Addressing the Needs of Culturally and Linguistically Different Students

In developing instructional approaches for students who are at risk of dropping out of school, special consideration should be given to cultural and linguistic differences. These differences are important to consider because students' learning and behavior are influenced by their cultural perspectives. *Culture* is defined as distinctive patterns of behavior, thought, and perception that are characteristic of a particular subgroup of students (Kagan, 1990). Good teaching must therefore consider cultural differences (Garcia, 1982). In addition, the successful use of some cognitive reading strategies appears to exhibit not only age and ability differences but also cultural differences (Waxman et al., in press). Furthermore, the reader's prior knowledge, experience, attitude, and perspective determine the ways in which information is perceived, understood, valued, and stored (Pearson, 1984).

Prior knowledge plays a powerful role in comprehension and learning. Students participating in both reciprocal teaching and KEEP are asked to make predictions to activate their prior knowledge. Differences in this knowledge base are likely to affect susceptibility to instruction (Stein et al., 1989). For example, expert comprehenders generally try to relate new material to personal experience (Campione & Armbruster, 1985). Differences in background knowledge or experience due to cultural differences may be an important source of variation for strategy use and outcomes (Steffenson, Joag-Dev, & Anderson, 1979). If a student has no prior knowledge about a particular topic being discussed, then the student may not be able to apply an appropriate cognitive reading strategy (Stein et al., 1989). In a classroom where students are not only of low ability but also have a culturally different background, strategy instruction becomes extremely complex. In these classrooms, the teacher has to deal with knowledge base differences that may arise out of having to read text from a cultural perspective different than that of the student. Therefore, if students are from certain populations, especially if they are young, low-ability, or culturally different students, they may not be able to tap into prerequisite prior knowledge without help and may need more teacher-directed instruction to help them accomplish the linkage.

Teacher Training

In providing appropriate reading comprehension instruction for students at risk, culturally sensitive and carefully structured staff development procedures are crucial. A key aspect to consider in the implementation of these approaches is the teacher. Teacher training can contribute to the effective instruction of at-risk students. Effective interventions have noted the importance of teacher values and beliefs. For example, in effective programs, teachers become accountable for students' success, teachers extend their role beyond the standard set of required teacher activities, and teachers have positive attitudes about students' potential for learning (Wehlage, Rutter, Smith, Lesko, & Fernandez, 1989).

From the teachers' point of view, the approaches outlined in this chapter are very demanding. Teachers of children who are at risk are presented with a complex classroom situation. First, teachers must diagnose students' needs in terms of the strategies that they know, those that they do not know, or those that students use inappropriately. In addition, teachers in these classrooms must also deal with different cultural backgrounds. In many instances, teachers also have to address different levels of language proficiency. The variety of languages found in many classrooms and the difficulty in assessing the students' levels of proficiency make diagnosis of strategies difficult. This classroom situation makes the teaching of strategies difficult. To help teachers readily diagnose students' strategy use, diagnostic instruments need to be developed.

Teacher training is an important part of all the programs that are described. Teachers need to be exposed to a variety of approaches (e.g., modeling, coaching, role-playing, discussions). Staff development procedures become crucial to the implementation of these programs because many teachers have not been exposed to strategy training procedures. Furthermore, teachers may not believe that strategy instruction is beneficial, particularly for low-achieving students (Padron, in press). Scardamalia and Bereiter (1989) explain that nonexpert teachers who do not continue on a developmental path during their teaching may develop strategies to help them cope with complex classroom situations. Consequently, teachers may tend to "problem minimize." Problem minimizing may have a greater probability of occurring in classrooms where students are disadvantaged and/or culturally and linguistically different. If students, for example, have not been exposed to some of the experiences or prior knowledge required by the content, teachers may problem minimize and decide not to teach the content or only teach the content to "those who know." As a result, there may be an overemphasis on repetition of content through drill and practice (Knapp & Shields, 1990; Lehr & Harris, 1988; Levin, 1987) due to teachers' lower expectations for these students.

Conclusion

This chapter reviewed several effective instructional approaches that are available to teachers of at-risk students for developing successful readers. Not all practices will work with every student. Nonetheless, considering research evidence of the positive effects that these programs have had in increasing students' reading comprehension, these procedures appear to have promise for improving the reading achievement of at-risk students.

Students are at risk of dropping out of school for a variety of reasons. Programs developed to enhance the academic achievement of at-risk students therefore need to address these differences (Wehlage et al., 1989). More specifically, instructional programs developed to improve reading comprehension of culturally and linguistically diverse students must match the students' cultural patterns. If reading instructional programs are based on a constructivist view of the reading process, then the students' cultural patterns play a significant role in the reading comprehension process. The programs outlined in this chapter are based on constructivist principles, yet, with the exception of KEEP, these programs have not addressed the relationship between the cognitive and social dimensions of the learning environment. In addition, although the programs discussed have a strong teacher training component, teachers must not only be trained in a variety of approaches (e.g., modeling, coaching), they must also understand students' cultures. Research has, for example, established the importance of students' discussing their experiences as they relate to the text and of allowing students to respond in culturally compatible styles (Au & Mason, 1981).

In conclusion, further research is needed in designing instructional programs that address not only the cognitive needs of the low-achieving students but also the students' self-concepts. Such instruction would assure that students acquire an acceptable level of achievement and that they develop appropriate thinking skills necessary for academic success.

References

Anderson, R. C., & Armbruster, B. (1990). Some maxims for learning and instruction. *Teachers College Record, 91,* 396-408.

Anderson, R. C., & Pearson, P. D. (1984). A schema-theoretic view of basic processes in reading. In P. D. Pearson (Ed.), *Handbook of reading research* (pp. 255-292). New York: Longman.

Applebee, A. N., Langer, J. A., & Mullis, I. V. (1988). *Who reads best? Factors related to reading achievement in grades 3, 7, and 11.* Princeton, NJ: Educational Testing Service.

Au, K. H. (1981). Participation structures in a reading lesson with Hawaiian children: Analysis of an appropriate instructional event. *Anthropology and Education Quarterly, 11,* 91-115.

Au, K. H., & Kawakami, A. J. (1986). Influence of the social organization of instruction on children's text comprehension ability: A Vygotskian perspective. In T. E. Raphael (Ed.), *The contexts of school-based literacy* (pp. 63-77). New York: Random House.

Au, K. H., & Mason, J. M. (1981). Social organizational factors in learning to read: The balance of rights hypothesis. *Reading Research Quarterly, 17,* 115-152.

Baker, L., & Brown, A. (1984). Metacognitive skills and reading. In P. D. Pearson (Ed.), *Handbook of reading research* (pp. 353-394). New York: Longman.

Campione, J., & Armbruster, B. (1985). Acquiring information from texts: An analysis of four approaches. In J. Segal, S. Chipman, & R. Glaser (Eds.), *Thinking and learning skills: Relating instruction to research* (Vol. 1, pp. 317-359). Hillsdale, NJ: Lawrence Erlbaum.

Charbonneau, M. P., & John-Steiner, V. (1988). Patterns of experience and the language of mathematics. In R. R. Cocking & J. P. Mestre (Eds.), *Linguistic and cultural influences on learning mathematics* (pp. 91-100). Hillsdale, NJ: Lawrence Erlbaum.

Cohen, S. G., McDonnell, G., & Osburn, B. (1989). Self-perceptions of at risk and high achieving readers: Beyond Reading Recovery achievement data. In S. McCormick & J. Zutell (Eds.), *Cognitive and social perspectives for literacy research and instruction: Thirty-Eighth Yearbook of the National Reading Conference* (pp. 117-122). Chicago: National Reading Conference.

Coley, J. D., & Hoffman, D. M. (1990). Overcoming learned helplessness in at risk readers. *Journal of Reading, 33,* 497-502.

Collins, A., & Smith, E. (1982). Teaching the process of reading comprehension. In D. K. Detterman & R. J. Sternberg (Eds.), *How and how much can intelligence be increased.* Washington, DC: Government Printing Office.

Escobedo, T. H., & Huggans, J. H. (1983). Field-dependence-independence: 778. A theoretical framework for Mexican American cultural variables? In T. H. Escobedo (Ed.), *Early childhood bilingual education: A Hispanic perspective* (pp. 119-135). New York: Teachers College Press.

Farr, M. (1986). Language, culture and writing: Sociolinguistic foundations of research on writing. In E. R. Rothkopt (Ed.), *Review of research in education* (Vol. 13, pp. 195-223). Washington, DC: American Educational Research Association.

Flood, J., & Lapp, D. (1990). Reading comprehension instruction for at-risk students: Research-based practices that can make a difference. *Journal of Reading, 33,* 490-496.

Forrest-Pressley, D., & Gillies, L. (1983). Children's flexible use of strategies during reading. In M. Pressley & J. Levin (Eds.), *Cognitive strategy research: Educational applications* (pp. 133-156). New York: Springer-Verlag.

Foster, G. E. (1989). Cultivating the thinking skills of low achievers: A matter of equity. *Journal of Negro Education, 58,* 461-467.

Gagne, E. (1985). *The cognitive psychology of school learning.* Boston: Little, Brown.

Garcia, G., & Pearson, P. D. (1991). Modifying reading instruction to maximize its effectiveness for "all" students. In M. S. Knapp & P. M. Shields (Eds.), *Better schooling for the children of poverty: Alternatives to conventional wisdom* (pp. 31-60). Berkeley, CA: McCutchan.

Garcia, R. L. (1982). *Teaching in a pluralistic society: Concepts, models, strategies.* New York: Harper & Row.

Kagan, D. M. (1990). How schools alienate students at risk: A model for examining proximal classroom variables. *Educational Psychologist, 25,* 105-125.

Knapp, M. S., & Shields, P. M. (1990). Reconceiving academic instruction for the children of poverty. *Phi Delta Kappan, 71,* 753-758.

Lehr, J. B., & Harris, H. W. (1988). *At risk, low-achieving students in the classroom.* Washington, DC: National Education Association.

Levin, H. M. (1987). Accelerated schools for disadvantaged students. *Educational Leadership, 44*(6), 19-21.

Lyons, C. A. (1989). Reading Recovery: An effective early intervention program that can prevent mislabeling children as learning disabled. *ERS Spectrum, 7*(4), 3-9.

Lysynchuk, L., Pressley, M., & Vye, N. (1990). Reciprocal teaching improves standardized reading comprehension performance of poor comprehenders. *Elementary School Journal, 90,* 470-484.

Mier, M. (1984). ERIC/RCS: Comprehension monitoring in the elementary classroom. *Reading Teacher, 37,* 770-774.

Moll, L. C. (1986). Writing as communication: Creating strategic learning environments for students. *Theory into Practice, 25*(2), 102-107.

Olshavsky, J. (1976-1977). Reading as problem-solving: An investigation of strategies. *Reading Research Quarterly, 12,* 654-674.

Padron, Y. N. (1989, April). *The effect of strategy instruction on bilingual students' cognitive strategy use in reading.* Paper presented at the annual meeting of the American Educational Research Association, San Francisco.

Padron, Y. N. (1991). Commentary. In M. Knapp & B. Means (Eds.), *Teaching advanced skills to at-risk students: Views from research and practice* (pp. 131-140). San Francisco: Jossey-Bass.

Padron, Y. N., & Knight, S. L. (1990). Linguistic and cultural influences on classroom instruction. In H. P. Baptiste, Jr., H. C. Waxman, J. Walker de Felix, & J. E. Anderson (Eds.), *Leadership, equity, and school effectiveness* (pp. 173-185). Newbury Park, CA: Sage.

Palincsar, A., & Brown, A. (1984). Reciprocal teaching of comprehension-fostering and comprehension monitoring activities. *Cognition and Instruction, 1,* 117-175.

Palincsar, A., & Brown, A. (1985). Reciprocal teaching: A means to a meaningful end. In J. Osborn, P. Wilson, & R. C. Anderson (Eds.), *Reading education: Foundations for a literate America* (pp. 299-310). Lexington, MA: Lexington.

Palincsar, A. S., & Klenk, L. J. (1991). Learning dialogues to promote text comprehension. In M. Knapp & B. Means (Eds.), *Teaching advanced skills to at-risk students: Views from research and practice* (pp. 112-130). San Francisco: Jossey-Bass.

Paris, S., Wixson, K., & Palincsar, A. (1986). Instructional approaches to reading comprehension. *Review of Research in Education, 13,* 91-128.

Peason, P. D., (1984). *Handbook of reading research.* New York: Longman.

Pearson, D. P., & Johnson, D. (1978). *Teaching reading comprehension.* New York: Holt, Rinehart & Winston.

Pinnell, G. S. (1990). Success for low achievers through Reading Recovery. *Educational Leadership, 48*(1), 17-21.

Saracho, O. N. (1983). Cognitive style and Mexican American children's perceptions of reading. In T. H. Escobedo (Ed.), *Early childhood low-achieving education: A Hispanic perspective* (pp. 201-221). New York: Teachers College Press.

Scardamalia, M., & Bereiter, C. (1989). Conceptions of teaching and approaches to core problems. In M. C. Reynolds (Ed.), *Knowledge base for the beginning teacher* (pp. 37-46). New York: Pergamon.

Slavin, R. E., & Madden, N. A. (1989). What works for students at risk: A research synthesis. *Educational Leadership, 46*(5), 4-13.

Steffenson, M., Joag-Dev, C., & Anderson, R. (1979). A cross-cultural perspective on reading comprehension. *Reading Research Quarterly, 15,* 10-29.

Stein, M., Leinhardt, G., & Bickell, W. (1989). Instructional issues for teaching students at risk. In R. E. Slavin, N. L. Karweit, & N. A. Madden (Eds.), *Effective programs for students at risk* (pp. 145-194). Boston: Allyn & Bacon.

Tharp, R. (1987, October). *Culture, cognition, and education: A culturogenetic analysis of the holistic complex.* Paper presented at the Conference of the Institute on Literacy and Learning, University of California, Santa Barbara.

Tharp, R. (1989). Psychocultural variables and constants: Effects on teaching and learning in schools. *American Psychologist, 44,* 1-11.

Tharp, R., & Gallimore, R. (1988). *Rousing minds to life: Teaching, learning, and schooling in social context.* New York: Cambridge.

Waxman, H. C., Padron, Y. N., & Knight, S. L. (in press). Risks associated with students' limited cognitive mastery. In M. Wang, H. Walberg, & M. Reynolds (Eds.), *Handbook on special education* (Vol. 4). Oxford: Pergamon.

Wehlage, G. C., Rutter, R. A., Smith, G. A., Lesko, N., & Fernandez, R. R. (1989). *Reducing the risk: Schools as communities of support.* New York: Falmer.

• 13 •

Implementation of an Urban School-Within-a-School Approach

DANIEL U. LEVINE

As I will use the term in this chapter, a *school-within-a-school* for intermediate-level or senior high students "at risk" of not graduating from high school or graduating without adequate academic skills refers to a relatively small unit to which (mostly) low-achieving, urban students are assigned for most or all of their academic classes, and their academic teachers also work mostly or entirely within the unit.[1]

A school-within-a-school (SWAS) unit defined in this way constitutes one category within a broader conceptual grouping of "alternative" approaches through which educators can provide at-risk urban students with opportunities that are more effective than participation in traditional intermediate schools (i.e., grades 5 or 6 through 8 or 9) or senior high schools. Other potentially effective approaches, which also can make education more meaningful for at-risk students by providing personalized assistance to enhance academic growth, include small magnet and/or alternative minischools, "storefront schools" and "street academies," and high school "outposts" (Levine, 1975; Levine & Havighurst, 1992; Wehlage, 1988).

There are many ways to organize and operate a SWAS unit for at-risk students. For example, one teacher can be appointed for each academic subject taught separately; two or more teachers can share responsibilities for instruction in English, history, or some other subject; or English and social studies as well as math and science can be block scheduled for instruction delivered by only two teachers who thus have considerably more personal contact than is usual with each student. In determining what SWAS model is best for a given school and groups of students, efforts should be made to adapt the organizational pattern (including the numbers and assignments of participating students and teachers) in terms of the school's history and current organization, faculty strengths and weaknesses, other alternatives available for at-risk students, level of students' performance, imperatives for desegregation, and other considerations (Keefe, 1986). Locations at which SWAS approaches have been implemented successfully include the following:

- South Boston High School, where most ninth and tenth graders (who had reading scores below grade level) were placed in reading and writing courses rather than traditional English; a minischool was established to emphasize experiential learning and individualized instruction for alienated students; and a school-within-a-school emphasizing academic learning also was established (Kozberg & Winegar, 1981)
- Washington High School in Los Angeles, where "magnet centers" have provided small classes for students particularly interested in a specific area of study such as communication (U.S. Department of Education, 1987)
- Wingate High School in Brooklyn, where SWAS units have provided concentrations of courses in labor studies, police science, mass media, and other high-interest or career-oriented themes (Schain, 1980)

The remainder of this chapter will provide a detailed description of the implementation and outcomes of the ninth-grade SWAS program operated since 1984 in the Kansas City, Missouri, School District. Having demonstrated considerable success, the SWAS program in Kansas City offers instructive lessons for educators who may want to implement a similar approach for at-risk urban students elsewhere.

The Ninth-Grade SWAS Program in Kansas City

The Kansas City School-Within-a-School program was established to help students with low reading scores improve their comprehension and to motivate and prepare them to succeed in academic courses. Operating at the ninth-grade level in all but one of the district's senior high schools, the SWAS program usually assigns 60 to 100 students to receive instruction from four of five teachers of English/language arts, math, reading, social studies, and, in some cases, science. A teacher coordinator serves at least half-time.

Placement in the SWAS is based on grades, teacher and counselor judgment, attendance, and other data, with special attention given to functional comprehension scores on the Degrees of Reading Power Test (see below). Students who are severely disruptive or are virtual nonreaders generally are not assigned to SWAS because they require an even stronger intervention. More than 70% of students in the SWAS program are low-income African Americans.

Staff appointed to SWAS are selected for their willingness and capacity to work with at-risk students. With four or five academic teachers instructing fewer than 100 students, class size is usually fewer than 20. Teachers are provided with training and other forms of assistance closely related to the objectives of the program.

Program Characteristics

Major characteristics of the SWAS program include the following:

- Teachers have common planning periods, which enables them to coordinate instruction to provide reinforcement across classes—a necessity for low achievers.
- Teacher teams agree on the selection and use of texts, on student grading policies and practices, on communication with parents, and on other matters.
- Highly motivating experiences are offered to students. These include academic competition between teams and schools, college visits, conferences with local community leaders, and cultural events.
- Intensive staff development is offered, including summer training, Saturday sessions, and seminars during the regular school day. Summer staff development time has been particularly valuable in providing teachers with the technical assistance to coordinate curriculum and instruction across subject areas and to share ideas and materials across schools.

Philosophical Premises

As stated in a SWAS program description, major premises underlying operation of the SWAS program include the following:

1. Students who have deficiencies now will fall further behind and will experience serious difficulty in achieving success in the adult world unless there is positive intervention.
2. A prerequisite to academic achievement is the development of a healthy self-image.

3. A program which includes the dual approach of improving academic skills emphasizing comprehension, cognition, and providing guidance to help students develop a positive image of self and positive relationships with others should eliminate some skill deficiencies and simultaneously assist the students in developing the self confidence necessary to pursue school goals with greater vigor and a greater probability of success (Gooden, 1985, p. 2).

Linking Learning Across Subjects

As mentioned above, one of the central components of the SWAS approach is to coordinate curriculum and instruction across subject areas to reinforce vocabulary, concepts, and other aspects of learning for participating students, who previously have experienced relatively little success in school. Referred to in the program description as "Linking Learning," this component also is intended to facilitate coordination of efforts of teachers in each SWAS team and to help students acquire appropriate "schema for thinking and comprehending" (Gooden, 1985, p. 10). One indication of the stress placed on this component and its importance in implementing the SWAS program is evident in the fact that nearly all teachers on SWAS teams functioning in 1984-1985 participated in a three-week (all-day) summer workshop at which approximately two weeks were devoted to the development of school-level policies, classroom lessons, and specific week-by-week plans for coordinating instruction during the school year across English, reading, mathematics, and social studies.

Emphasis on Comprehension-Improvement Strategies and the DRP Approach

Stress in SWAS has been placed on instructional strategies for improving students' comprehension since the second year of the program in 1984-1985. During the first year, SWAS staff had worked very hard to coordinate teaching across classrooms, refine student selection criteria, motivate students, and implement other aspects of the program's philosophy as described above. Data collected at the end of the 1983-1984 academic year indicated, however, that, although student attendance and motivation apparently improved markedly, virtually no gains were registered in academic performance (Levine & Campbell, 1984). After a one- or two-month period during which staff attempted to recover from this debilitating outcome, decisions were made to concentrate more systematically and meaningfully on instructional-improvement aspects in subsequent years.

Accordingly, the Degrees of Reading Power (DRP) approach was emphasized in 1984-1985 and has been a basic focus for instruction and continuing staff development in SWAS since that time. The DRP approach, in its broadest outlines, is based on a three-step set of components that have been briefly summarized (Koslin, Koslin, Zeno, & Ivens, 1989, p. 1) as follows:

1. Administer the DRP Test in order to "measure students ability to comprehend English prose".
2. Analyze the difficulty-level (i.e., "readability") of instructional materials and select materials in accordance with their match with students' current comprehension levels (see below).
3. Provide instructional materials and support services to help teachers acquire and use instructional strategies for improving students' comprehension.

The DRP Test. Developers of the Degrees of Reading Power Test have described it as measuring

> what might be called minimally inferential comprehension—a necessary though not sufficient, prerequisite to other higher order cognitive abilities. In other words, [the] Primary and Standard DRP tests are single-objective tests measuring how well students understand the surface meaning of what they read. (Koslin, Zeno, & Koslin, 1987, p. 1)

The manual for the DRP cites the following characteristics as constituting "properties which distinguish" the DRP from other tests:

1. DRP test items are designed so that the paragraph or passage in which they are embedded must be read and understood in order for the student to answer correctly.... [W]hen the meaning of the paragraph is taken into account, only one response is plausible.
2. All of the content information that is needed to select the correct response is contained within the DRP paragraph or passage. No prior familiarity with the subject matter is required to answer the embedded items correctly....
3. Regardless of the difficulty of the prose paragraph or passage, all response options are common words . . . [thus] failure to respond correctly . . . can be attributed unambiguously to a failure to comprehend the text in which they appear.

4. DRP paragraphs and passages are designed to reduce the likelihood that guessing strategies, associative processes, and other nonreading activities can be used to respond to items correctly....
5. Item difficulty is linked to text difficulty. The student should be able to respond correctly to most of the items in the text up to the point at which the student cannot understand . . . well enough to decide which word is correct. (Koslin et al., 1987, p. 4)

Developers of the DRP Test also have cited (Ivens & Koslin, 1989, p. 4) additional "important features of the Primary and Standard DRP tests" as follows:

1) they are untimed; 2) the paragraphs and passages form a linearly ordered scale, i.e., all paragraphs and passages, from the easiest to the hardest, measure the same construct of reading; 3) the results can be interpreted in terms of what students can read; and 4) the tests are particularly sensitive to the assessment of growth in reading across grades.

Furthermore, there is "no evidence that teachers can circumvent successfully the instructional process by teachings to the format" of the DRP (Ivens & Koslin, 1989, p. 9).

Students' scores on the DRP are reported on a scale ranging from 15 to 99 units. Converted from raw scores, the scale units represent the readability of materials for which a student registers a particular probability of success. For example, a student with a raw score of 41 on Test Form E-9 receives a mid-instructional level scale score of 70, indicating that he or she can process prose at this level of difficulty/readability (see below) with a "probability of success" of 75%. Similarly, this student receives an "independent-level" comprehension score of 59, indicating that he or she comprehends material at this reliability level with a 90% probability of success (Koslin et al., 1987, pp. 17-18).

DRP matching of students and texts. As mentioned above, students' DRP scores are reported in scale units that can be aligned with readability/difficulty scores for prose materials identified as being at a level of difficulty at which a given student will have a 50% probability of success (frustration level), a 75% probability of success (instructional level), or a 90% probability of success (independent level). Text categorization according to students' comprehension levels has been summarized briefly by educators in the Orange County, Florida, Public Schools (Monahan, 1988) as follows:

Frustration level: Student's ability to comprehend the text is improbable.
Instructional level: Students can understand the text with good instructional assistance in the classroom.
Independent level: Students can read the text without help.

The DRP measure of text difficulty is derived from the Bormuth Mean Cloze Readability Formula, which is based on the length of words, the length and complexity of sentences, and the proportion of commonly used words. The DRP readability formula is available as a computer program that can be installed on microcomputers and uses an "abbreviated set of coding rules" that makes it relatively easy to obtain a readability estimate for a passage or set of passages teachers may want to use in instruction (Koslin et al., 1987, p. 21). In addition, the College Board and Touchstone Associates have calculated and distributed DRP values for thousands of textbooks and trade books that are used frequently in U.S. schools. Because teachers then have information denoting students' comprehension scores and text readability values that are measured in the same functional metric, they can proceed to improve the match between students' current comprehension capacities and the materials assigned for instruction.[2]

The philosophy underlying matching of students' comprehension levels and text materials has been described at some length in materials published by the College Board and Touchstone Associates. According to a recent DRP publication (Koslin et al., 1987, pp. 29-32):

> In order to increase student ability to comprehend . . . the materials assigned should be sufficiently difficult to require that the student expends efforts to comprehend them. At the same time, the materials must be easy enough to ensure that the student will experience success. . . . The balance between "challenge" and probable success is thought to be provided by materials that are beyond, but not too far beyond, the student's current comprehension ability. . . . [However], if the difficulty of the materials greatly exceeds the ability required of the student, then instruction will flounder.

Teachers' use of comprehension-improvement strategies. The most extensive and far-reaching component in the DRP approach involves the introduction and dissemination throughout a school of instructional strategies to improve students' comprehension of textbooks and other prose materials used in the classroom, homework, libraries, media centers, and other educational locations and assignments. Because virtually all teachers use prose materials selected to facilitate learning of the subject being taught, the effectiveness of instruction in nearly all classrooms depends in part on students' capacity to comprehend these materials. From this point of view, every teacher is or ought to be a teacher of comprehension in his or her subject field. Use of instructional strategies to help students understand what they are being asked or required to read thus is an important part of each teacher's job.

Numerous instructional strategies have been developed to enhance students' capacity to comprehend materials used in the classroom and elsewhere. Widespread development during the past two decades of comprehension-improvement strategies and of understanding in how to use them effectively in the classroom and throughout the school has constituted what amounts to a "revolution" in educators' capacity to enhance the comprehension abilities and performance of their students (Pearson, 1985). Strategies emphasized in the SWAS program are designated and described briefly in Appendix Table 13.A of this chapter.

Problems and Deficiencies in Implementation

As one would expect with reference to a difficult intervention intended to help hard-to-reach students across a number of differing schools, implementation of the SWAS program sometimes has been problematic and inadequate. To begin with, school-within-a-school approaches are vulnerable to various kinds of misimplementation. Indeed, principals and other administrators who are not vigorously and completely dedicated to improving the performance of low achievers are prone to allow one or more of the following (or numerous other) developments that undercut possibilities for success:

- Some of the teachers selected to participate demonstrate or themselves conclude that they are not suitable for this type of assignment.
- Instructional methods are not suitable for working with alienated urban students.
- Expectations and requirements for students are minimal because teachers are not willing to make the strenuous effort needed to maintain high standards or do not believe students can learn or can overcome difficulties in their environment.
- Alternately, expectations and requirements are inflexible and do not take into account students' learning problems and preferences.
- Too many or too few students are selected to participate.
- Teachers and/or students are overloaded with assignments and responsibilities beginning in the early stages.

An Urban School-Within-a-School Approach 241

- Key supplies and equipments are not available on a timely basis.
- Staff development is too theoretical or, alternately but less frequently, entirely fails to provide an appropriate intellectual framework.
- Organizational units to help low achievers become a "dumping ground" or "warehouse" for students and/or teachers not welcome in "regular" school units and activities.
- Inadequate help and attention are provided by key administrative and support personnel who devise schedules, counsel students, implement school responses to behavioral infractions, allocate schoolwide incentives for students, or otherwise are at least partly responsible for important services that affect the project.

Efforts to implement the ninth-grade SWAS program in the Kansas City school district have been hampered by predictable difficulties such as those enumerated above, particularly during the first two years when staff at each school were struggling to determine how to proceed and what instructional approaches to implement. Thus some units have had unstable or unsuitable teacher teams, have received little direction or assistance from administrators, or otherwise have failed at times to function successfully. Formal evaluations (Pink, 1986, 1990) conducted by district personnel during the first few years specifically identified the following considerations that reduced the effectiveness of one or more units:

- Staff initially received inadequate orientation and staff development.
- The full-time coordinator at the district level could provide assistance only when invited.
- Direct coordination and assistance from the superintendent's office were unavailable; instead, reliance was placed on bureaucratic directives.
- Arrangements were not made to provide teachers with systematic feedback on their classroom performance.
- Insufficient time was provided for teachers to acquire appropriate skills.
- Insufficient attention was given to issues involving teacher and student schedules.
- Administrators failed to adjust program delivery in accordance with evaluation data.
- Too little technical assistance was provided.

Indications of Successful Implementation and Positive Outcomes

Although several of the SWAS units have mostly floundered in trying to cope with the kinds of problems enumerated above, most have functioned adequately after the initial two-year "shakeout" period. Based on extensive contact with district personnel throughout this period and based on review of district evaluation reports and other data, I can estimate that three or four of the eight units have been functioning very well most years, and another three or four have had some successful years interspersed with problematic periods. In particular, data from DRP testing indicate that average annual gains at well-functioning units typically are about eight to ten points per year, which is equivalent to two to three years of growth using norms published by the College Board. Overall, the history of the ninth-grade SWAS program in the Kansas City School District indicates that very positive outcomes can be attained using this approach for improving the education of low-achieving adolescents in big city districts.

District evaluation. Recent evaluation reports prepared by the Evaluation Office of the School District of Kansas City, Missouri, Department of Research, Evaluation, and Testing generally have provided encouraging information regarding the effectiveness of the ninth-grade SWAS. For example, the last full evaluation (Gassman, 1988) reported that average attendance in 1987-1988 was 88%—five percentage points higher than districtwide ninth-grade attendance. In addition, evaluators found that 484 of 491 students enrolled in ninth-grade units in 1985-1986 were still in the district's high schools in 1987-1988. The 1988 evaluation report also included the following information:

> The data indicate an increase in the efficient use of classroom time. Instructional activity time versus managerial time increased and more of an emphasis on curricular components was observed. . . . The perceptions of those associated with the program indicated the program was accomplishing its goals. Generally, the teachers in the program responded positively to questionnaire items concerning the program (Gassman, 1988, p. iv).

The latter conclusion was based partly on data reporting the percentages of SWAS teachers who responded positively to various questionnaire items, which can be seen in Table 13.1.

In addition, classroom observations carried out by district evaluators have indicated that SWAS staff are systematically emphasizing development of students' comprehension skills and related instructional goals dealing with oral expression, writing, and higher-order cognition. As reported in the

Table 13.1 SWAS Teachers' Responses to Questionnaire Items

Response	1986-1987	1987-1988
1. Satisfied with the program	93	89
2. Satisfied with student selection process	67	53
3. Satisfied with site administrative support	90	64
4. Feel SWAS is an asset to the school	100	89
5. Feel students enjoy being in the SWAS program	65	94
6. Feel SWAS in-service sessions have been helpful	90	83
7. Regularly use SWAS instructional strategies	87	86
8. Have appropriate instructional materials	58	61
9. Have sufficient planning time for SWAS classes	61	44
10. Feel the SWAS resource teachers have been helpful	90	97

Table 13.2 Comprehension-Related Activities Present in Lessons

Comprehension-Related Activity	Percentage of Lessons Coded as "Present" by Observers
Comprehension skills	92
Oral expression	72
Written expression	58
Higher-order thinking skills	64

district's 1988 SWAS evaluation, these comprehension-related activities were coded as being present in a majority of lessons observed by evaluators, as shown in Table 13.2.

Teacher Assessment and Use of Comprehension-Improvement Strategies and Other Program Characteristics

As mentioned above, students' reading comprehension scores on the DRP Test did not improve during the first year of the SWAS program in 1983-1984, but comprehension-improvement strategies have received systematic emphasis since 1984, and impressive gains in student performance have occurred regularly at the well-functioning units. To obtain information on teachers' evaluation and use of comprehension-improvement strategies, a colleague and I (Levine & Sherk, 1990) administered a questionnaire that was completed and returned by half of the 30 teachers who served as ninth-grade SWAS staff in 1988-1989. One of the sections on the questionnaire asked respondents to designate how frequently they used 13 comprehension-improvement strategies that had been emphasized in staff development. (Strategies selected for inclusion were designated by the SWAS Resource Teacher and several other persons familiar with the program. A description of these strategies is provided in Appendix Table 13.A.) Average frequency of use of the strategies was designated by responding teachers on a scale on which 1 = "very often," 2 = "often," 3 = "sometimes," 4 = "hardly ever," and 5 = "never." For 8 of the 13 strategies, the average score indicated that teachers reported using the strategy at least "sometimes" (as indicated by a score of 3 or lower).

Regarding perceived effectiveness of the comprehension-improvement strategies they had used, respondents were asked to designate effectiveness on a four-point scale on which 1 = "very," 2 = "some," 3 = "little," and 4 = "hardly any." The average effectiveness for the 13 strategies was 2.0—exactly at the "some" effectiveness point on the four-point scale, and 6 of the 13 strategies received average designations of 1.8 or lower.

Because coordination of instruction across classrooms has been an important activity in planning and implementing the SWAS program, we also asked respondents: "To what extent have you been able to coordinate introduction of vocabulary, use of comprehension strategies, or similar aspects of your day-to-day instruction with instruction in other SWAS classrooms?" Among the 14 teachers who responded, 3 designated the response category "nearly all the time," 2 selected "most of the time," 7 selected "some of the time," and 3 designated either "once in a while" or "hardly at all." Thus the large majority indicated that they have been able to coordinate instruction with other SWAS teachers at least some of the time. In a subsequent part of the questionnaire, a large majority of the respondents indicated that this type of coordination had been an important consideration contributing to the success of the SWAS program.

Other conclusions from the questionnaire administered to SWAS teachers included the following:

- Of the 15 respondents, 9 said they had been able to make use of students' DRP scores "very often" or "often" in planning instruction.
- Of the 15 respondents, 5 selected "very much" when asked: "To what extent have you been able to match materials with DRP scores?"; 7 others selected "somewhat" and 3 selected "not very much."

An Urban School-Within-a-School Approach

- Among the 12 respondents who said they had been very or somewhat successful in matching materials with students' DRP scores, all but one responded that matching had been at least "somewhat helpful" in improving learning.

For both questions cited above regarding use of DRP scores, new SWAS teachers understandably accounted for most of the responses indicating relatively little use.

In addition, respondents indicated that their students spend an average of 35% of classroom time in cooperative learning activities, which are heavily emphasized in SWAS planning and staff development, and that the Learning Partners approach was the cooperative activity they used most frequently and effectively. And, finally, in rating 17 "considerations" that "may have been most important in contributing to the success of the SWAS program," a plurality of respondents designated each consideration except "assistance from counselors in your school" as "very important" or "moderately important." Considerations cited most frequently as being very important included "small class size," "willingness of SWAS faculty to work hard," "faculty enthusiasm," "flexibility in implementing SWAS," "assistance from SWAS coordinators," "students' willingness to accept help," and "students' willingness to ask for help."

Conclusions

The most obvious conclusions to be drawn from this account of the ninth-grade SWAS program in the Kansas City, Missouri, School District are that well-functioning units can substantially improve the performance of previously low-achieving and alienated urban students and that effective implementation of systematic approaches for improving students' comprehension skills should be a central part of such an effort.

In addition, one can infer that success depends on steps taken to address problems that predictably hamper effective implementation. Enumerated earlier in this chapter, such problems include tendencies toward inappropriate selection and assignment of teachers and students, failure to provide adequate staff development, and lack of strong leadership to ensure satisfactory arrangements regarding instructional materials, student schedules, common planning time for teachers, and other prerequisites for successful operation of a school-within-a-school. From this point of view, improving education for urban students through a school-within-a-school approach depends on the same considerations that make the difference between success and failure in improving school effectiveness in general, namely, outstanding leadership, committed and capable teachers, and incorporation of instructional strategies that have demonstrated effectiveness for improving the performance of low-achieving students.

Notes

1. From some points of view, the term *school-dependent students* is more useful than *at-risk students* because it emphasizes the school's responsibilities to succeed with students who require unusual amounts of guidance and support to learn.
2. Koslin et al. (1987, p. 32) also emphasize the point that "while challenge is an important variable in planning lessons, variables such as the amount of help teachers will provide, student interest and student need for success also should be considered" in decision making. In addition, the authors caution that users should "avoid selecting a single level of comprehension . . . to effect *the* mechanical match of materials with ability for any instructional purpose."

References

Gassman, G. W. (1988). *Longitudinal evaluation of the school-within-a-school program.* Kansas City, MO: School District of Kansas City, Evaluation Office.

Gooden, F. E. (1985). *A school-within-a-school.* Kansas City, MO: Kansas City School District.

Ivens, S. H., & Koslin, B. L. (1989). *DRP: Decade of change.* Paper delivered at Florida Reading Council Conference, Sarasota.

Keefe, J. W. (1986). How do you find the time? In H. J. Walberg & J. W. Keefe (Eds.), *Rethinking reform: The principal's dilemma* (pp. 1-3). Reston, VA: National Association of Secondary School Principals.

Koslin, B. L., Koslin, S., Zeno, S. M., & Ivens, S. H. (1989). *DRP teacher's manual.* Brewster, NY: Touchstone Applied Science Associates.

Koslin, B. L., Zeno, S. M., & Koslin, S. (1987). *The DRP: An effectiveness measure in reading.* New York: College Entrance Examination Board.

Kozberg, G., & Winegar, J. (1981). The South Boston story: Implications for secondary schools. *Phi Delta Kappan, 62*(8), 565-567.

Levine, D. U. (1975). Educating alienated inner city youth: Lessons from the street academies. *Journal of Negro Education, 44,* 139-148.

Levine, D. U., & Campbell, V. (1984). *Evaluation of school-within-a-school units at Central, Northeast, Paseo, Southwest, and Westport high schools.* Kansas City, MO: Center for the Study of Metropolitan Problems in Education.

Levine, D. U., & Havighurst, R. J. (1992). *Society and education* (8th ed.). Boston: Allyn & Bacon.

Levine, D. U., & Sherk, J. K. (1990). *Effective implementation of a comprehension-improvement approach in secondary schools.* Kansas City: University of Missouri, Kansas City, Center for the Study of Metropolitan Problems in Education.

Monahan, P. (1988). *The new look in secondary reading in Orange County, Florida.* Orlando, FL: Orange County Public Schools.

Pearson, P. D. (1985). *The comprehension revolution* (Report No. 57). Urbana: University of Illinois at Urbana-Champaign, Center for the Study of Reading.

Pink, W. T. (1986). *Evaluation of the school-within-a-school (SWAS) program.* Kansas City, MO: School District of Kansas City, Evaluation Office.

Pink, W. T. (1990). Staff development for urban school improvement: Lessons learned from two case studies. *School Effectiveness and School Improvement, 1,* 41-60.

Schain, R. L. (1980). *Ninth annual report to the parents.* Brooklyn, NY: George W. Wingate High School.

U.S. Department of Education. (1987). *Schools that work educating disadvantaged children.* Washington, DC: Government Printing Office.

Wehlage, G. G. (1988). *Dropping out: Can schools be expected to prevent it?* Paper presented at the annual meeting of the American Educational Research Association, New Orleans.

Table 13.A1 Mean Effectiveness and Frequency of Use Ratings for 13 Comprehension-Improvement Strategies*

Strategy	Description	Mean Effectiveness Rating	Mean Frequency of Use Rating
Anticipation Guides	A series of statements to which students respond individually before reading, connecting their existing knowledge to the text.	2.6	2.0
Concept Mapping	Usually has four components: (a) core questions or concepts; (b) strands, subordinate ideas; (c) strand details; (d) strand relationships.	2.5	1.7
DRA	Orientation designed to develop vocabulary and comprehension during silent or oral reading and follow-up.	2.5	1.7
KWL (Know/Write/Learn)	After brainstorming and discussion, students generate questions that they want to answer during reading. As students read, they ask additional questions and record information.	3.2	2.2
Prediction	Speculation about the topic to be studied, followed by reading to confirm or disconfirm the predictions.	1.9	1.4
PREP (Prereading Plan)	An assessment/instructional strategy used to estimate students' levels of background knowledge.	2.9	1.7
Questions Only	Students ask questions about the topic, while the teacher provides information only in response to questions.	3.3	2.7
Request	After silent reading, the teacher and student take turns asking and answering questions. The teacher models mature questioning.	3.9	3.0
SQ3R	A study procedure involving the steps: survey, question, read, recite, review.	3.0	2.0

Table 13.A1 (Continued)

Strategy	Description	Mean Effectiveness Rating	Mean Frequency of Use Rating
Story Map	Helps teachers analyze the story so that questions during discussion will create a coherent framework for understanding and remembering.	3.3	2.0
Structured Overview	The teacher arranges preselected vocabulary from text into a schema or diagram that depicts key relationships among the terms. Students and teacher verbalize reasons for the diagrammatic arrangement.	2.4	1.7
Three-Level Guides	Teacher-made questions to accompany the study of textual material. Students respond to literal, interpretive, and critical/applied questions.	4.2	2.6
Writing/ Summarizing	Self-explanatory.	2.2	1.8

• 14 •

Accelerated Schools for Students in At-Risk Situations

JANE McCARTHY
HENRY M. LEVIN

It is often said that you can tell what a school is like by the greeting you get as you walk in the front door. That is certainly the case as you walk through the door of Hollibrook Elementary School in the Spring Branch Independent School District in Houston, Texas. You are greeted by pleasant smiles and warm hellos on the part of staff and students. People at the desks in the school lobby consist of paid professionals as well as parent volunteers. It is difficult to tell them apart. There are comfortable sofas and chairs and reading materials available. The principal peels herself away from a group of students hugging her and comes to greet you. A team of trained student guides arrives to take you on a tour of the building. It is evident from their words and actions that these fifth graders love their school and take pride in it. They want their visitors to see every aspect of life in the school.

As you tour the bewildering maze of hallways and corridors, of temporary buildings and outside walkways, you are struck by something that you haven't seen very often in public elementary schools. Students and teachers in every classroom—and there are many classrooms in this school, which has more than 1,000 students—who are actively involved in learning. They scarcely notice the visitors in their midst. They are happy, and smiles are everywhere. You are overwhelmed by the colors, the richness of the materials, the activity—orderly but exciting—taking place in each room.

In one room, students are studying the concept of measurement by measuring all types of objects in the room, including each other. Another room has adopted a nautical theme this year. You must walk across the gangplank to enter. Activities and curriculum revolve around ships and the sea. Many classrooms have mailboxes at their doors. Hallways have street names and students deliver mail to each other. On the stage in the center of the building is a miniature grocery store, complete with shelves stocked with groceries. Freezer bins hold fake frozen goods while vegetable bins hold fake produce. There is even a flower cart. A class is in the store studying weights and measures by weighing the produce on the grocery scales. A local store has donated all the equipment, including an old cash register. It is a colorful, stimulating setting. The adults in our tour group don't want to leave.

In another room, the second graders are tallying their money from the day's sale of popcorn in the cafeteria. These ambitious students have incorporated and formed "Only Popcorn." Their corporation issues stock certificates and holds shareholders' meetings using Robert's Rules of Order. There are plans to franchise to the fifth grade this year. Profits are used for field trips and school supplies.

The center foyer has exhibits of letters to students from their armed forces pen pals in the Persian Gulf. There are maps showing that region of the world. Classes incorporate the history and geography of the region into the curriculum. Students clip out articles from newspapers and discuss issues regarding the situation with teachers and each other. Servicemen have sent students many artifacts—pins, patches, pictures, and letters written in both Spanish and English. The students are very excited about their pen pals and have sent them packets for Christmas. A teacher tells us that a parent of one of the servicemen called the school to thank them for writing to her son. No other mail had gotten through to him but theirs.

In the kindergarten wing, older students can be seen sitting on the floor reading to their "little buddies." Some have their arms around their little friends and all are engrossed. Bilingual kindergarten classes are situated next to English-speaking kindergartens and the classes have many activities together. Students learn to communicate with each other quickly, each learning the language of the other in the process.

The parent lounge is off-limits to visitors today. The father of two of the students has been tragically murdered and the social worker and parent volunteers are helping the family plan the funeral today. The counselor is in the classrooms of the two students helping their classmates deal with the tragedy.

The cafeteria is full but orderly. Each class has students, called the "Sparkle Squad," in charge of cleaning up the area. They have little aprons, sponges, and buckets. After the area is clean, the game boxes come out and students can play checkers, Parcheesi, Scrabble, or other board games until it is time to go outside.

In the teacher workroom, the Parent Involvement Committee is meeting. The members are examining data from the recent parent-teacher conferences. The data confirm the attendance of 98% of the Hollibrook parents at these conferences. The committee members discuss ways to find out why the other 2% didn't attend.

The student guides bring the visitors back to the teachers' lounge area where refreshments have been set out. The students shyly tell the guests that they have prepared the food themselves. The principal and a teacher come into the room to answer any questions the guests may have about what they have seen in the school today. There are many questions.

From the description of Hollibrook Elementary, one would assume that it is an affluent school in an affluent area. Certainly, it has resources that other schools don't have—a social worker, an abundance of instructional materials and equipment, a spotlessly clean interior, a nicely landscaped exterior. Reality, however, is quite different. Hollibrook is situated in a predominately Hispanic working-class neighborhood composed of large apartment complexes. Approximately 85% of the students come to school speaking only Spanish. Most receive subsidized lunches because of financial need. Many students are newly arrived immigrants from Central and South America. Until last year, test scores at Hollibrook were in the bottom 25th percentile. The turnover rate of students was 104% as students moved in and out of the area, sometimes several times in one year. Both student and teacher morale was low, and few students thought of themselves as intelligent. Classrooms were very traditional—lecture, drill, recitation. Materials used were predominately textbooks and work sheets. The building was drab and colorless. There was virtually no landscaping outside of the building. Discipline was a major concern of teachers and administrators. Vandalism was high, with thousands of dollars worth of damage done to the buildings and grounds each year. Parents seldom, if ever, came to school, and few turned out for PTA or parent conferences.

The new principal and the teachers decided that something drastic had to be done to improve things at the school. The vehicle for change that they selected was the approach of the Accelerated Schools Project, established at Stanford University in 1986.

Since implementing the Accelerated Schools approach, with no major infusion of funding, Hollibrook has experienced dramatic changes. Test scores have soared, turnover has dramatically decreased, vandalism has disappeared, parent attendance at conferences has risen to 98%, attendance at PTA meetings has grown too large to be accommodated in the school cafeteria, and morale and self-esteem have risen among students and teachers. All of the new materials and equipment have been made by teachers and parents or donated by local businesses. Landscaping was provided by a cooperative effort of businesses and community, with labor donated by parents and teachers. The social worker was secured after faculty voted to give up one teaching position at the school to get a full-time social worker on campus. All of the changes at Hollibrook were decided upon by teachers and faculty working collaboratively to solve problems and govern the school.

Other accelerated schools across the nation are experiencing the same kinds of successes. Daniel Webster School in San Francisco, for example, had the highest percentage gain in language on standardized tests in the district of 72 elementary schools for the 1989-1990 school year and the second highest gains in math. One of Daniel Webster's teachers won the "Teacher of the Year" Award for the 1989-1990 school year. She developed a curriculum using artifact trunks filled with historical clothing, cooking utensils, art, literature, toys, and so on. Lessons are built around the contents of the trunk.

Hoover Elementary School in Redwood City, California has dramatically increased parent participation at school: 98% of all parents attended their most recent back-to-school night. At Briar Crest Elementary School in Missouri, the student and teacher school attendance rate went from being the lowest in the district to the highest.

More than 50 accelerated schools in California, Missouri, Illinois, Texas, and other states have also experienced similar growth since committing themselves to a program that replaces remediation with acceleration and academic enrichment. Designed to bring at-risk students into the educational mainstream by the end of elementary school and to support their accelerated progress in middle schools, accelerated schools offer a unique approach to schools and schooling.

The Need for Intervention

At-risk students currently account for approximately one third of all elementary and secondary students in our nation, and the number is rising (Pallas, Natriello, & McDill, 1989). Students are in at-risk situations for many reasons—poverty, cultural or linguistic differences, dysfunctional families, or recent immigration. In some states such as California, more than half of the state's public school students are members of ethnic minorities. These students enter school with unique needs. Schools that operate in the same manner that they did when the typical student was from the White middle class are finding that the old solutions no longer suffice.

Traditional responses to the at-risk student have been remedial classes and pullout programs, which slow down learning. This causes students to fall further and further behind their peers. By the end of sixth grade, many at-risk students are at least two years behind grade level. In later years, as many as half drop out of school. The social and economic consequences of these failures are enormous, both to the individual students and to the nation as a whole. The premise of accelerated schools is that at-risk students must actually learn at a faster rate than more privileged students. Their educational program needs to be one of enrichment rather than remediation. This premise will be discussed in greater detail later in this chapter.

The numerous reform efforts of the past 20 years have failed to meet the needs of those individuals most at risk of failure. In fact, reforms that raise competency standards or requirements for graduation may actually contribute to an increase in the number of students who drop out of school (Levin, 1987). Although expectations are an important variable, simply raising the standards while changing nothing else does not cause test scores to rise or at-risk students to achieve.

We believe that the failure of many reform efforts can be traced directly to their piecemeal approach. They address only a few aspects of school or schooling and ignore the rest. The Accelerated Schools process follows an integrated approach to restructuring—curriculum, instruction, and school organization are all affected at the same time. This simultaneous approach is a central feature of accelerated schools. Only a total restructuring effort offers a chance for success.

What Are Accelerated Schools?

What are accelerated schools and how does the process produce dramatic changes in schools with high percentages of students in risk situations? Developed by Henry M. Levin and a team of educators at Stanford University in 1986 (see Levin, 1986, 1987, 1988), after an exhaustive study of school reform efforts of the past 20 years, accelerated schools were a response to the failure of those efforts to effect any meaningful long-term change in the education of at-risk students. *At-risk students* refers to those who are unlikely to succeed in school because their home resources and experiences differ from the expectations on which school experiences are built.

Schools today, as they are currently structured, often use organizational, curricular, and instructional strategies that contribute to the labeling and isolation of at-risk students, lowered expectations, frustrating and unidimensional school experiences, and a lack of awareness of the strengths of students, parents, and teachers (Levin & Hopfenberg, 1991). These students are caught in a mismatch situation between homes and schools. Accelerated schools are designed to bring these children into the educational mainstream and make them academically able by the end of elementary school. This goal is accomplished by transforming the current structure of schools according to three basic schoolwide principles: unity of purpose, building on strengths, and school-site empowerment with responsibility.

Unity of Purpose

The design and implementation of educational interventions that have the potential to successfully address the needs of all children require the active involvement of parents, community, teachers, and administrators. The Accelerated Schools process empowers the entire school community to forge a vision of an effective school that focuses on bringing about the academic and social success of all students. This unified vision occurs after much thought and interaction. The vision is the dream for the future and represents what the members of the school community want the school to be and what they think the school needs to be to facilitate the optimal educational and social development of its students. This dream is then captured in a written vision statement. This vision then serves as the focal point for all actions and is the standard by which all actions are held and evaluated.

This unified purpose is in sharp contrast to the typical school where teachers and administrators often work independently and sometimes at cross-purposes with each other. In an accelerated school, all participants combine efforts and resources to make the vision come to life in the everyday activities of the school. They share a common language, a common set of goals, and a common dream that drives their daily behavior.

Building on Strengths

The philosophy of the accelerated school is one that identifies deliberately and builds on the positive characteristics and talents of all participants—students, teachers, administrators, and parents. The identification of these strengths and the use of them in the instruction and governance of the school are crucial components of the process. Too often, schools have become so demoralized that it is difficult for them to see anything but the weaknesses of all involved. This new process enables people to expand their focus and to see assets rather than debts. For example, many students in at-risk situations bring with them a natural curiosity about life, abilities in oral and artistic expression, ability to use their hands to create and learn, and creativity and imagination. The accelerated school uses these strengths to develop curricular and instructional strategies that are appropriate. This is an approach that, in the past, has usually been reserved for gifted and talented students.

Parents also are untapped resources in most schools. Because parents love their children and want them to succeed, they can be the school's most powerful allies and can show their support in a number of ways from doing volunteer work to fund-raising to working with their children at home to support the learning taking place in schools. Some accelerated schools have established Parent Rooms, where parents can meet and feel welcomed at school. Community and business leaders are also sources of support. In many instances, they would like to be of assistance but don't know how to go about it. Creative accelerated school personnel find ways these groups can contribute time, money, and support.

School-Site Empowerment With Responsibility

Accelerated schools offer teachers, parents, and administrators the opportunity to make important educational decisions dealing with the school's curriculum, instructional strategies, and governance system, which facilitates educational processes. Decision making is collaborative, and responsibility for implementing decisions is also shared. Task forces or cadres composed of teachers, parents, administrators, and, in some instances, students use an inquiry process to suggest solutions for challenge areas in the school. They report their findings to a steering committee, which serves as a clearinghouse for proposals presented to the school as a whole. The steering committee also evaluates proposals in light of the school vision.

Not only do participants plan and implement together—they also take responsibility for the outcomes of those decisions. The central school district office collaborates with the school by providing necessary services such as technical assistance, staff development, evaluation, or information.

Accelerated Schools at Work

Accelerated schools are not just conventional schools that have added special programs. The three principles of *unity of purpose, building on strengths,* and *school-site empowerment with responsibility* form the foundation for comprehensive change in schools. Everyone is involved and every aspect of the school is affected. Change doesn't just occur in one grade level or in one area of the curriculum. The entire process is opened up for examination and changes are made to move the school closer to its agreed-upon vision. The goal of all changes is the academic and social achievement of all students.

The Accelerated Schools Project encompasses a comprehensive process rather than a set of instructional or curriculum packages. All participants adhere to the philosophy and a process for implementation called *collaborative inquiry.* Through the inquiry process, school community members take stock of all aspects of the school and create a nonjudgmental baseline from which to proceed. Special attention is devoted to student, staff, parental, and program strengths that can serve as a basis for action and enrichment. Then the school determines priorities, or areas of challenge, where the vision is not being met. This process requires deliberation and consensus building on the part of all school community members. Once the key areas are targeted and a small list of initial priorities (usually three or four are workable) is generated, school members establish cadres to design strategies for investigating each area of challenge. Within those parameters, each school creates its own unique environment as all participants work toward the vision. Curriculum, instruction, and organizational practices are integrated into initiatives that address the school's vision. Let's take a brief look at each of these areas.

Curriculum

The curriculum of an accelerated school provides a rich framework within which teaching and learning take place. The accelerated curriculum embodies what we know about the ways in which all children learn and provides opportunities for maximized intellectual and personal growth. The curriculum is a carefully integrated whole that flows from a unified vision of what it is that children in at-risk situations should know and be able to do by the time they leave the school. The curriculum is designed to enable students to think and act at high levels of complexity by providing them with relevant, motivating, and challenging experiences and materials. The curriculum builds on children's strengths and is predicated on the belief that all children are capable of complex learning when provided with the appropriate curriculum and instruction.

Curriculum is equitable to all groups—racial, ethnic, gender, and socioeconomic class. It is broad in scope and is interdisciplinary in nature. The curriculum includes more than textbooks and work sheets, although it may use those as jumping-off points. Heavy emphasis is placed on the use of manipulatives, student research, and school-based instructional materials. The curriculum builds on the culture, experiences, and environment of the children as well. The community and home are integral elements of the curriculum in the accelerated school. This year, for example, one of our schools chose "family" as the central focus for their curriculum. All types, styles, and shapes of family are studied in all subject areas.

The accelerated school incorporates language into every aspect of the curriculum. Students are immersed in language all day long. Basic skills are not taught in isolation but are woven into the very fabric of all concepts. The curriculum is *not remedial* but enriched and challenging. The gifts of all children are built upon, and all children are viewed as potentially gifted and talented.

The curriculum of an accelerated school is not a piecemeal list of facts and concepts. It is a carefully planned, holistic entity that integrates accelerated principles throughout. All accelerated schools develop their own curriculum in keeping with their personal vision. There is no packaged program or set of materials that all must use. We believe that this ability to develop unique solutions to specific challenges is one of the strengths of the process.

Instruction

The instructional strategies and practices in accelerated schools are designed to provide students with a rich and varied learning environment. Strategies are diverse so as to build on the unique gifts of each child and teacher. There is much involvement of the senses, and active learning is the rule rather than the exception. The emphasis is on problem solving. Because most children learn best by doing, the strategies used provide them with many opportunities to use new skills and concepts in meaningful ways. The learning environment is not chaotic—structure is provided as needed. But the environment is stimulating to the mind and natural curiosity of children. Students are engaged in active and exploratory discourse in all subjects to stimulate their thinking and understanding as participants in constructing the learning process.

Experience at many accelerated schools has shown that building on student strengths leads to more efficient and effective learning. Thus teachers present instruction in many different ways to build on the diverse strengths of learners in the classroom. The teacher's job becomes one of arranging learning environments, selecting materials, and providing activities that allow students to use several modalities, such as listening, looking, touching, or manipulating. Teachers also develop alternative ways to assess student progress, which gives valuable information, which then informs instruction.

Instruction in accelerated schools tries to help at-risk students learn at a faster rate than their more privileged peers. Current remedial practices, relying on drill and repetition, cause these students to fall further and further behind. Accelerated programs have usually been reserved for gifted and talented students who perform at the top on all standardized measures of success. Yet, doesn't it seem strange to channel so much enrichment to help our top students get even better while deliberately slowing down the learning process for those children who lack educational advantages (Levin & Hopfenberg, 1991)?

Research shows that accelerated instruction works for at-risk students. A recent study, for example, randomly assigned at-risk students to remedial, average, and honors seventh-grade mathematics classes. At year's end, the at-risk students in the honors classes—which provided prealgebra instruction—outperformed those placed in the other two groups (Peterson, 1989). As one Hollibrook teacher puts it,

> An important part of building on children's strengths is simply raising our expectations for them. We did that here and the kids just amazed us all. They rose to the level of our expectations . . . on test results, on the papers they turned in. They just did it!

In reality, however, the teachers did more than just raise their expectations—they changed instructional strategies at the same time, thus providing the opportunity for more students to achieve mastery.

Organization

The organization of the accelerated school is based on a broadened definition of the members of the school community and the expanded role they play in the decision-making process. Teachers, administrators, parents, students, and community all play a part in collaboratively determining the activities the school undertakes in quest of its vision.

Parental involvement, in particular, is seen as a critical factor in the success of the process. Parents are a visible presence in the school and serve in a number of roles. They may join task forces, serve on the school steering committee, do volunteer work, and attend training sessions designed to strengthen their ability to help their children academically.

The roles of administrators and central office personnel change as they become facilitators of the school renewal process. They may provide staff development and technical assistance or help with assessment or waivers from restrictive regulations.

The organization of the school facilitates and supports the curriculum and instructional activities. Change in one area demands change in all other areas. Creative and flexible scheduling may be needed, for example, to support changes in instructional strategies. The school governance structure, guided by the *collaborative inquiry process*, and consisting of task forces or cadres, the steering committee, and the school-as-a-whole decision-making body, supports the changes implemented by the school community in all areas of challenge.

Integrated Change

The Accelerated Schools process is not a piecemeal approach to educational reform. We believe that change must occur in *curriculum, instruction,* and *organization* simultaneously. Change in each one of these areas is a necessary but not sufficient condition to produce lasting success. It is the mutual supportiveness of change in all three that gives the accelerated school its strength. Change in curriculum, for example, is enhanced and facilitated by corresponding changes in instruction and organization. The goal of all change, of course, is to strive toward the school vision, the acceleration of the learning of students in at-risk situations.

The Cost of Becoming an Accelerated School

People always like to know what the bottom line is. How much will it cost to become an accelerated school? An unusual feature of the Accelerated Schools Project is that it starts with schools as they are rather than setting special conditions such as getting a different set of teachers or students or a large increase in budget. Although our research shows that there is a considerable economic return to increasing financial investments in the education of at-risk students, the current political economy of schooling does not suggest that those resources will be immediately forthcoming.

Meanwhile, the challenge of meeting the educational needs of our at-risk students cannot wait. We are currently underusing the enormous talents embodied in our existing teachers, students, parents, and communities. Through unity of purpose, responsibility for educational decisions and their outcomes at the school site, and building on the strengths of the participants, accelerated schools marshall all available resources and reallocate existing resources to bring at-risk students into the academic mainstream efficiently and effectively. The lack of additional funding does not serve as an impediment to the process. Many accelerated schools have found creative solutions to financial needs.

Summary

Accelerated schools are young and developing, not a finished product. We estimate that the process of transforming a school into an accelerated school will take approximately six years. Our pilot schools have been using the process for three years and already have seen some dramatic changes. We are just now expanding the process to the middle school level (see Hopfenberg, Levin, Meister, & Rogers, 1990). Such systemic reform, however, must be implemented thoughtfully, and we must avoid looking for the "quick fix." Patience is a necessary virtue as all members of the school community adjust to their new and expanded roles as decision makers. The good news is that we believe that accelerated school results are not transitory. The integrated approach to change—affecting *curriculum, instruction,* and *organization* simultaneously, and building on the principles of *unity of purpose, building on strengths,* and *empowerment with responsibility*—holds promise for lasting and meaningful educational reform.

References

Hopfenberg, W., Levin, H. M., Meister, G., & Rogers, J. (1990). *Toward accelerated middle schools.* Paper prepared under a grant from the Edna McConnell Clark Foundation, Stanford University.

Levin, H. M. (1986). *Educational reform for disadvantaged students: An emerging crisis.* West Haven, CT: National Education Association.

Levin, H. M. (1987). New schools for the disadvantaged. *Teacher Education Quarterly, 14*(4), 60-83.

Levin, H. M. (1988). *Accelerated schools for at-risk students* (Research Report Series RR-010). New Brunswick, NJ: Rutgers University, Center for Policy Research in Education.

Levin, H. M., & Hopfenberg, W. (1991). Don't remediate: Accelerate! *Principal, 70*(3), 11-13.

Pallas, A., Natriello, G., & McDill, E. L. (1989). The changing nature of the disadvantaged population: Current dimensions and future trends. *Educational Researcher, 5,* 16-22.

Peterson, J. M. (1989). Remediation is no remedy. *Educational Leadership, 46*(6), 24-25.

• 15 •

Conclusion: Future Directions for Educating Students at Risk

JUDITH WALKER DE FELIX
H. PRENTICE BAPTISTE, JR.
JAMES E. ANDERSON

The authors of the chapters in this volume have argued convincingly that America is losing a valuable resource in the children who are currently labeled "at risk." Lou Carroll Campbell, Jr., noted that students at risk are putting America at risk (*All Children Can Learn,* 1983). Kenneth Clark concurred, stating that youth at risk really means society at risk (*All Children Can Learn,* 1983).

Our social institutions, including education, are based on a set of assimilation ideologies and monocultural perspectives. The principal theories and elements of these ideologies have been Anglo-conformity, social and economic middle-classism, and the perennial melting pot philosophy (Gordon, 1964). Thus schools, as well as other institutions, have always been "at risk" of not serving the children of U.S. society. It is the children who do not fit within the assimilative theories of our society that are immorally and illegally "disadvantaged." But it is the foundation and the structure of the U.S. society that is actually "at risk."

In this concluding chapter, we will present some hunches on future educational trends. As several authors mentioned, the educational neglect of large portions of U.S. society is not new. There are also new developments in education. Perhaps these will guide concerned educators in arenas where change may be forged.

Power of Population

The growth of the educationally neglected population has been the topic of many reports. There is even a rap song, "Hispanic Panic," that points to the fears evoked as popular magazines, school in-services, and scholarly reports point to the growth of the Spanish-speaking population. It is interesting that this fear represents a fear of change. As one Mexican American scholar told us, "That might be his panic; it's not mine" (Tatcho Mindiola, personal communication).

To the multiculturalist, the growth of the Hispanic populations represents growth in diversity. There are some 20 diverse Hispanic populations, the largest of which is the Chicano. Each group within the umbrella of "Hispanic" needs specific educational treatment. Cuban students generally are not at risk of school failure because of the availability of bilingual programs where Cuban Americans are concentrated. On the other hand, Mexican Americans represent the cultural group that needs the most educational attention. The large numbers living in Texas, especially, are apt to be neglected. The Texas Education Agency (1988) reported that only 20% of the Spanish-speaking students in that state receive programmatic support. Recent Central American immigrants also need specific educational interventions that they generally do not receive. It is not uncommon for these students to be illiterate in Spanish. Learning English under those circumstances is extremely cognitively demanding.

The government agencies that keep statistical profiles have exaggerated the numbers of any one particular Hispanic group by using the umbrella term *Hispanic*. The bureaucratic convenience has, however, helped focus national attention on the grave educational situation for most Spanish-heritage students. In short, if each cultural group were reported independently, there would probably be no "Hispanic panic."

Asian Americans have a similar advantage. If the numbers of Filipino, Korean, Vietnamese, Chinese, Pacific Islanders, and so on were reported independently, probably few would be "concerned" about the growth of the Asian population. The real concern, however, is the lack of attention to those Asian-heritage groups that do not fit the stereotype of the hardworking, successful Asian student. Filipino students in California, for example, usually have more in common with their Chicano/Latino peers than they do with their Chinese American classmates. This is overlooked by the umbrella term *Asian American*.

Similar governmental groupings of Native Americans, White ethnics, and even African Americans have helped to draw attention to the big picture of educational neglect. Even while enlightened educators attempt to respond to cultural differences within these large groups, the population growth alone gives educators the attention-getting device necessary to motivate conservative school districts and other agencies to act.

The growth of minority populations may even be underestimated. Pallas, Natriello, and McDill (1989) have reanalyzed Census Bureau figures using what they believe to be more appropriate assumptions. For instance, they projected that the Hispanic birthrate will not decline as rapidly as the Census Bureau predicted. Hispanics will, they project, account for most of the overall population growth expected between 1982 and 2020. The African American population is expected to grow from 14.7% of the U.S. population in 1982 to 16.5% in 2020. These scholars note that, while this increase appears small, the population shift means that, whereas in 1982, almost three of every four children were White, in 2020, only about one of two children will be White. One in ten children in 1982 were Hispanic, while one in four will be Hispanic in 2020. Another aspect of Hispanic fertility not considered in Pallas et al. (1989) is the youth of the Hispanic mothers, especially when compared with the family-delaying practices among the White middle-class population.

Changing demographics may mean that political changes may occur. African Americans have been somewhat successful in bringing change through the ballot box. Hispanics, especially Mexican Americans and recent immigrants, do not have a history of voting as cohesively as African Americans. With more Chicano/Latino politicians and greater numbers of registered voters, it may be possible to elect more culturally sensitive school boards, state legislators, and congressional representatives.

Better Understanding of the Learning Process

Educators have a very good idea of what works. Andrew Hahn, for example, wrote in 1987 that educational research has identified programs that work to prevent dropouts and to give current dropouts a second chance. He claimed it was time to quit analyzing the situation and begin thoughtfully implementing that research.

Ronald Edmonds (1978), guru of effective schools, stated the following:

We can whenever and wherever we choose, successfully teach all children whose schooling is of interest to us. We already know more than we need, to successfully teach all children. Whether or not we do it must finally depend on how we feel about the fact that we haven't so far. (p. 35)

Another recent trend has been the understanding of the school as a learning context. Brown, Collins, and Duguid (1989) described situated cognition as an optimal learning setting. In such contexts, schools would provide authentic tasks in which students would act as apprentices to learn everyday cognition. To Brown et al., the ordinary practices of the culture are what need to be included in schools. The Cognition and Technology Group at Vanderbilt has been developing similar contexts. More fully described by Richard Johnson in this volume, the Vanderbilt group creates authentic tasks on videodisc. They believe that visual formats, rather than text materials, allow children to develop pattern recognition skills. Such a rationale has appeal for educators of language-minority students or of students with weak literacy skills. The Cognition and Technology Group also sees knowledge as tools. Citing Dewey (1933), they note that, when people learn to use a tool, they learn not only what it is but also how and when to use it.

The entire winter 1990 issue of the *Review of Educational Research* is dedicated to the exploration of situated cognition. Generally, the authors in that volume point to the importance of interactive settings in which students focus on authentic tasks in a context mediated by experts in that task. Novices generally confront new information or new processes without involvement (Shuell, 1990). New concepts and theories appear to be facts to be memorized unless the setting requires some interaction with the material (Cognition & Technology Group, 1990). Additionally, if learners are not required to act on the material, they are unlikely to monitor cognitions and so cannot even use strategies they have found useful before (Garner, 1990).

Traditional classroom approaches can also interfere with higher-level thinking. Productive, well-practiced routines can inhibit deep processing. School routines, ingrained after only a few years, have been used so frequently that they have become automated (Garner, 1990). To children who are not of the dominant cultural group, some of the school routines are the source of misunderstanding (see Saracho & Gerstl in this volume). It is no wonder that these children frequently fail to achieve deep processing while in school.

The classroom's affective environment must be conductive to higher-level thinking as well. Garner's (1990) review of the literature found that, when students in competitive classrooms succeed or fail, they attribute their performance to innate ability. In classrooms that build self-esteem and learning strategy use, students ask, "What can I do to succeed?" In a nonsupportive classroom, students may ask, "Am I stupid?" Learners asking the ability question generally assume that learning is out of their own control.

Classrooms that provide for internal self-regulation of learning appear to be optimal (Iran-Nejad, 1990). Such classrooms would provide a variety of contexts, help students adapt to these contexts, assist them in looking at both the details and the whole. Learning thus becomes "a change between qualitatively different conceptions" (Marton, 1988, p. 73). Students can approach learning deeply with hope for success and intrinsic motivation (Iran-Nejad, 1990).

This movement to active, authentic problem solving provides great hope for children from groups that have not fared well in U.S. schools. They can learn the academic tools within a context that allows for adjustments to individual learning style differences. Students can "own" the material as they conduct research and collaborate to solve problems. Cultural and linguistic similarities and differences can be explored in an integrated fashion rather than as a separate activity (such as those developed for "Black History Month").

Some Future Concerns

The picture is not all rosy for children whose progenitors did not succeed academically. One of the major concerns has been the so-called reform movement. Schools have been "reformed" so often now that the public and some educators want to return to the peaceful time when schools could run themselves as they saw fit. Cuban (1990) analyzed the patterns of reform and found that few reforms actually make differences in classrooms. Yet, there have been significant changes. The history of federal intervention in the schools, for example, reminds us what *at risk* meant before *Brown v. Board of Education.* Yet the large numbers of children who are not succeeding academically warn us that we must move beyond the rhetoric of reform.

In spite of the reform movement, schools are philosophically, psychologically, and structurally no different than they were in the industrial era of the 1800s.

> Some schoolmen [sic] liked what they saw in the textile mills of New England in the 1840's and sought to pattern school organization after them. This was an appealing idea, for it was to be mass education, it meant order and discipline, graded systems, good management, a concern with productivity (usually measured in terms of the number of students who were channeled through the system), and specialization of teachers and supervisors. The factory model permitted the schools to deal efficiently with large numbers of students. Individual attention was not needed; children could be grouped according to ability, level of aptitude, age or all of these, and a single teacher could work with hundreds. The children could progress in logical and orderly fashion upward through the system. The schools could, of course, teach those things necessary to make cultures into one. The whole system was designed to replicate the demands of the industrial system. Its emphasis was on bells, punctuality, time[d] completion of assigned facts, and hierarchical power structure—all of these things existed in the modern factory. Thus the masses could be socialized to the factory system in the school. Even the rewards were similar. The grading system became the "paycheck" for satisfactory completion of a task, ordered as it were, by one's boss. (Selakovich, 1978, p. 35)

This lack of change in schooling is also supported in Toffler's *The Third Wave* (1980) and Naisbett and Aberdeen's *Megatrends 2000: Ten New Directions for the 1990's* (1990).

Assimilative theories and ideologies generate paradigms in education that reflect the embedded values that make up these theories. To adequately respond to the educational challenges that exist in a multicultural society, schools and educational institutions must unlock themselves from dysfunctional educational theories and paradigms and align themselves with policies, practices, and programs that are multicultural in nature.

Current models of educational leadership and teacher training programs are likely to be incapable of preparing competent educational professionals for today's diverse schooling environments because those programs are embedded within paradigms that are incongruent with the conditions they must address. This leads to the long stream of reform, restructuring, and retraining efforts that never really solve problems such as the "at-risk" concept. Each wave of reform merely "retitles" and "recasts" it year after year using a new name.

A second concern deals with the continuation of the research agenda described above. With large numbers of students pushed out of academia, who will be conducting the educational research of the future? Because a high proportion of the current university faculty will retire within the next 10 years, there is a window of opportunity for an unprecedented number of new faculty members (Western Interstate Commission for Higher Education, 1987). This need for faculty is occurring at the same time that the percentage of minority Ph.D.s is decreasing.

Educational faculty have generally been considered immune from shortages of minority faculty, as the largest proportion has historically been housed in education. In fact, three trends make such a stereotype outdated. First, there is a dwindling number of African American doctoral graduates each year (Mooney, 1989). African Americans experienced an 18% decline in master's degrees between 1975-1976 and 1980-1981. By 1984-1985, the number had decreased 31.5% from 1975-1976. In that same period, African American doctoral students declined from 1,095 to 909. Today, except in historically Black universities, less than 3% of full-time faculty members are of African heritage.

In 1985, Hispanic faculty constituted 1.7% of full-time faculty in all U.S. universities. While the percentage of Hispanic doctoral graduates has increased, the numbers are still quite small, even in education. Furthermore, the trends for Chicano/Latino graduate students are somewhat different than those for African American students, probably due to the advantages the latter have had in their own schools and universities. Citing negative experiences in elementary and secondary schools, fewer Chicano secondary students choose to major in education as undergraduates than do Black students. In fact, 43% of Hispanic high school graduates go to two-year colleges, and most do not continue to a four-year institution.

This trend away from education majors is noted in graduate degrees as well. In 1984-1985, there were 521 Black doctoral graduates in education while there were only 163 Hispanic doctorates. On the other hand, in the physical and life sciences, there were 88 Black doctorates but 110 Hispanics. In 1987, the National Latino Faculty Study found that 41% of all Hispanic faculty were concentrated in Chicano Studies programs (Garza, 1988). Furthermore, those who were classified as university administrators were in fact directors of programs that were concerned exclusively with areas such as language, minorities, studying abroad, affirmative action, and so on. In short, those faculty were in positions that did not promote their careers as researchers.

Additionally, professional careers other than university research and teaching, because they are more lucrative (Brazziel, 1988), have been able to recruit more minority members. For example, several programs have increased the number of minorities in engineering and law (Western Interstate Commission for Higher Education, 1987).

The National Research Council (1989) asserted that the extent of underrepresentation of minorities in higher education is in direct proportion to the amount of mathematics needed in the field of study. Because they lack a sound foundation in math, many African Americans and Latinos are shut out of most professional careers. Thus the cycle of poor schooling continues.

The concept of "at-riskness" is currently being defined as a deficit and deprivation notion, with the deficit on the part of the children. It is the latest version of William Ryan's "blaming the victim" rationale. The problem of "at-riskness" is a social and political issue, not really an education issue. As Ron Edmonds (1978) and numerous others have said, we already know enough to educate everybody. It is really a question of social integrity and moral commitment, not a question of educational development. If this indeed is true, then it is unlikely that those individuals who maintain their current philosophies, paradigms, and programs can be expected to change or solve the problems. What is needed are new philosophies, new paradigms, and new leadership.

In this volume, we have seen some indication that some changes are making a difference for some children. New paradigms put the old ways at risk. Ineffective policies and programs must give way to innovations that meet the educational needs of our increasingly more diverse society.

References

All children can learn, all schools can be effective. (1983). [Videotape of Urban Education Scholar Series presentation]. College of Education, University of Houston.
America's shame, America's hope: At risk students. (1989). [Videotape].
Brazziel, W. F. (1988). Black Americans find road blocks at graduate school. *Educational Record, 68,* 1.

Brown, J. S., Collins, A. S., & Duguid, P. (1989). Situated cognition and the culture of learning. *Educational Researcher, 18*(1), 32-41.
Cognition and Technology Group at Vanderbilt. (1990). Anchored instruction and its relationship to situated cognition. *Educational Researcher, 19*(5), 2-10.
Cuban, L. (1990). Reforming again, again, and again. *Educational Researcher, 19*(1), 3-13.
Edmonds, R. (1978). *A discussion of the literature and issues related to effective schooling* (Vol. 6, pp. 1-39). St. Louis: CEMREL.
Dewey, J. (1933). *How we think.* Boston: D. C. Heath.
Garner, R. (1990). When children and adults do not use learning strategies: Toward a theory of settings. *Review of Educational Research, 60,* 517-530.
Garza, H. (1988). The "barrioization" of Hispanic faculty. *Educational Record, 68,* 1.
Gordon, M. M. (1964). *Assimilation in American life: The role of race, religion, and national origins.* New York: Oxford University Press.
Hahn, A. (1987). Reaching out to America's dropouts: What to do? *Phi Delta Kappan, 69,* 256-263.
Iran-Nejad, A. (1990). Active and dynamic self-regulation of learning processes. *Review of Educational Research, 60,* 573-602.
Marton, F. (1988). Describing and improving learning. In R. R. Schmeck (Ed.), *Learning strategies and learning styles* (pp. 53-82). New York: Plenum.
Mooney, C. J. (1989, August 2). Affirmative-action goals, coupled with tiny numbers of minority Ph.D.s set off faculty recruiting frenzy. *Chronicle of Higher Education,* p. 1.
Naisbett, J., & Aberdeen, P. (1990). *Megatrends 2000: Ten new directions for the 1990s.* New York: William Morrow.
National Research Council. (1989). *Everybody counts: A report to the nation on the future of mathematics education.* Washington, DC: National Academy Press.
Pallas, A. M., Natriello, G., & McDill, E. L. (1989). The changing nature of the disadvantaged population: Current dimensions and future trends. *Educational Researcher, 18*(5), 16-22.
Selakovich, D. (1978). *Ethnicity and the schools: Educating minorities for mainstream America.* Danville, IL: Interstate Printers & Publishers.
Shuell, T. J. (1990) Phases of meaningful learning. *Review of Educational Research, 60*(4), 531-548.
Texas Education Agency. (1988). *Report: Data and information on the educational condition of limited English-proficient students in Texas.* Austin: TEA.
Toffler, A. (1980). *The third wave.* New York: William Morrow.
Toffler, A. (1990). *Powershift.* New York: Bantam.
Western Interstate Commission for Higher Education. (1987). *From minority to majority: Education and the future of the Southwest.* Boulder: Self.

Index

Accelerated schools, 23, 56, 200, 250, 253-254
  collaborative inquiry, 257
  cost, 261-262
  curriculum, 258, 261
  instruction, 259, 261
  organization, 260-261
  principles, 200, 255-257
  program description, 200, 255
Acculturation, 113
African Americans, 106, 114-118, 148-149, 177, 179, 189, 266, 270, 271
  perceptual style, 114, 115
  See also learning styles
Alienation
  student, 2, 5
  teacher, 2, 5
Asian Americans, 107, 124-127, 148, 179, 265
  cultural influences, 126-127
  See also cognitive styles
At-risk
  defined, 3, 4, 11, 43-44, 55, 61-63, 87, 105, 147, 175-176
  educational policy, 20
  educational ramification, 18
  effective programs, 27, 63, 196, 224, 233
  instructional practices, 91, 94
  profile, 48-51, 53, 88, 94, 113, 254
  role of community, 15, 28, 29, 31
  role of educators, 12, 28-29, 31, 35, 37, 38-41
  role of parents, 14, 28, 37-38
  role of schools, 13, 31, 35, 39
  stigma theory, 19, 20
  students, 2, 6, 11, 17, 22, 34, 53, 87, 105, 127, 138-141, 143, 145, 156, 160, 163, 167-168, 195, 199, 209, 219, 222-223, 233, 254, 260, 264, 268-269

Bilingual/bicultural education, 69-71, 215
Bilingualism, 190

Chapter I/Title I programs, 21, 22, 196, 197, 203, 212
  effective programs, 204, 207-209
  federal government, 216-217, 219-220
  history, 203-204, 207-208
  instructional practices, 211-212
  organizational/leadership, 209-210, 218
  TIERS model, 212
Classroom environment, 13
Cognitive strategies, 223
Cognitive style, 64, 108, 117, 128, 152
  Asian American, 124-125
  definition, 109, 112
  Mexican American, 118
  Native Americans, 119

273

Compensatory education, 21, 22, 23, 27
  programs, 195, 204, 213, 215
Cooperative learning, 14, 23, 69
Cultural politics, 161-163, 166, 168, 170-171
Culture, 146-150, 161-162, 165-166, 198, 224, 226-227, 267
  definition, 162-164

Degrees of Reading Power (DRP) Approach, 199, 237, 239, 242-243
Degrees of Reading Power Test, 235, 237-240
Disadvantaged, 22, 197, 207
  educationally, 3, 176
  students, 4
Drop outs, 23, 27, 148
  discipline, 12
  interventions, 16, 53-56
  rates (status), 2, 11, 44-49, 52, 57
  school size, 13

Educational leadership, 166, 169, 269
Effective schools, 154, 196, 204, 266-267
English as a second language (ESL), 72, 208
Equity, 140, 146, 161, 172

Field dependence, 109-112, 113, 116, 118-120, 123
Field independent, 109-112, 113, 116, 120, 123-125

Grade retention, 22, 23

Higher-level thinking skills, 222-223, 267-268
Hispanics, 66, 67, 70, 74, 75, 148, 149, 252, 265-266, 270
Home culture, 68, 76

Home environment, 25, 63

Inner city school, 2, 7
Interactive videodisc, 63

Kamehameha Early Education Program (KEEP), 198, 224, 226, 227, 229

Language minority students, 65-77
  instructional practices, 69-77
  perceptions of, 65-67
Learning, 150-153, 164
Learning styles, 110, 113, 116, 128-129, 268
  African Americans, 116
  Native Americans, 119-123
Limited English proficient, 87-88, 138, 176
Low achieving students, 4

Magnet schools, 29
Marginality, 34-35
Marginal student, 15, 33-41, 50
Mastery for All, 86
Matthew effects, 4
Mediocrity paradigm, 141, 174-175, 171
Melting pot theory, 137
Mexican Americans, 106, 117-118, 265
Multicultural
  education, 176-179, 183-185, 189
  literacy, 186-190
  teacher education, 174, 176
Multicultural environments, 138, 141
Multicultural literacy, 141

Native Americans, 107, 119-123, 148, 266
  See also learning styles

Progressive retardation, 4

Index

Public policy
  deficit model, 2

Reading recovery, 198, 224, 225
Reciprocal teaching, 198, 224, 227
  teacher training, 228-229
Reforming/restructuring
  schools, 3, 25

School-based programs, 196
School environment, 4-7, 35, 36, 38, 40, 112, 119, 201
Schools-Within-a-School Approach (SWAS), 199, 233, 234
  characteristics, 235

  implementation, 240-243
  philosophy, 235-236
  program description, 234

Teacher education
  professors, 180-182, 191
  programs, 175-176, 183, 188, 191
Teacher training, 269
Technology, 13, 63, 89, 100, 195
  videodiscs, 89-95
  videodiscs lesson formats, 95-100

Underachievement, 2
Underachieving students, 3
Urban schools, 2, 18